Alcoholic to Alchemist

The Art of turning wine into water

By Paul Henderson

A CIP record for this book is available from the British Library

ISBN 978-1-4709-6218-0

This book is dedicated to
my beloved family,

Stanley, Brenda
and **Barbara Henderson,**

without whose love, understanding, and
support my life would have surely
ended prematurely, and
these pages would never
have materialized

Contents

Author's Note

This book is divided into ten sections. Each section is designed to deepen your understanding of the principles involved in the Twelve Step Philosophy for Optimal Living (which comes towards the end). The earlier sections focus on identifying and alleviating the underlying psychological mechanisms that give rise to your destructive tendencies, whilst the later sections concentrate on personal growth and spiritual development.

At times you may feel that the material is veering away from the topic of alcoholism – and so it is! *Alcoholism is a destructive mind-set; the answer to which is a radical shift in thinking.* The **Twelve Step Philosophy for optimal Living** is designed to initiate and sustain this shift: *it concentrates on the answer, not the problem.* The eclectic mix of psychological tools and spiritual practices aim to raise your self-awareness, awaken your Higher-Self, and reveal your ultimate purpose in life.

For optimal effect, read and digest the sections preceding the Twelve Step Philosophy. Complete the exercises and contemplate the ways in which they can enhance your quality of life. Note your shift in thinking. Then work your way through the Twelve Steps in chronological order, absorbing each one and applying its teachings to your life.

It is important to remember that this is not a *'programme'* with a start, a middle, and an end – *it is an on-going philosophy:* **a way of life.** Absorbing and applying the principles to your life on a daily basis will bring about the radical shift in consciousness needed to reach your true potential.

The Spirit of Alchemy

Peter was sitting outside a youth club totally demoralized when a spirit descended. 'What's wrong?' the spirit enquired.

'I'm lonely,' Peter replied. 'I haven't got the confidence to go inside and mix with the others.'

The spirit promptly informed him that if he went into the garden and stood under the Banyan tree he'd be granted anything he desired.

Somewhat sceptically, Peter trudged into the garden and stood under the huge tree. Having heard that alcohol was the antidote to all life's problems, he wished for some beer. In a flash, a crate appeared. He took it to a secluded part of the garden and began to drink. Within a short space of time his confidence rose and his mood began to lighten. He entered the youth club and mingled easily with his peers. 'This is it!' he exclaimed. 'Alcohol's what I've been looking for all my life. Let's have another beer!'

Next morning, Peter's mood was sombre once again. The liberating effects of alcohol had worn off and he felt rough. After some quiet deliberation, he concluded that the desired effects hadn't lasted because the alcohol was in short supply and the beer wasn't strong enough.

Returning to the Banyan tree, he wished for a larger supply of stronger alcohol. In a flash, twelve bottles of wine appeared before him. Again, he began drinking and within an hour he was frivolous and carefree.

For the next few months the cyclic pattern of feeling

rough, drinking, and socializing continued. The downs were rough, but Peter realized that if he drank in the mornings the adverse effects subsided and he soon pepped up. So he began to top himself up regularly.

With his confidence riding high and his inhibitions at bay, he started dating a pretty young girl named Laura. Life was good and, so long as he had a permanent supply of alcohol, there was no reason it shouldn't remain that way.

The liberating effects of the wine remained for a few months, but he found himself having to gradually increase his consumption to sustain them. After a few months, his tolerance became so high that it had very little effect. Even after drinking several bottles he failed to rise above his problems and insecurities. His self-esteem and confidence began to plummet and he found it difficult to maintain his social persona. He needed a new plan: urgently!

'Maybe wine is too weak, but spirits are sure to work,' he deliberated.

Optimistically, he ventured back to the Banyan tree. Wish. Flash! A crate of whisky appeared. As he drank it, his problems and insecurities were quickly suppressed and he felt liberated once again.

The years elapsed and the pattern perpetuated: drinking whisky, forgetting his problems, withdrawing, wishing for more whisky, and getting high again. During this time Peter's personality started to decline. Continuous drinking not only caused his problems to disappear, but his morals, values, ethics, and standards vanished too: the placid Doctor Jekyll frequently changed into the menacing Mister Hyde. One minute he was an amicable, sociable person, the next, an unpredictable menace. During black-out he argued and fought with his friends and family, leaving a trail of destruction in his wake. On emerging from these drunken escapades he had no recollection of what had happened. He was mortified when told of his bizarre and destructive antics.

Filled with guilt, remorse, and paranoia, he rushed back to the Banyan tree. The only way to escape this unbearable life was to drink himself into oblivion, he deduced. Flash! The whisky appeared. After gulping it down, sure enough, he crashed out. But rather than slumber in a silent sanctuary, he kicked, punched and screamed as his inner turmoil manifested as horrendous nightmares.

Desperate and beaten, he traipsed back to the tree and wished for a supply of alcohol that would alleviate the sweats, shakes, nightmares, paranoia, unpredictability, aggression and persecuted sleep. Flash! An array of spirits promptly appeared: whisky, brandy, gin and vodka. Peter started to drink, but this time, rather than his problems abating, all hell broke loose. His mind became a battleground in which every thought was a weapon of mass destruction.

His destructive habit continued for years, during which time he deteriorated drastically. He experienced family dysfunction, divorce, imprisonment, sectioning, delirium tremens, hallucinations, liver damage, loss of bladder and bowel control, premature aging, homelessness and poverty: drink relieved him of his friends, his family, and his dignity.

Destitute and suicidal, he returned to the wish fulfilling tree. Death was surely his only option now. Standing dispassionately under the verdant canopy, he made a wish for a deathly cocktail of alcohol and painkillers. Whoosh! It appeared. As he gulped it down, a haze descended and he slipped into a dark abyss.

On crossing to the *other side* a spirit appeared to greet him. '*Remember me?*' he asked.

'Yes,' Peter replied, somewhat agitatedly. 'Why did you allow me to destroy my life?'

'*I simply offered you a choice, dear one. You are in sole control of your life. The faculty of choice is the greatest gift bestowed on the human race; without it they would be merely slaves. Your mind is a wish fulfilling tree filled with infinite opportunities. Every choice you make is a wish which will be granted.*

'*Somewhat misguidedly you chose alcohol, deeming it to be the magical panacea for all life's problems...but it isn't. Alcohol doesn't cure anything; it simply dulls your conscience and renders your memory inactive. So you temporarily forget about your problems or simply don't care. But using alcohol to suppress your problems is self-defeating. They don't disappear when you discard them - they build up in your unconscious mind until the pressure gets to such a magnitude that they blow. When this eruption occurs, you and alcohol become incompatible for life. Every subsequent bout leads to dysfunction – a downward spiral to destruction.*'

'So what was the solution? What was I supposed to do about my problems?'

'*You came here in search of Heaven, did you not?*'

'Yes.'

'*Well, Heaven is not a place, my friend; it is a state of mind. By transforming your emotional and mental debris into the treasures of insight, inspiration, fulfilment, and enlightenment you will enter the kingdom of heaven and access the infinite possibilities it beholds. To succeed in life you must become like fire. Consume any obstacles that stand in your way and utilize them as fuel for yourself.*

'....You have a mission, my friend. Abusive alcohol consumption has now reached pandemic levels on Earth [1]*. Your mission is to help alleviate it. Life is precious, Peter. Embrace it. Leave your impression on the world. Go and help these people back to dry land where they can embrace the wonderful gift of life.'*

Peter looked perplexed. 'How am I supposed to do that now: I'm dead?' he retorted.

'Every death is simply a rebirth, my friend.'

As these words reverberated through Peter's mind, the surroundings took on an iridescent glow. The spirit evaporated into the ether and a bright light permeated the air.

Epilogue

First light pierced the dorm of the rehabilitation centre. One bleary-eyed occupant yawned and stretched, before walking over to the window. Starring ruminatively at the huge tree in the garden, he contemplated a strange dream he'd had during the night. The veil of darkness that shrouded his internal world had seemingly lifted. He was infused with a renewed sense of optimism. He felt as though his old self had died and given rise to a new one – and so it had: the *Spirit of Alchemy* had arisen from the depths of his psyche and his life was about to change forever.

---

[1] Recent statistics show that an estimated **40,000 people in England and Wales lose their lives through alcohol abuse every year,** costing the economy fifty five billion pounds annually. One in five people are currently affected in some way by the habit. These figures are rising rapidly around the globe.

Part One

The Origins of the Twelve Step Philosophy for Optimal Living

The Author's Journey

'Don't walk behind me I will not lead,
Don't walk in front of me I will not follow,
Just walk beside me and be my friend.'

Anon

Torrential rain battered my emaciated body as I lay slumped on the rat infested railway embankment. Emotionally bankrupt, bereft of meaning, homeless and penniless, I'd resigned myself to a liquid last supper. Catching a glimpse of myself in a broken mirror revealed the extent of my deterioration. The twenty-five year old former fun-loving entertainer had been replaced by a decrepit old man: eyes sunken, yellow complexion, jittery and unkempt. Death seemed imminent: almost welcoming.

Images of my beloved family flooded my beleaguered mind, intensifying the disabling guilt that dogged me on a daily basis. They couldn't bear it any longer; they asked me to leave the family home to avoid the pain of watching me slowly committing suicide.

I reached for the bottle of Vodka beside me and hoped the amnesic effects would kick in quickly. I needed to obliterate all traces of reality and retreat into oblivion. I took a swig. My body suddenly arched and went into spasm. I sank into a dark abyss.

On coming to, my head felt like home to a swarm of bees. Dazed and confused, I attempted to re-orient myself. The stench of sweat and urine filled my nostrils - the after-effects of yet another fit. As tears rolled down my cheeks and dissolved into the driving rain, I longed for the return of the happy-go-lucky lad who vanished as my drinking escalated, but all that I could see was the decrepit old man. How had this nightmare started?

I was born at the beginning of the sixties in Liverpool. My parents, Stanley and Brenda, held several jobs to keep the roof over our heads and put food on the table. My sister, Barbara, came along two and a half years later. We were a very close unit.

Childhood was quite normal for the inner city; a mixture of fun and fear - close knit communities; gangs hanging around on street corners; children playing in the streets; and neighbours in and out of each other's houses: sharing, caring and sometimes squabbling!

I became streetwise at a very early age. My clown persona carried me through the nuances of childhood and adolescence. Having the ability to make people laugh proved a valuable asset, enabling me to integrate well with my peers and deflect the wrath of the bullies.

During my formative years my love for animals kept me occupied. The family home was a menagerie: birds, hamsters, rabbits, dogs, fish, tortoises, terrapins and frogs occupied many of the rooms. I had aspirations to become a vet back then; but alas, my dreams were dashed when I realised I couldn't stand the sight of animals in pain!

Aged eight, the second love of my life emerged - music. I became entranced by my dad's guitar. I'd strum the strings and listen with intrigue and fascination. Unlike many children, my interest in the guitar was not a short-term fad. Over the next few years, I practiced relentlessly and became an accomplished guitarist.

On reaching my teenage years, a school friend and I formed a duo. Within a year we were performing at social clubs and community centres. I'll never forget our first gig. The venue was a small social club in close proximity to our house. For some unknown reason Robbie and I decided to change into our stage outfits at home and walk to the club. Adorned in pink shirts, black bow ties and violet trousers, we marched past our friends who were playing football on the street corner – I still cringe when I recall the jeers and ridicule we were subjected to! Still, the gig was a great success and proved to be the start of a magical era.

Music became my passion. Within a couple of years, the duo expanded into a five piece band. Rather than advertise for musicians, Robbie and I decided to invite our friends to join us – none of whom were musicians or vocalists! I took on the arduous task of learning all the instruments: drums, bass guitar, and keyboard. I'd then relay my knowledge to the other band members. It wasn't unusual for me to be up until three or four in the morning, learning the various parts. Mum would be yelling down the stairs, *'Paul, do you know what time it is? You've got school in the morning!'*, but I was oblivious, totally immersed in the magic of my mind.

The band was very successful. We travelled the country performing gigs at clubs, private functions and festivals. The lads bonded like brothers – often fought like them too! I'd arrived – or so I thought - earning money pursuing my passion and travelling with friends to exciting places. Not to mention the attention we received from the girls! I was living my dream.

Around this time I was introduced to alcohol. I guess it was bravado at first. At fifteen I felt grown up when I drank. However, bravado soon became secondary to the liberating feeling alcohol instilled within me. As soon as I drank, my inhibitions dissolved and an unexplainable edge was put on life. My worries, anxiety and self-doubt gave way to a wonderful sense of liberation and invincibility. Consequently, the seductive effects started to get a strangle-hold very quickly.

Within a couple of years my commitment to the band began to wane in favour of drinking. My irate friends were frequently left awaiting my arrival at rehearsals, whilst I knocked back pints of lager with vodka chasers in the local pub.

During one of these bouts I met a trainee nurse who moonlighted as a barmaid to earn some extra cash. We started dating and after a year planned to get engaged. Trying to inject some stability back into my life, I renewed my commitment to the band and mended my relationships with the lads.

The band travelled down to Birmingham for an audition with an agent who booked acts to work abroad. The audition went very well; we secured a three month contract to perform at the American Army bases in Germany. Around the same time, we also secured a recording contract with a small label here in the North West of England. Our future looked extremely promising.

As the date for the German tour approached, however, I felt torn apart. I wanted to perform at the army bases and spend time with the lads, but I didn't want to leave my girlfriend. After much deliberation and heartache, I pulled out. Sadly, a few months later, the group disbanded and the tour and recording never materialized.

The absence of music in my life began to take its toll. A cavernous void opened up and I became miserable and restless. The novelty of my relationship had worn off and my interest was beginning to wane. Life seemed meaningless. Needing an escape route, I turned back to alcohol. Within a very short period I became prone to unpredictable and irrational behaviour and my girlfriend left.

I managed to secure a low-paid job in a garage, driving and cleaning cars. Although I curtailed my drinking during the week, I binge-drank at the weekends. Black-outs and brawls ensued, and I was locked up on numerous of occasions. Doctor Jekyll was quickly turning into Mister Hide.

I dreaded the mornings after. I'd wake up full of paranoia and remorse, shaking, sweating, and vomiting, waiting for someone to tell me what I'd done the night before. The border between reality and fiction became vague. I often couldn't distinguish between the things I'd done and the things I'd imagined I'd done. I'd jump out of my skin every time the phone or door bell rang. My nerves were shot.

Aged eighteen, I lost my driving license for drink-driving and my job in the garage went. Thinking a geographical move would sort me out, I secured a job as a Bluecoat in a holiday camp and moved down south. Working from 7.30am to 1am the following morning could be draining, but the social arena I worked in meant alcohol was freely available.

Drinking was no longer a luxury: it was a necessity. My day started with vomiting, sweating and shaking, accompanied by severe paranoia – *what had I done the night before? Did I insult anyone? Did I embarrass myself?* I had absolutely no recollection. Struggling to hold a bottle in my trembling hands, I'd take a large swig of vodka - then another – and another. The first few gulps would inevitably come back up, so I'd make sure there was a bowl at hand. When the retching and shaking calmed to a point where I could walk to the bathroom without feeling faint, I'd take the bottle to the shower. A few more gulps of Vodka whilst the hot water poured over me and I started to stabilize. My paranoia would subside as alcohol began to work its magic and life became an adventure again. On went my blue-coat and a smiling face and off I went to entertain the campers.

The summer season ended and life became a barren wasteland again: totally meaningless. The void inside became greater than ever, and I drank faster than ever to try and fill it. The following few years saw me deteriorate very quickly: three drink-driving charges, suspended jail sentences, probation, rehabs and numerous admissions to hospitals.

The latter drink-driving offence was serious: drink-driving whilst on a drink-driving ban. Prison seemed imminent. Arriving at court, topped up with alcohol, I thoroughly expected to go to prison. However, Legal Aid provided me with a very talented barrister who pleaded I would lose my career if I was imprisoned (I was due to take an entertainment manager's post that summer). Consequently, my sentence was suspended. On leaving the court I headed for the nearest off-license, stuck half a bottle of vodka in my pocket, and headed for the nearest pub. The truth is I was already imprisoned.

By this time my family were distraught. Witnessing the sadness and despair in their eyes crippled me. To relieve the guilt I drank and drank and drank. I'd sneak bottles of spirits into my bedroom and hide them in readiness to drink throughout the night. Oblivion was now my only goal. But even sleep had ceased to bring respite. I'd shout, scream and sweat in a drunken stupor as the contents of my disturbed psyche expressed itself as horrific nightmares.

The onset of hallucinations saw gargoyle-like faces appearing at my bedroom window. Terrified, I'd flee into my parents' room to get help. They quickly realized what was happening and tried to reason with me, but their attempts were to no avail. The hallucinations were so vivid I was convinced they were real.

During one particularly bad experience, I ran into my sister's bedroom and ordered her to make her way to my parents' room as quickly as possible. *'Why?'* she enquired, startled.

'I've just seen two gunmen going into our bathroom.' I replied.

More frightened of me than the two illusory gunmen, she headed for my parents' bedroom.

Another night I hallucinated thieves breaking into my dad's van which was parked outside our house. I rushed to call the police, only to be cut off by my mother.

'They're gonna get away with the van!' I ranted.

After numerous attempts to reason with me, she backed off and I called the police. When they arrived, our road was desolate; not a soul in sight. My mum had a quiet word with the puzzled officers and they turned to leave. As they returned to their car, I hallucinated heads popping out of the neighbours paths and shrieked at them to arrest these people, but they left in the knowing that these criminals existed only in the domain of my screwed up psyche.

Things continued to deteriorate drastically. Unable to determine reality from the alcohol fuelled delusions of my warped mind, I became terrified. I pleaded with my doctor to get me help. To this day I owe him my life. He had me admitted to hospital and rehabs on numerous occasions. Although I would often sign myself out and return to drinking, his faith never waned.

On hitting rock bottom, I'd go to any lengths to be admitted into hospital – it was the only place I felt safe. I'd take lethal cocktails of alcohol and painkillers and then tell someone. Although this destructive behaviour was a cry for help, not a serious attempt to kill myself, I almost ended my life on two occasions. On one occasion, after being rushed to hospital and having my stomach pumped, I was lying in bed fatigued and paranoid when an emergency team came hurtling in and inserted numerous drips into various parts of my body. They promptly informed me that a toxic level of painkillers and alcohol remained in my bloodstream. My life was saved only by the swift response and expertise of these people.

But did I learn from the experience? Was it enough for me to quit drinking? No - I was to repeat this procedure time and time again. I'd go to any lengths to obtain drink: beg, steal, or borrow. The first possessions I parted with were my guitar, microphone and other musical equipment. To walk past the local second-hand shop and see them for sale was heartbreaking, but drink was a necessity I couldn't live without.

After selling all my possessions, I reverted to theft and deceit. My father was a milkman at the time and used to collect a large sum of money on a Friday night. Although he and my mother selflessly cared for me throughout my withdrawals, tending to my every need as I convulsed and vomited - and, although I loved them dearly - one Saturday morning I stole the whole contents of my father's cash bag and fled. When I eventually emerged from that bender, the guilt was unbearable: I hated myself with a vengeance.

Finally, I reached bottom. My emaciated body gave the appearance of an old man, though I was still only in my twenties. When I ran out of alcohol, I'd revert to drinking surgical spirits, methylated spirits, after shave, and even squirting body deodorants into my mouth hoping they'd bring some relief.

...And so I ended up on that railway embankment, homeless, penniless, and totally exhausted; several rats scurrying past seeking shelter from the driving rain; the faces of my beloved family appearing vividly in my mind. Surely this was the end of the road?

As darkness eclipsed any flicker of hope I had left, something extraordinary happened. Emerging from the depths of my psyche, a loving voice whispered the words *'you weren't born to live this way.'*

Was it another hallucination? Was I schizophrenic? Had I lost it completely? No – none of these explanations rang true. If I suffered from any of these conditions, I wouldn't have had the faculty of reason to challenge them – and I did.

That experience proved to be the start of an enlightening and fulfilling journey. Rocky, admittedly, as relapse followed sobriety in cycles - but so worthwhile. Although I stumbled and fell, I no longer viewed relapse as failure; it became a feedback system from which I learned.

The wise inner voice remained my companion throughout. *If you don't get the results you want, preserve the learning, refine your techniques and try again*, it whispered to me – and I adhered to the advice. This voice I came to know as the *archetypal alchemist:* my inner friend, mentor and genius. There's one lying dormant inside you right now. Call on him/her now; be guided from the wilderness and transform enslavement into enlightenment.

Epilogue.

Documenting these events from my life has been a surreal experience; like a bad dream from which I've now awoken. Today, it's a totally different story. I don't think about drink, whatsoever. I don't fear it, avoid it, or have a healthy respect for it – quite honestly, it's insignificant. What an amazing turn-around considering *my* history.

Alcoholism is a mind-set, the answer to which is a radical shift in consciousness. Through adherence to the philosophy outlined in this book, I achieved this shift. Today, my mind is a creative kingdom that gives rise to feelings I could never attain through the bottle: ecstasy, euphoria – literally, heaven! Now I'm free, liberated and master of my own destiny, every day is an adventure providing the opportunity to embrace the infinite possibilities that life has to offer.

The loser that once spent his days on rat-infested railway embankments has given way to a therapist, author and inspirational speaker! Since quitting alcohol, I have travelled the world on various quests for knowledge, attained a degree in psychology, trained in many different facets of therapy, and spoke to large audiences about my experiences. Can you believe it? That homeless, pathetic, down-and-out now teaches psychology and holds seminars and workshops throughout the country: people actually pay to hear what he has to say! From having no bus-fare or bed to sleep in at night, he now stays in some of the most luxurious hotels in the world and drives a brand new Mercedes Benz!

Seriously, transforming the mental and emotional debris that gave rise to my destructive tendencies has become my wealth. Through the process, I realised my ultimate purpose in life – *to evolve my understanding of the mind and spirit and relay my findings to others.* I now know beyond a shadow of a doubt that there isn't anything that lies beyond the realms of possibility: I can achieve anything I want in life. To date, I have penned a novel – *Spirit of Adventure: Signposts from the Sacred Singularity* - and you are currently reading my second book. In the future I have plans to write a musical and various plays, write and record music, and continue to travel the world on my quest for knowledge. What an absolute joy it is to be alive! My sustained happiness and fulfilment stems from the knowing that I am a limitless, inexorable bundle of potential, capable of achieving anything I choose to focus on - and guess what? So are you!

As for the family, well, our bond has grown in a beautiful way. The pain and sorrow that once was, has been supplanted by laughter and joy. My parents and sister are my best friends today. Past experience served only to bring us much closer together.

Then, of course, there's my extended family - a wealth of close and intimate friends with whom I intend to walk hand-in-hand for the remainder of life's journey. I'd like to extend that invitation to you, my friends. I am a privileged guy, someone who found a way out of the denizens of despair to a life beyond his wildest dreams. I'd like you to come and join me on the journey **from Alcoholic to Alchemist** and realize your dreams too: it's a wonderful adventure.

Namaste, my friends,

Paul

Steve's Story

The best mind-altering drug is truth
Lily Tomlin

My drinking days seem like a lifetime ago now. Funny, isn't it, while you're in the throes of alcoholism there seems no way out, and then you release the habit and find it almost impossible to remember! I suppose that's comforting for those of you reading these words. Can you imagine going through the day without thinking of a drink? I always thought it impossible, but I've been free of those thoughts for almost twenty years now. That's what this book has to offer you: *freedom*.

I sincerely hope my story helps, particularly those of you who are apt to blame the past for abusive drinking. If, like me, you had a turbulent childhood, you should be seeking to avail yourself of all those things you missed out on: love, nurturance, encouragement, meaningful relationships, adventure, joy and happiness – instead of blaming the past. Holding the past responsible for current dilemmas simply results in further punishment: self inflicted punishment.

The unique philosophy outlined in the forthcoming pages taught me that it's never too late to have a happy childhood: *the child within is forever present and never ages*. The **Alcoholic to Alchemist Philosophy for Optimal Living** will help you process unresolved issues and set you free from the bondage of the past, enabling you to embrace the infinite possibilities life has to offer.

I was born in Liverpool, 1949. Abandoned at birth, I was placed in the care of a local Salvation Army children's care home. Two years later I was fostered out to an elderly couple who were brother and sister. After an initial settling in period, I found myself grateful for the stability my new home provided - at last, I had a place to belong.

Throughout school, however, I harboured an underlying sense of alienation from the other children. Wearing hand-me-down clothes that were more appropriate for someone five years my senior didn't help. Neither did being issued with a different coloured meal ticket from the rest of the pupils, advertising the fact that I was in receipt of free meals - it was highly embarrassing. As a result, I became a social outcast and the target of cruel ridicule.

As my foster parents were much older than the parents of other children my age, they were unable to participate in the normal leisure activities associated with family life. So I spent much of my time away from school alone, too.

My introduction to drink came very early in life. Every fortnight my foster parents received a delivery of Guinness and brandy from the local supermarket. When they weren't looking, I'd sneak the dregs from their glasses. I'll never forget the warm glow those dregs gave me; they lit up my insides. I was hooked from the very beginning.

Though life wasn't perfect, it was the best it had ever been. I had a roof over my head, I was well fed, and I had the dregs to lift my mood. Then, just after my eighth birthday, another bombshell descended: my foster-father started to sexually abuse me. Though it was wrong and obscene and I hated him for it, I never told anyone for fear of reprisals. I didn't want to be removed from the only home I'd ever known. Rather than risk being taken back to the children's home, I decided to suffer in silence. I'd also heard of other kids who'd been abused and no-one believed them; rather than being helped, they were punished. So I decided to keep it quiet. When things got tough, I hid some alcohol in my bedroom and that used to relieve the pain a little.

Two years later my dilemma deepened when my biological mother reappeared on the scene and demanded visiting rights. I was terrified: she was a total stranger. Nevertheless, she was granted rights.

On visiting days, my social worker would come to collect me. But, convinced my biological mother was going to take me away, I'd often run away and hide.

Alas, my fears were never recognised. My mother's actions only served to reinforce the underlying sense of rejection that constantly dogged my life. She'd promise me the earth: presents, cinema, holidays - then not even bother showing up for the visits. At the time, I wished I'd never set eyes on her again.

On reaching my teenage years the sexual abuse stopped abruptly. I'd had enough and vowed never to carry it out again. The look in my eyes was enough for my foster-father to back off. The subject was never again broached. I pushed it deep down into my unconscious and forgot all about it. Those experiences were not dead and buried, however: they were buried alive, and would manifest as destructive tendencies in the years to come.

The next few years were spent hanging around on street corners, drinking with some newfound friends - obliterating the memories of the past. We were rebels. As we put the world to rights, we justified our entitlement to get 'blitzed' and let off steam.

During this period I met Carol, my future wife. She was the friend I'd always wanted; we did everything together. With her by my side, the next few years were okay. I managed to get a few jobs here and there and earn some money for us to go the cinema and the beach. Still riddled with insecurities and low self-esteem, however, my drinking became progressively worse. I needed it to obliterate the past.

Aged eighteen, I found work as a refuse collector. Drinking and the job went hand-in- hand. I drank at lunch times then resumed for another heavy session after work. The more I drank, the more I wanted to drink: I'd never had enough. The downward spiral had started and there was seemingly no basement.

In 1970 my foster-mother died and it had a devastating effect on me. I drank relentlessly to obliterate the event from my mind. I didn't even remember getting married, and the kids coming along was a blur too – all five of them! Whilst Carol was at home tending to the kids, I'd be down some back alley, in a cemetery, or slouched in some other obscure place, getting out of my mind.

My behaviour had started to change radically. I'd always been a passive person, but now I was picking fights and arguments. My aggressive and unpredictable behaviour got me barred from most of the pubs I frequented, which is why I drank in back alleys. My only claim to fame is that I never won a fight in my life! I always ended up on the receiving end. I was hospitalized on numerous occasions. Bruised and battered after being beaten up or carrying other injuries sustained through drink. If I wasn't in hospital, I was usually in court or locked-up (for my own safety).

My predisposition to wet myself – a phenomenon stemming from a turbulent childhood – escalated with drink. I'd often awaken from a drunken stupor to find my trousers saturated in urine. This lack of control escalated rapidly, to the point where I'd be in a bar or club and someone would point out that I'd wet or soiled myself, but I just didn't care; I'd lost all self-respect and dignity.

Brawls, black-outs, family dysfunction, hospitals, court appearances, prison cells, and hard drinking were to be the story of my life for many years to come.

Epilogue

I met Paul in august 1992, when I entered a twelve step treatment programme. He was group leader and had a couple of years' sobriety under his belt at the time. From our first meeting an inexplicable bond materialized. The best label I can give to it is that of *'soul brothers'* – two kindred spirits destined to share the trials and tribulations of life together.

What transpired over the subsequent years was a wonderful, insightful adventure. I've never taken a drink in the nineteen years I've known Paul, which is a wonderful testimony to the effectiveness of the philosophy outlined in this book.

Today, I'm still employed in the same job I started all those years ago, that of refuse collector. I don't know how, but I must have been doing something right! Choosing to serve the public in such a humbling way keeps me grounded. Every time I remove rubbish from the streets, I'm reminded to keep my mind free of mental and emotional debris. The shift in conscious that transpired as a result of the self development work I underwent with Paul is nothing short of phenomenal. Not only do I embrace life to the full today, but I also have a remarkable relationship with my three sons, two daughters, and now, ex-wife, Carol, after earning back their love and respect.

Paul documented the psychological and spiritual techniques, as well as the interventions and practices we used to bring about the shift in consciousness needed to attain our true potential. During this work he identified several important factors that had been overlooked by many treatment programmes; new ways of being that *not only alleviated alcoholism, but enabled people to reach their true potential.* He always maintained that quitting drink was not enough. Alcohol is an escape vehicle used to flee from a life that's deemed unbearable. If we transformed our lives in such a way that they became exciting and alluring, there is no need for escape and the vehicle becomes redundant.

Paul was relentless in his mission. Not only did he travel the world talking to wise and enlightened people, he embarked on an in-depth exploration of his own inner domain. His commitment and dedication led to the revolutionary new philosophy you're now holding in your hands.

You are a miracle waiting to happen. If you adhere to the ideas set out within this book with equal fervour as that which you expended on the pursuit of alcohol, I guarantee your life will change beyond recognition. Believe me, it's a wonderful experience to see the light return to the eyes of your loved ones as they re-unite with the person they lost to alcohol many years ago. It's a joy to get up of a morning and know that the day will be filled with purpose and meaning. It's a joy to be alive and embrace the infinite possibilities this world has to offer.

Good luck, my friends,

Steve

The Twelve Step Philosophy for Optimal Living

The Twelve Step Philosophy
for Optimal Living

Step 1: Admit having developed a destructive alcohol habit as a consequence of attempting to escape the curriculum of life.

Step 2: Having crossed the Abreactive Threshold, we need to abandon the idea that alcohol provides a means of escape and supplant it with the following belief: *'The most effective way to escape our problems is to solve them.'*

Step 3: Come to accept that the locus of the problem was a mind infected with fear, futility, guilt and pain – the answer to which is a profound shift in consciousness.

Step 4: Aspire to invoke a major shift in consciousness by allowing life to unfold from the wisdom of our Indwelling Divinity.

Step 5: Live Life Consciously:

Step 6: Develop and sustain self-love through regular communion with our inner child.

Step 7: Make an inventory of all the kind and caring acts we've carried out throughout the course of our life - and/or – make an inventory of all the future kind and caring acts we intend to carry out.

Step 8: Forgive and be Free

Step 9: Identified our life's purpose.

Step 10: Daily meditation

Step 11: Continuing Development: This step is comprised of the following five components:
   i. Stay on purpose and continue to utilize our unique talents to serve the highest good of all we encounter.
   ii. Commune with our Indwelling Divinity on a daily basis
   iii. Frequently absorb inspirational literature with the objective of re-programming our mind.
   iv. Regularly transmit our intentions
   v. Continually affirm positive statements

Step 12: Having radically transformed our lives and actualized our optimal potential, we aspired to assist others in making the journey from Alcoholic to Alchemist.

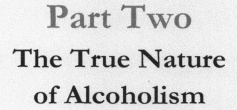

Part Two
The True Nature
of Alcoholism

The True Nature of Alcoholism

Understanding the true nature of alcoholism and exposing the unconscious forces that sustain it is the key to freedom.

The unconscious, as the term suggests, is that which lies beyond our conscious awareness – mental strategies that are so ingrained that they run independent of our conscious control. Mastering these forces is liberating; but how can we disarm an adversary we cannot see? The following topics are designed to bring your unconscious programming into the light of consciousness, thereby raising your awareness of the underlying psychological mechanisms that perpetuate your desire to escape:

- **What Causes Alcoholism?** (Chapter 1)
- **Alcoholism – the true nature of the phenomenon** (Chapter 2)
- **The underlying mechanics of addiction** (Chapter 3)
- **Crossing the invisible line** (Chapter 4)
- **The impact of unconscious programming** (Chapter 5)
- **The power of the labels we attach to ourselves** (Chapter 6)
- **A simple structure of the mind** (Chapter 7)

Chapter 1

What Causes Alcoholism?

The range of theories proposed to explain why certain people develop problems with alcohol is extensive. Although there's some evidence to support certain facets of these ideas, their impact is negligible: *there is absolutely no evidence to suggest a predeterminate for alcoholism.* By dispelling the myths surrounding alcoholism, this chapter will free you of all negative indoctrination.

To ascertain the underlying beliefs and influences that underpin destructive drinking is important. Far too often people subscribe to negative beliefs such as '*I've got an addictive personality*' or '*I suffer from the **illness** of alcoholism,*' without realizing the dire consequences.

Beliefs are powerful; they shape our lives. By identifying with these beliefs, you are inadvertently ushering yourself into a mind-set of powerlessness: ***I am ill or diseased, therefore I have no choice but to drink; it's an affliction.*** What rubbish! Internalizing negative ideas can, and often does, lead to self-fulfilling prophecy.

> ## Believe it and you'll achieve it

Your mind will always attempt to actualize what you continually impress upon it. So stop convincing yourself that you're diseased, ill or have an addictive personality, and start convincing yourself that you're a limitless bundle of potential, capable of attaining anything you desire.

Dispelling the Myths...

Internal Factors

The ideas examined here relate to the belief that some people develop problematic drinking as a result of some intrinsic abnormality; something that distinguishes them from '*ordinary people.*'

MYTH: **Alcoholism is a Psychiatric Illness or Disease**

Over the past twenty years the view that alcoholism is a disease or illness has been discredited; mounting evidence suggests that all the fundamental tenets are incorrect.

I appeal to the individuals and organisations who insist on supporting this view to think again. *What criteria is your view based on? What purpose does it serve?* From personal experience I am convinced that defining alcoholism as a disease or illness serves only to exacerbate the problem and place unnecessary mental obstacles in the way of sobriety.

To define alcoholism in terms of a disease or illness is both ludicrous and damaging; both terms denote something over which we have very little control; something that is inflicted upon us. If alcoholism is a disease or illness then the tens of thousands of people who have resolved their destructive drinking patterns must have had a disclaimer written into their anatomy; something along

45

the lines of: *if this person gets fed up with the illness of alcoholism then they can simply choose not to have it anymore!* Why else would they suddenly become exempt? They didn't undergo surgery or take a course of medication; they simply decided to resume control of their lives and dismiss all the negative doctrine that's irresponsibly bandied about.

For years, I too claimed to have a disease called *alcoholism:* a terminal disease, of course! What an ingenious way to relinquish all responsibility and wallow in self pity for the rest of my life. Wasn't I clever! Hadn't I pulled the wool over everybody's eyes? So clever, in fact, that I'd denied myself of an excellent quality of life - a life filled with adventure and infinite possibilities.

> ## Deceiving others simply denies *YOU* an excellent quality of life

Plying your mind with ideas of *illness* or *disease* simply reinforces the unconscious strategies that are destroying you. Your words act as bars that keep you imprisoned in a dungeon of denial. These theories are simply excuses masquerading as reasons. If you want to continue drinking, then do so - but don't delude yourself into believing that you are compelled to: *it is a choice.*

After changing my perspective and rejecting the illness and disease theories, I came to accept alcoholism as simply a polluted mind; a mind infected with fear, guilt, futility and pain. Subsequently, I set about re-programming the negative mental patterns that kept me bound and, quite magically, my life transformed beyond all recognition. I guarantee yours will too if you follow the guidelines laid out in the rest of this book.

FACT:
You do not have an illness or disease called alcoholism

FACT:
You are not abnormal

MYTH: **Alcoholic Personality Predisposes a Person to Drink**

Here it is supposed that there is a type of personality which predisposes some people to develop a problem. Although in-depth research has been conducted over a wide spectrum of areas, there is no evidence or consistent results to prove a *'pre-alcoholic'* personality. Claiming to have an *alcoholic or addictive personality* is simply another excuse to defend a habit that denies you of a wonderful life. Give it up!

FACT: You do not have an alcoholic personality: there is no such thing!'

MYTH: **Alcoholism is a *Physical* Allergy**

This view suggests that some people have an allergic reaction to alcohol; it suggests that *'alcoholics'* are *'normal'* until they consume alcohol - once they do, they trigger an allergic reaction which ignites a craving to drink more and more.

Although this theory is at the heart of the disease model of alcoholism, there is not one shred of evidence to back it up. Granted, once a person with an alcohol habit takes a drink, they do tend to crave more and more alcohol. But this is not the result of a physical abnormality; it is a symptom of an overwhelming need to escape: *a malfunction of the mind - not the body.*

FACT:
You do not have a physical allergy to alcohol;
You have an overwhelming desire to escape life.

Factors within the Social Context

The ideas presented in this section advocate the belief that people develop alcoholism as a result of learned behaviour or peer pressure.

Modelling Parents

There is some evidence to suggest that dysfunctional drinking can be handed down from generation to generation; approximately 40% of problem drinkers report having one or both parents who drink abnormally.

Parental behaviour is the single biggest influence on the long-term development of children. Parental attitudes and behaviour create values to which children adhere. Depending upon the degree of identification with the parental drinker, a child is more likely to follow in their footsteps.

Yet, with alcoholism there are innumerable exceptions to this rule. In fact, statistics show that most people with drinking problems do not have parents who abuse alcohol; and many people without a problem have parents who drink destructively. Therefore, problematic drinking is not predetermined by having parents with an alcohol problem.

FACT:
We don't have to accept what we have inherited!

FACT:
Any learned behaviour can be easily unlearned

FACT:
Most people with drinking problems do not have parents who drink abusively, and many children of such parents do not develop drinking problems.

FACT:
Dysfunctional drinking is not handed down from generation to generation - it is a choice made by the individual concerned

Genetic Vulnerability

Research in this area is fraught with problems and ambiguity. Although there is some evidence to suggest a possible genetic influence, the link can only be applied to a small percentage of problem drinkers. The research implies an increased risk of people developing a problem, but it certainly does not imply a predisposition to drink abusively.

I have personally facilitated the transformation of many people who have come from parents and grandparents who drank heavily. Without exception, they were able to recover in exactly the same manner as people who didn't have the so called *'genetic inheritance'*.

So what's the big deal? We can argue indefinitely as to the influence of genetic inheritance, but surely that would mean we were living in the problem. The Alchemist's objective is to live in the answer, and the fact remains that genetic inheritance does not affect the capability of a person to radically transform their life.

FACT:
Genetic inheritance does not predetermine alcoholism

FACT:
Genetic inheritance does not impede radical transformation

Unstable Home Environment

There is increasing evidence to support that an unstable home environment contributes to the likelihood of alcoholism. Parental conflict, parental absence, or early parental loss resulting from marital break-up can be major catalysts. Once again, however, there are innumerable cases that do not lend themselves to this theory; therefore, an unstable home environment is not a pre-determinate of alcoholism. Even in the cases where alcoholism does transpire as a result of people escaping negative childhood experience, it does not preclude them from radically transforming their lives.

Remember my friend, Steve? Left on a door-step at birth; ridiculed at school; sexually abused by his foster-father. He now lives a life beyond his wildest dreams. If he can radically transform his life, then so can you.

> **FACT:**
> **An unstable home environment does not pre-determine alcoholism**

> **FACT:**
> **People who have experienced unstable home environments often excel on our Twelve Step Philosophy for Optimal Living**

Peer Pressure

Peer pressure has a very strong influence on a person's development, especially during adolescence. People often model themselves on their peers, developing their attitudes and mimicking their behaviour. Alcohol has a wide range of socially ascribed meanings: maturity, masculinity, sexual desirability, and strength - all of which can be alluring to a young person desiring to be accepted by his peers. However, in reality, *abusive alcohol consumption leads to vomiting, diarrhoea, impotence, accelerated ageing, and brain deficiencies.* Alluring? I think not. Get real kids. Excessive use of alcohol will see you ostracized by your peers. Who wants to associate with an unpredictable menace, reeking of stale ale, urine and faeces?

FACT:
Peer pressure does not predetermine alcoholism

FACT:
Abusive alcohol consumption leads to diarrhoea, vomiting, and impotence not maturity, masculinity, sexual desirability, and strength

National and Cultural Conditions

So far our attempts to understand the origins of problematic drinking have been based on alleged predispositions or external influences. The ideas in this section change the focus, suggesting that people succumb to alcoholism due to the trials and tribulations of society as a whole.

Availability and Portrayed Image

This view suggests that the problem is simply the availability of the substance. It states that we are all at risk of developing alcohol-related problems simply by being exposed to alluring advertisements. Indeed, there exists some evidence to support this view. The number and range of alcohol-related problems within any given country appears to be directly proportional to the amount of alcohol consumed by its population. Holders of this view argue for reducing the positive profile of alcohol within our society.

However, if the positive profile of alcohol consumption was a pre-determinate for alcoholism then most of the population would succumb. *We are all exposed to advertisements for alcohol yet most people do not develop problems as a result.*

FACT:
Alcoholism is not predetermined by exposure to advertisements that portray alcohol in a positive light

Societal Problems

This final view suggests that social problems give rise to abusive drinking. Society is viewed as competitive, hostile and unfair; hence, it is argued that people drink excessively to escape their social conditions. They seek escape from things such as violence, unemployment, deprivation and poverty.

This proposal is perhaps the closest to the truth in that it identifies an inability or refusal to meet life's challenges as the root cause of alcoholism. Escapism is undoubtedly the underlying cause of all abusive drinking, but often it is a person's *perception* of life, not life itself, that poses the problem.

> **FACT:**
> **People do turn to alcohol to escape life's challenges, but often these problems are distorted interpretations of the mind. Alcohol doesn't provide a means of escape from such mental phenomena, it exacerbates it. If you are unhappy with your life, there are myriad of other choices available to you.**

Conclusion

Although these theories are useful in ascertaining certain factors that contribute to heavy drinking, none of them identify and address the root cause of alcoholism. They are all riddled with inconsistencies. Even in the cases were alcoholism has been linked to such 'causes', the process of transformation remains exactly the same. By adhering to these ideas you place the locus of control outside of yourself and become disempowered. In truth, they have very little credence. You can dispel alcoholism any time you choose. These theories constitute *excuses* not *reasons*.

> ## Live in the answer – not the problem.

Chapter 2

Alcoholism:
The True Nature of the Phenomenon

Defining Alcoholism

To date, explanations of the term *alcoholism* have been extremely
vague, misleading or ambiguous; some have even served to
compound the problem. As we have seen, definitions such as illness
and disease have been bandied about to describe the phenomenon;
if you use them, stop it now! You don't realise the damage you are
inflicting on yourself. Repeatedly telling yourself that you are
suffering from an impairment or deficit will programme your mind to
accept limitation and thwart your growth. This topic is of such
magnitude that I have addressed it at length in the forthcoming
pages, but for now let's continue defining and analysing the term
alcoholism.

Alcohol is a common term for ethanol, a compound produced
when glucose is fermented by yeast. The amount of yeast and
length of fermentation determines the alcohol content. Cider and
wine are made from fruit, while cereals such as barley and rye form
the basis of beer and spirits. Beer, wine, and spirits have the
capacity to alter a person's state of mind, which is why they are
categorised as *mind altering drugs.*

The suffix '*-ism*' denotes a distinct system of beliefs surrounding a topic. Therefore, the precise definition of the term *alcoholism* is as follows:

A distinct system of beliefs relating to alcohol

No mention of illness? No disease? No recovery? No dependency? No addiction? In fact, no direct reference to the abusive consumption of alcohol?

Alcoholism is in the mind: not in the bottle

Paradoxically, the failure of science to determine the root cause of alcoholism is indicative of its true nature - alcoholism cannot be measured or quantified simply because it is a maladaptive function of something which lies beyond the scope of scientific instrumentation: the mind. More specifically, it is an ingrained set of maladaptive beliefs that give rise to a constant cycle of destructive tendencies. The *symptom* - abusive alcohol consumption - is but a by-product of a deep underlying need to escape. Alcoholism is a mind-set - a destructive way of thinking - the answer to which is a profound shift in consciousness.

Alcoholism is an ingrained set of maladaptive beliefs that give rise to a constant cycle of destructive tendencies. Alcohol abuse is a mere symptom of an overwhelming desire to escape from a life that's deemed unbearable. Removing alcohol alone bears no fruits. To address the root problem one has to transform their world into a place that is alluring and purposeful, thereby removing the need to escape. The answer to alcoholism lies in educating and cultivating the mind so it recognises life as a journey of limitless possibilities.

The catalyst for alcoholism is an urgent need to escape, supported by a set of beliefs that erroneously deem alcohol to be the magic antidote to all life's problems. Alcohol is misconstrued as a vehicle that transports us from a state of mental persecution to a problem free, elevated state of mind. What rubbish! Let's stop deluding ourselves! The fact that you're reading this book refutes that myth:

When did alcohol last solve any of your problems?
Also
When did the removal of alcohol alone solve your problems?

The Seductive Illusion

Alcohol does not alleviate problems; it temporarily masks them. By impeding the transfer and consolidation of information in long-term memory, it induces temporary amnesia. However, temporarily suppressing our problems has an adverse cumulative effect. Continually denying our troublesome issues results in repression, a mechanism whereby problematic thought processes are banished to the realms of the unconscious mind. Although hidden, they are not dead and buried: *they are buried alive.*

Unresolved issues that have been banished to the realms of the unconscious are not dead and buried:
They are buried alive.

Suppressed energy must find a means of expression. These banished issues gather momentum in the realms of the unconscious and continue to impact our lives in ways that are both bewildering and destructive: phobias, mood swings, irrationality, paranoia, unpredictability, aggression, neuroses and psychosis. Alcohol abuse is symptomatic of an unsteady mind; a mind beleaguered with unresolved issues. Without a stable mind a person is unable to control their actions and is therefore prone to the following destructive cycle:

unresolved issues > repression > distorted thinking > severe moods swings > unbearable life > need to escape > consume alcohol > black-outs > irrational behaviour > paranoia and remorse > need to escape > consume alcohol

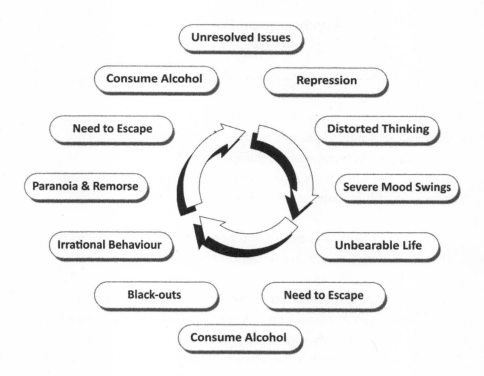

The Great Escape

People constantly deviate from their resolution to abstain from alcohol because they have a powerful incentive: **ESCAPISM.** But what are they escaping from? What is this force that they are unable to contain; the force that disables their firm resolve to quit?

Underlying all occurrences of alcoholism are what I have termed the Sobriety Saboteurs; destructive forces that manifest in four guises:

> **Fear**
> **Futility**
> **Psychological Pain**
> **Guilt**

You can expend energy on manipulating and controlling external events, but in doing so you are treating an *effect* or a *symptom* - not a *cause*. Until you have conquered the internal saboteurs, all efforts to transform your life will be to no avail. The external world is simply a reflection of the contents of your mind.

If you stood in front of a mirror and noticed a figure approaching with a knife, you wouldn't try to disarm the mirror image. Yet, metaphorically, this is exactly what people experiencing alcoholism tend to do - expend tremendous amounts of energy on trying to manipulate external circumstances in order to subvert a problem that lies within. Once they have yielded to their inner adversaries; when the sobriety saboteurs have drained their will-power and good intentions, they declare themselves powerless. But they are not powerless; they are misguided. They need to focus their energies within, not without.

Get into your mind: not out of it!

In the formative stages of alcoholism, alcohol consumption is akin to throwing water on a fire, it douses the flames of fear, futility, guilt and pain. However, this effect is extremely short lived; continuous abuse sees alcohol become the fuel which ignites unresolved issues; these, then spiral out of control. Don't delude yourself; don't fall into alcohol's seductive trap. Alcohol offers NO solution to your problems whatsoever:

The only way to escape your problems is to solve them

Chapter 3

The Underlying Mechanics of Addiction

The journey from **Alcoholic to Alchemist** is one of insight and understanding. We have to challenge the old doctrines in order to evolve our understanding of the fundamental mechanisms that underlie addiction. I get extremely angry when I see addiction defined in the following ways:

- Addiction is slavery.
- Addiction is a state in which one is powerless and out of control.

Language and thought are inextricably linked. Internalized vocabulary converts to linguistically structured thought, and thought is the software that programmes our minds. In the words of George Orwell:

"If thought corrupts language, language can also corrupt thought."

Alcoholism is a malfunction of the mind, and the mind is composed of thoughts. Since most of our thoughts result from internalized language, then it is imperative that we use language effectively. Deficient language is transposed into corrosive inner dialogue (which is the basis of negative programming).

When addiction is defined in terms of slavery and powerlessness, it subtly *instructs* our unconscious minds to *become* slave-like, relinquish power and surrender control. Addiction feeds on this kind of negative labelling.

Addiction isn't a process whereby a person cannot stop taking a substance: it is the person's *belief* that they cannot stop that is the problem.

> ## The locus of the problem is in the mind – not in the substance.

Our unconscious mind is akin to a faithful servant; we place an order and it responds without question. It doesn't determine whether our request will enhance or inhibit our lives; it has no analytical function whatsoever; it simply internalizes the words we impress upon it and responds accordingly, thus:

> ## Negative language gives rise to negative thought, which initiates life-denying action.

As our thought processes directly influence our body's chemistry, and subsequently, our body's chemistry determines both our health and our behaviour, mastery of language is a key variable in the art of radical transformation. We can re-programme our minds and radically change our thought processes by using language effectively. And since we are in the process of becoming what is prominent in our mind, we need to honour the power of the spoken word.

> ## As a man thinketh in his heart, so *is* he.
> Proverbs 23v7

The power of language is further compounded when we realise its influence on belief. Most beliefs stem from adhering to ideas that have entered our minds in the form of language. And beliefs are powerful; they shape our lives. Whatever we believe in whole-heartedly will come to pass. Whatever we hold prominent in our mind will actualize. This law has been known since time immemorial. Believe in failure and poverty and experience it. Believe in success and abundance and manifest it. Believe you are an alcoholic and severely restrict your potential. ***Belief is the midwife of actuality***. So cultivating our minds through supportive and nurturing language is essential for success and well-being.

"There is a law in psychology that says if you form a picture in your mind of what you would like to be, and you keep and hold that picture there long enough, you will soon become exactly what you have been thinking."

William James (1842 – 1910)

This insight also applies in reverse; that is, if you form a picture of what you *don't* want and keep it there long enough, it too will actualize. The problem is that most people do this unconsciously. Unaware of the consequences of holding a negative focus, they concentrate on the things they *don't* want in life and inadvertently birth them into existence.

The information above can be condensed and translated as follows:

- **Talk slavery – think slavery – become a slave.**
- **Talk of powerlessness – think powerlessness – relinquish your power.**
- **Talk of alchemy – think radical transformation – actualize your true potential.**

So now, with your newfound knowledge, let's re-define the exact nature of addiction and remove the power-loaded vocabulary that keeps you stuck.

Addiction isn't something we've been afflicted with; it is not something that has been unwittingly thrust upon us; it is not a process by which we are enslaved to a substance; it is not an illness; it's not a state of powerlessness: **it is a HABIT**. By definition, rather than being something we are powerless over, a habit is something *we* have formulated: something we have taught ourselves to do. If we have taught ourselves to do it, then, unequivocally, we have the power to change it.

A habit is something we have taught ourselves to do; if we have taught ourselves to do something, then, unequivocally, we have the power to change it.

Earlier on I posed the question – *how can we disarm an adversary we cannot see?* This question is indicative of the reason why many people mistakenly believe they are powerless over alcohol. The mental software that propels our addictive actions operates from beyond the conscious threshold; mental strategies that are so deeply ingrained that they no longer require mental deliberation or conscious control. The absence of conscious control creates the illusion that *something* or *someone* other than ourselves is responsible for our actions: they happen despite using our will-power to oppose them. But will-power is no match for the power of our unconscious mind. The strategies etched into our unconscious are rigidly ingrained after years of use, so they will always override our conscious intent. But we must remember that as we were responsible for programming our unconscious mind in the first place, we *can* re-programme it.

Rather than being at the mercy of some mysterious disease, illness, or personality defect, we have fallen victim to our own negative self talk. Through ineffective language we have programmed our unconscious mind to execute strategies that drive us to drink; strategies that operate automatically, without intervention from the conscious mind. This process is called **habituation.** A habit is a set of unconscious instructions which are executed automatically whenever a specific stimulus is encountered (these stimuli will be discussed in chapter 15, p.144). Remember all those vows you made never to drink again, only to find yourself back in the depths of despair after experiencing yet another relapse? The process crept up on you so subtly that you were totally bewildered as to how and why? This is the work of maladaptive unconscious programming: baffling and destructive. Let's look at an example.

Example:

On his last bender, Geoff, who was usually a placid person, went into work and physically abused his boss; he was immediately dismissed. Two days later, full of remorse, he returned home to face his wife and children. After seeing the deep sadness and fear in their eyes, he made a solemn vow never to drink again. The following day, when the anaesthetic effects of alcohol had worn off, his guilt accentuated to such an extent that he couldn't bear it any longer. The next half hour was a whirl of confusion; his mind blitzed by persecutory thoughts. To his utter despair, he found himself in an alley knocking back half a bottle of vodka.

When faced with intense guilt (a Sobriety Saboteur), Geoff needed a means of escape. Although he vowed in all earnestness never to drink again, and although he loved his family dearly, his mind reverted to an escape strategy that had been firmly impressed upon it over many years. Geoff's conscious will-power – his vow not to drink – was no match for the power of his unconscious programming, so he relapsed.

But do not despair; do not be duped into thinking you are powerless to prevent relapse. The underlying strategies that drive you to drink are still under your jurisdiction; don't forget – *you devised them in the first place*. These mental processes were originally installed *by you* with a positive intention. They served to enhance amiability and sociability, instil confidence, aid relaxation, and relieve stress – seducing you into progressively consuming more alcohol. But once you crossed that invisible line - the *Abreactive Threshold* (see next chapter) - these strategies became destructive and life-denying. Having such a large investment in escapism, however, you have never reviewed and revised them. But now that time has arrived. To change these negative strategies you need to heighten your awareness and identify the triggers, consciously change your response, and consequently, begin to re-programme your unconscious mind.

Chapter 4

Crossing the Invisible Line

The Abreactive Threshold

People often say *'I've crossed the invisible line'* to describe their demise into alcoholism; but what exactly are they referring to?

Habitual abuse of alcohol leads to greater tolerance. As tolerance increases, the harder it becomes to attain respite from the persecutory thoughts that warrant escape. The feelings of liberation, relaxation, peace, omnipotence, ecstasy and euphoria once attained through alcohol are lost forever.

The objective of alcohol abuse is to *get out of your mind;* a statement that highlights the real problem: *an urgent need to escape the chaotic contents of your psyche.* Many individuals misguidedly move house, change jobs, go on holiday, and embark on new relationships in an attempt to escape their troubles, but they forget: *they take their heads with them.* Diversions such as these are futile: problems located in the mind have a tendency to follow people wherever they go! When their distractive ploys fail, they seek asylum in alcohol. Initially, it appears to work; their troubles magically abate. The seductive trap has been set and their drinking escalates. But alcohol hasn't alleviated anything; it has simply suppressed the troublesome contents of their mind – hidden them out of sight.

At this stage alcohol acts as a damn pushing back the polluted reservoir of their mind. As drinking progresses, however, alcoholic amnesia escalates and gives rise to instability. As a consequence, their unconscious mind is replenished with more and more emotional and mental debris. Eventually the pressure becomes so great that alcohol can no longer contain the build-up of unresolved issues and they come flooding from the unconscious to the conscious with the might of a tsunami. This is the point of no return. The Abreactive Threshold has been compromised and the effects are irreversible. Alcohol no longer gets them *out of their minds*: it locks them into them. Now, with their escape route cut off and nowhere to run, they become unpredictable entities. Driven by the persecutory tactics of their turbulent minds they lose control. All subsequent bouts of drinking lead to abreaction: severe mood swings, paranoia, intense guilt and suicidal tendencies are very common.

Out of the thousands of people I've met who have abused alcohol, not one has crossed the Abreactive Threshold and returned to drink normally. The phenomenon is very similar to an allergy that remains dormant for years and is then activated when a person crosses the Abreactive Threshold. After crossing this *invisible line,* all subsequent bouts of drinking lead to abreaction on a physical, emotional and mental level – or any combination of the three.

It always intrigues me to observe that a person with an allergy to nuts doesn't decide to control his nut consumption for fear of death by anaphylactic shock. Yet so many people who have crossed the Alcoholic Abreactive Threshold insist on trying to control their consumption of booze, despite the obvious threat of destruction, insanity or death.

The Abreactive Threshold is a phenomenon whereby alcohol ceases to contain your mental pollution and it comes flooding from the unconscious to the conscious with the might of a tsunami.
Once compromised, there is no reverse engineering - the invisible line has been crossed and you and drink remain incompatible for life.

Chapter 5

Stop HARMing Yourself

The Habituated Automatic Response Mechanism (H.A.R.M)

Addiction can be described as a **H**abituated **A**utomatic **R**esponse **M**echanism; the cyclic execution of a set of subliminal mental strategies that are designed to transport us from inner turmoil to a psychological sanctuary – the chosen method of transportation being the substance of choice (e.g. heroin, cocaine – or in our case, alcohol). Our H.A.R.M. operates as follows:

> Feel *fear* - drink
> Feel *guilt* - drink
> Feel *pain* - drink
> Feel *bored* - drink

On encountering one of these primary triggers, our unconscious strategies are automatically executed and propel us towards oblivion. To illustrate how the process works, let's take the example of flying an aircraft.

At the flick of a switch a pilot can put an aircraft into auto-pilot mode – a navigational mechanism that automatically maintains a preset course. The course is governed by a set of instructions that have been programmed into the aircraft's computer system. Although the aircraft is under the temporary control of the computer system, the pilot maintains ultimate control. To avert disaster, he can turn off the auto-pilot system *and resume manual control at any point in time.*

Metaphorically speaking, the same principle applies to addiction. Our **H**abituated **A**utomatic **R**esponse **M**echanism is a preset list of mental instructions that sets us on a pre-determined course of destruction. It is comprised of the following three components:

> **A Trigger.**
> **Maladaptive core beliefs.**
> **Desired outcome.**

1. **A Trigger** (the auto-pilot switch): **a stimulus that switches a person from rational, conscious processing to destructive, unconscious processing.**

   Alcoholism is triggered by an internal or external event which activates a need for escape. Triggers manifest in four fundamental ways: fear, guilt, pain or futility (see sobriety saboteurs p.144), all other manifestations are derivatives of these.

> *Example – Fear trigger. First light pierces the curtains. Robert fidgets restlessly in his sweat saturated bed. He is paralyzed with fear as persecutory thoughts bombard his mind: What happened last night? Who did I insult? Did I embarrass myself? Was I aggressive? Did I get into trouble? Fear and paranoia escalate and his shaking hands reach for his trousers which are strewn beside his bed. Has he got any money? He needs to banish the persecution from his mind; he cannot bear it. He needs to escape: he needs alcohol.*

In this example, Robert's need for escape is a direct result of alcoholic amnesia (black-out). He cannot remember the previous night which gives rise to persecutory thoughts that warrant escape. Fear acts as the auto-pilot switch, handing control of his rational, conscious mind over to an adversely conditioned part of his unconscious mind which houses the next stage of the H.A.R.M. – the maladaptive core beliefs (the '-ism').

2. Maladaptive Core beliefs – the ('-ism'):

Remember, the suffix '-ism' means *a set of beliefs relating to* whatever precedes it; in our case – alcohol. So alcoholism is defined as **a set of beliefs relating to alcohol**. Understanding this stage of the H.A.R.M. is crucial in our quest to alleviate alcoholism. As a fruit never re-ripens once it has decomposed, so the core beliefs of alcoholism never return to fruition after a person has crossed the Abreactive Threshold. If you consume a fruit that's past its sell-by date, it is liable to poison you. Likewise, if you adhere to the maladaptive beliefs central to alcoholism once you have crossed the Abreactive Threshold (the point at which alcohol induces an abnormal reaction), they will poison your mind. Herein lies the problem: *people* **do** *adhere to these beliefs after crossing the threshold.*

When people encounter a situation that warrants escape, they regress to the past and remember the impact that alcohol **used** to have on their minds: *not the impact it has* **now**. This is why I refer to the core beliefs as maladaptive; they have never been *adapted* to reflect the destructive impact of alcohol on the mind *currently*. After crossing the Abreactive Threshold, these beliefs no longer hold true: they become destructive myths that seduce you into relapse.

Destructive Myths

- Alcohol will improve the way I feel.
- Alcohol will improve my state of mind.
- Alcohol will eradicate my pain, fear, and guilt
- Alcohol will put the excitement back into my futile life
- Alcohol will instil confidence and enhance my sociability
- Alcohol will relax me
- Alcohol is a cure for all problems

So now we have the trigger (an event that warrants escape), which leads to the seductive lure of the core beliefs, which leads to the third stage of the H.A.R.M. - the desired outcome.

3. **Desired Outcome:** alleviation of problems – ESCAPE. Every mental strategy has an intended outcome. The final mission of the H.A.R.M. is to transport the mind to a better place: a psychological sanctuary. This pursuit can be summed up in one word: ESCAPISM. Thus, the person reaches for the bottle. Unfortunately, however, after crossing the Abreactive Threshold, the promise of escape via the bottle turns out to be nothing other than a seductive scam. Drink no longer transports the person from the undesirable state evoked by the trigger, to the psychological sanctuary promised by the core beliefs: it transports them into hell.

**The goal of every addiction is to transport the mind to a better place: a psychological sanctuary.
In the formative stages it may succeed; however, habitual use leads to the initiation of dormant forces, which on awakening, transform heaven into hell.**

Summary

Addiction and auto-pilot mode are very similar; both are comprised of a set of programmed instructions that are designed to transport you from one place to another. With addiction the destination is psychological and the instructions are programmed into your unconscious mind. Alcohol is a vehicle that is designed to transport you from inner turmoil to a psychological sanctuary. Whenever you encounter fear, futility, pain or guilt (the triggers), you *switch* from conscious functioning to a preset list of unconscious instructions. These subliminal directives then act as a navigational system to steer you towards the goal of *escape*.

However, after crossing the Abreactive Threshold, the system begins to malfunction and you find yourself being transported into the past when alcohol functioned in a different way – a time when the core beliefs held true. You drink in the belief that alcohol will alleviate your problems, but it exacerbates them and mental mayhem ensues. However, as a pilot can resume manual control of the aircraft at any point in time, so *you can regain control of your life at any time*. By bringing your hidden destructive patterns out into the light of consciousness, you can process and eradicate them.

**Are you ready to avert disaster,
turn off the auto-pilot system,
and resume control of your life?**

Chapter 6

The Impact of Unconscious Programming

The mind is composed of two interrelated components: the *conscious* and the *unconscious*. The conscious element is responsible for processing the continuous stream of information that bombards us each day: pictures, sounds, feelings, tastes and smells; it analyses and evaluates this information then devises strategies for responding to it.

A strategy, in this context, is a sequence of internal representations (sounds, images, feelings etc.) that lead to an action. For example, you may see food and feel a hunger pang; a mental image of your favourite food then appears on your internal screen. This, in turn, leads to a voice in your head saying '*I must eat*,' and your taste buds start to water. This sequence of events then propels your body to take action and you seek out the nearest restaurant. Thus, thought undergoes a sequence of unfolding to become action.

Example: Strategy

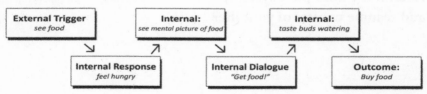

The stimulus, the hunger pang, initiates a sequence of internal representations – feelings, sounds, pictures, tastes – that propel your physical body to manifest your desire (i.e. eat). Because of the conscious mind's limited capacity to handle information, when a strategy has been tried and tested repeatedly, control is handed over to the unconscious mind. When we execute a strategy without any conscious deliberation; that is, when a strategy initiates automatically, it is said to be ***habituated*** or a **habit**. Every habit has a desired outcome. Unconscious strategies are servomechanisms that automatically steer towards their targets. With alcoholism the target is invariably escape, but the strategies that drive it are outdated and give rise to despair and destruction.

Example: Joan

Due to excessive alcohol abuse, Joan's children were put into care. Initially, she clung to sobriety for three months, desperately wanting to be re-united with her family. Each day, however, images of her distraught children bombarded her mind, accompanied by the shouts of 'mummy, mummy' as they were being chaperoned away. Eventually, it all got too much for Joan and her destructive strategies began to seduce her. An image of a bottle of whisky entered her mind, along with an internal voice that whispered 'all your problems will disappear if you drink.' Her mind became fixated on these outdated strategies. As the internal images became more pronounced, and the inner voice became more prominent, a feeling of desperation arose. Consequently, Joan pawned her bracelet, purchased a bottle of scotch and proceeded to purge the problems from her mind.

Epilogue:

Alcohol never solved Joan's problems: it exacerbated them. Her children were in care for a further two years. In the interim period, she was hospitalized on eleven separate occasions after experiencing alcohol induced fits. She was also evicted from her accommodation for rent arrears. With no home and escalating irrational behaviour, there seemed little hope of ever re-uniting with her children. However, when Joan hit rock bottom, the internal alchemist emerged. Once again she was admitted to hospital for detoxification. This time, however, on being discharged, she vowed to transform her life. Using many of the techniques outlined in this book, Joan's life improved beyond all recognition. She trained as an alternative therapist with the view to working from home. After two years sobriety she proved to the authorities that she was more than capable of taking care of her children. Mother and family were re-united and took up residence in a new home - a rented house with a garden close to the sea. Joan built up a steady client base for her business which provided her with stability, fulfilment and enough finance to treat the children to a couple of holidays a year. With commitment and determination, Joan secured the love of her children and they are extremely happy today. Three years ago, Joan met Peter, who became a father-figure to the children. Later this year the couple will marry.

The negative strategies driving Joan's alcoholism - internal pictures and negative inner dialogue - kept her locked into the problem. As she sought escape from the painful contents of her mind, her awareness regressed to a time when alcohol anesthetized her pain; she was seduced by the '-ism' – the out-dated set of beliefs which promised salvation. This destructive strategy constantly persecuted her, recycling in her mind until she eventually relented and relapsed. However, in the midst of major crisis came a moment of sanity. The Sobriety Saboteurs gave way to the Alchemist and Joan aspired to radically transform her life. Subsequently, she set about re-programming her mind and formulating new life-enhancing strategies.

Joan formulated a vision of where she wanted to go in life and devised the mental strategies to support it. She practiced and habituated these new strategies. As a consequence, her corrosive inner dialogue gave way to the 'Wise Witness Within' and her new life was actualized.

Joan is one of our numerous success stories – *are you are next?*

Chapter 7

Check the Label
Is It Past the Sell-By Date?

The labels we attach to ourselves have the power to programme our unconscious mind. The unconscious mind doesn't question the commands and orders it receives, it simply executes them. If you continuously impress upon it the idea that you are stupid, then it will respond by formulating and executing the necessary mental strategies to ensure that you look stupid! Remember, the majority of your thoughts have arisen from internalizing conversations; therefore, *words form the basis of your cognitive (mental) programming.* The words you are reading write now are revising your thought processes and installing new cognitive strategies in your mind. So words are extremely powerful: they cause a shift in your thinking. With this in mind, let us now consider the effects of identifying with the following labels:

- **I am an alcoholic**: By identifying the whole of your personality - *I am* - with a deficit or impairment – alcoholic - you are instructing your unconscious mind to impose strict limitations on your potential as a human being. **Dispense with this negative self-talk: it feeds alcoholism.**

- **I am alcohol dependent:** This statement reaffirms to your unconscious mind that, in order to get through the day, you must imbibe alcohol. And what happens when you imbibe alcohol? You embark on a journey of unpredictability that usually leaves behind a trail of devastation and heartache. **Stop telling yourself you need alcohol: you don't!**

- **I am in recovery:** I still hear people making this statement after twenty and thirty years' sobriety – and they believe it whole-heartedly: I did it myself for many years. The consequences are plainly evident: stagnation and restriction. Although these people have abstained from alcohol for many years, they have inadvertently programmed their unconscious minds to accept limitation. The term 'in recovery' translates to *not yet capable of my full potential*. Remember, the unconscious mind is a faithful servant: it doesn't discriminate or analyse; it doesn't discern what's best for you; it just accepts your beliefs – negative or positive. As belief is the midwife of actualization - the process by which the contents of your mind become reality (actual) - then you need to align your belief system in accordance with your desires.

Impressing negative terminology on your mind will place boundaries on your true potential. Why compromise your true essence which is boundless and beyond restriction.

> ## Negative labeling is the glue that keeps you stuck

May I be as bold as to suggest a substitute for the aforementioned negative labels?...

I am an Alchemist

By identifying with this label you are informing your unconscious mind of your boundless nature and limitless potential; plying it with ideas of optimum functioning and transformation. You are suggesting that the best way to escape your problems is to solve them. When problems are perceived as challenges, the world is transformed into an adventure playground filled with opportunities to evolve.

Are your labels past their sell-by date?
Remember:

> **A negative label will disable**
> **A positive label will enable**

Chapter 8

Will Power Versus Won't Power:
The Basis of Relapse

Millions of people have made a solemn vow never to drink again, only to find themselves back in the depths of despair after yet another relapse – Totally bewildered, they ask themselves '*How has this happened, again?*' Well, there's quite a simple explanation. The vow they made is dependent on *will-power* – a function of the conscious mind based on intent. Although their pledge to abstain is made in all earnestness, conscious intent is no match for the power of the unconscious mind. Unconscious strategies will always preside over conscious intent, unless conscious intent is empowered with the propulsion force of *motivation*.

If sufficient motivation fuels the conscious intent to implement a new strategy, and the new strategy is practiced repeatedly, then the negative strategy will be overridden and a positive mental shift will take place. To clarify the procedure, let's take the example of driving.

When learning to drive, we expend a considerable amount of conscious effort on learning the procedures necessary to propel the car: dip the clutch, choose gear, press the accelerator, and so on. After practicing continuously, the process becomes automated – *second nature*. This is because the procedures have now been transferred to the unconscious mind, freeing up the conscious mind to attend to other things. Now, imagine that for some reason, the law changed so that the clutch and accelerator pedals exchanged places on all vehicles. Inevitably, drivers would be thrown into disarray; once again they would have to expend much conscious effort on coordinating the movements necessary to propel the car. Inevitably, mistakes would be made as people reverted to the way in which they'd driven for years. However, with perseverance, their conscious effort would eventually establish a new norm and supplant the existing unconscious programme.

Relapse operates according to the same principles. Conscious intent – **will-power** - is prone to be overridden by ingrained unconscious strategies which have been in place for years – **won't power.** Couched in terms of alcoholism, the conscious intention to quit after abusive drinking is prone to failure unless we have sufficient motivation to propel us into a new mind-set.

Motivation: The Force that Directs Our Behaviour

Motivation can be defined as a driving force which initiates and directs behaviour; it is an intrinsic energy that propels a person to take action. Motivation is directional; it either propels you **towards** what you *want,* or **away from** what you **don't** *want.*

To override the rigid conditioning of your unconscious mind, you need to fuel your will-power with both **toward** and **away from** motivation. Most people who pledge to give up drinking utilize *away from* motivation only; that is, they want to move away from hurting their loved ones; or they want to move away from constantly feeling ill; or they want to move away from being constantly broke. But *away from* motivation alone is rarely enough to sustain sobriety; at best, it may produce some short-term success. When the family has been appeased or good health restored, then lack of direction normally results in stagnancy - and stagnancy and futility are invitations to relapse. They have *moved away* but they have nothing to *move toward.*

To successfully transform your life you need direction and purpose; a plan for the future that will provide the motivation to propel you forward. Let's look at another of our incredible success stories.

> ### Example: Andrew's Story
> - **motivation plus will power leads to success.**
>
> Andrew had relapsed on many occasions. Although he tried his best to abstain from drinking, he found himself returning to the bottle (he was constantly overpowered by the destructive programs of his unconscious mind). It seemed that whenever he felt afraid, guilty, anxious, or that life wasn't worth living (Sobriety Saboteurs), his old habits (Habituated Automatic Response Mechanism) would kick in and initiate the stinking thinking (corrosive inner dialogue) that would put him back on the road to destruction. Eventually, he admitted defeat and turned up at my office.
>
> After chatting to him for a while, it became plainly evident that he adored his wife and their two young daughters. To date, these had been his sole source of his motivation; he wanted to move *away from* hurting them. On several occasions he'd stopped drinking for periods of six months to one year. Initially, the joy and relief on the faces of his family had sustained his motivation to stay away from alcohol. Lack of direction, however, would eventually leave him feeling inadequate and incapable of giving his family the niceties he thought they deserved. Being unemployed for six years had also left him lacking in confidence. So although the *away from* motivation gave him some success, the lack of *toward motivation* would eventually take its toll and he would relapse.
>
> Andrew needed something to aim toward; something to develop his self worth and breathe inspiration into him: he needed a *purpose*. I suggested that he complete the values elicitation exercise on p.231 in order to identify the attributes,

concepts and qualities that were most important to him. After completing the exercise, he discovered that the thing he valued most was the respect of his family; something he hadn't had in years. This objective became the *toward* motivating force that was absent in his earlier attempts to quit drinking.

Andrew had always been interested in Information Technology, and, when sober, he was a logical man and a good mathematician. These two attributes seemed to be his strength, so he decided to put them to use by embarking on an Open University Degree in computer science. He thrived on the challenge and attained excellent grades. On graduation, he secured a job in a local University as a programmer. Over a number of years he rose to the position of team leader with an annual income of forty thousand pounds plus! Not only did he gain the respect of his colleagues for the compassion and understanding he showed in his role, but he gained the much desired respect of his family.

Andrew is a classic example of someone who used ***away from*** and ***toward*** motivation to support his will power and overcome the rigid programming of his unconscious mind: he is a true Alchemist.

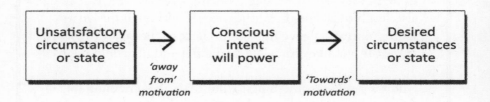

Chapter 9
Why Dr Jekyll becomes Mr Hyde

Now we have educated ourselves as to the mechanisms of the mind that give rise to conditioning and habituation, it's time to look at the impact of alcohol on our ability to sustain an acceptable way of behaving.

Alcohol is a *mind altering drug*. Consequently, it is capable of changing a mild-mannered, honourable person into an unpredictable, aggressive menace.

This chapter will investigate the underlying mechanisms involved in this process.

How Exactly Does Alcohol Alter the Mind?

I have addressed this question from two perspectives; firstly, through neurology - the study of the brain - and secondly, through psychoanalysis, using a structural theory of the mind proposed by eminent psychoanalyst Sigmund Freud – so prepare yourself for a psychology lesson!

Alcohol and Our Neurology

The brain has a filtering system designed to protect us from drugs by allowing only water to cross the blood-brain barrier. However, as the molecular structure of alcohol is similar to that of water, the filtering system is easily compromised and alcohol enters the brain. Since the brain controls essential functions such as speech, judgment and perception, the results can be hazardous. The longevity and intensity of the effects vary, depending on the amount of alcohol in the bloodstream.

Once alcohol reaches the frontal lobe of the brain, loss of reason and inhibitions occur. Initially, this can feel liberating, masking the troubles that warrant escape and leading to a temporary and illusory sense of well-being. However, don't be seduced by this mirage; it is fraught with problems. Without the faculty of reason to marshal our behaviour, we lack self-restraint and become unpredictable entities. One minute we're amicable, social people, the next, aggressive, irresponsible nuisances – a phenomenon often referred to as the *Jeckyll and Hyde syndrome.*

After the effects of alcohol wear off, many people cannot cope with the consequences of their previous bizarre behaviour. Their subsequent anxiety usually creates a need to escape again – and so the destructive cycle continues.

Alcohol and the Id, the Ego and the Superego

Eminent Psychoanalyst, Sigmund Freud, devised a theoretical structure of the mind that consists of three components: the **Id**, the **Ego** and the **Superego**. As the mind is abstract and intangible, such models are very useful in attaining a workable understanding of the possible mechanisms involved. Freud's Structural Theory is extremely useful for aiding our understanding of the imbalances involved when the mind is saturated with alcohol.

The Id

According to Freud, the Id is that part of the mind that houses our basic drives and instincts. One important aspect of his findings, in relation to our investigation of alcoholism, is that the Id is said to act in accordance with the ***pleasure principle***: *seeking to avoid pain or displeasure and attain instant gratification.* For example, when we're hungry the Id will seek to eat. Being instinctive and animalistic in nature it is not considerate of other people or context. If you were hungry and another person passed by eating food, the Id may well respond by snatching the food from their hands, instantly satisfying its own craving. As this sort of behaviour is socially unacceptable, the Id needs to be policed by another component of the mind.

The Superego

The Superego is that part of the psyche that is often referred to as the ***conscience.*** Freud referred to it as the internalised parental figure, having the primary function of instilling discipline. The Superego houses the morals, ethics, laws, rules and standards which have been impressed upon us by our parents and society as a whole. For obvious reasons, the Superego or conscience is often in direct opposition to the animalistic disposition of the Id. The Superego's job is to tame the basic instinctual drives of the Id so that civilized behaviour is maintained. Returning to the example I used earlier, when the Id is intent on taking food off the by-passer in the street, the Superego will impose its moral standards and intervene.

The Ego

The Ego is that part of ourselves that we often refer to as *I;* our concept of ***self.*** The primary function of this part of the mind is to interface between the primary instincts of the Id, the moral standards of the Superego, and external reality. The ego operates based on what has been termed the ***reality principle,*** which strives to satisfy the Id's desires in socially acceptable ways (i.e. in accordance with the standards set by the Superego). The Ego discerns the costs and benefits of an action before deciding to act upon or overrule the impulses.

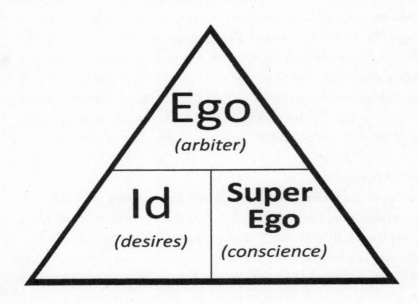

Putting it all together

To illustrate the way in which the three constituent components of Freud's theory interact, let's refer back to the example of the by-passer on the street:

You feel hungry and a person passes you in the street eating food. The Id springs into action and says *'grab it off him - quick. I'm starving. I need food: now!'* To which the Superego replies *'now, now, you know that's wrong. That's stealing; it's unacceptable behaviour.'* The Ego listens carefully to the two conflicting elements and takes arbitrary measures, *'okay'* it says, *'you're hungry, Id, but let's do this the correct way — a way that's acceptable to the society we live in. We'll go to the bank, draw out some cash, and find the nearest café.'* Hence, the Id's primary instinct of hunger has been satisfied by the Ego with adherence to the moral code set out by the Superego.

Relating the Theory to Alcoholism

Alcoholism invokes an imbalance of this system in which the instincts of the Id predominate over the social standards of the Superego and negatively manipulate the Ego. The Id's primary function is to avoid pain and displeasure and seek instant gratification. It has learnt that alcohol is extremely efficient when it comes to alleviating displeasure in the form of pain, futility, guilt and fear. In the early stages of alcoholism, the Superego will play a role in influencing the Ego to obtain alcohol through moral and ethical means; it will also ensure that the behaviour of the person conforms to socially acceptable standards. However, as alcohol consumption escalates, the system becomes imbalanced and dysfunctional. The influence of the Superego diminishes and is overridden by the Id's preoccupation with avoiding displeasure.

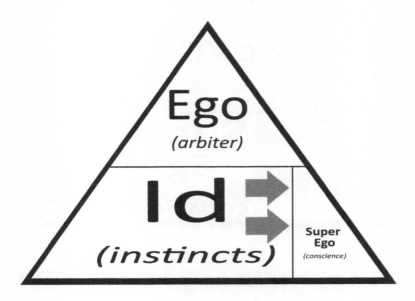

The Ego is then consumed by the antisocial influence of the Id and all hell breaks loose. The person no longer cares how he/she obtains alcohol: beg, steal, or borrow. Without the guiding force of a conscience and the evaluative expertise of the Ego, self-restraint breaks down and behaviour becomes irrational and unpredictable. When the effects of inebriation wear off, the consequences are difficult to face, and so the need to escape heightens.

The Consequences

As inebriation subsides, the Superego is reinstated. The return of the conscience is often a daunting time for the drinker: a time of intense guilt and remorse. As the Superego forcefully reaffirms its position in the psychic triad, it has a tendency to over-compensate for its absence by becoming over-active and oppressive.

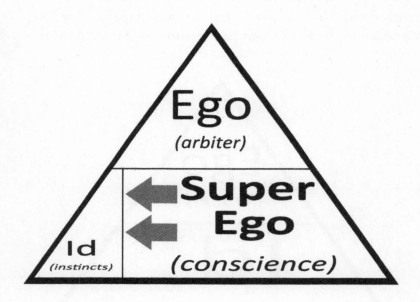

This often leaves the individual concerned with an overwhelming sense of regret. The accompanying guilt is often all-consuming, propelling the drinker back to the bottle. This subject is of such importance that I have dedicated a whole section to it – see Sobriety Saboteurs (p.144).

Chapter 10
Don't Fight or Fear Alcoholism –
Understand the Mind

Before we press on with the remainder of the philosophy, I would like to discourage you from developing a *fight* or *flight* attitude towards alcohol. There is no need to set your mind up for a war or be terrified of alcohol; it will impede your progress. Simply intending to understand the mechanisms of the mind will suffice.

No Fighting

Words are powerful tools for programming the mind. When we affirm to ourselves that we are going to *fight alcoholism*, we plant ideas of battles and difficulties in our mind; this is liable to bring about a self-fulfilling prophecy. We don't have to fight anything, we just need to understand. The word *understand* primes the mind in a way that promotes open-mindedness and wisdom – it puts the mind at ease and consequently makes it more efficient. Understanding involves no resistance, whereas *fighting* does; and resistance places strain on our resources. To illustrate the significance of this fact, read (and feel the full force), of the following two statements:

'I will fight my alcoholism and survive'
'I will understand my mind and radically transform my life'

Did you feel yourself getting up tight when reading the first statement? Jaw clenched? Make a fist? Did the second statement imbue you with a sense of relaxed optimism? Don't set yourself up for an unnecessary war; choose your words wisely.

No Fearing

Relapse is often associated with the myth that alcohol is cunning, baffling and powerful – no! No! No! it can't be: a liquid is not endowed with such capabilities. It is the unpredictability of your mind that's cunning, baffling and powerful.

> *The adage that alcohol is cunning, baffling*
> *and powerful is a myth;*
> *a liquid is not endowed with such capabilities:*
> *It's your mind that's cunning, baffling and powerful*

Let's get this absolutely clear! Your mind initiates the mental strategies that lead to the physical action of drinking; it does this in response to threats of fear, pain, guilt and futility. When the Sobriety Saboteurs reach an unbearable threshold, your desire to escape outweighs your desire to stay with reality. Misguidedly, you assume that alcohol will transport you to an inner sanctuary where all problems abate (as it once did). But once you have crossed the Abreactive Threshold there is no escape. Psychological sanctuary is supplanted by mental mayhem as alcohol hurls you into the Abreactive Abyss. When thoughts of escape arise, recognise that your awareness has regressed to what *used to be*, not to *what is currently. To address the root problem you have to dissolve the underlying mechanisms that warrant escape, instead of fleeing from them.*

Paradoxically, each manifestation of the Sobriety Saboteurs has a positive intention, you just have to identify and honour it. In the interest of using neither fight nor flight, we can overcome such saboteurs by using their own energy against them. This is rather like

Ju-Jitsu which neither meets force with force, nor runs. Instead, useful energies are channelled to positive conclusions.

The following section highlights the ways in which you can utilize the Sobriety Saboteurs to your advantage, preparing you to transform your mental and emotional debris into insight, inspiration, wisdom and creativity – like a true alchemist!

Section Two Summary

1. Although there are numerous theories proposed to identify why certain people develop problems with alcohol, all are inconclusive. There are no internal, external, social, cultural or genetic determinants of alcohol abuse. There is, however, one major theme that runs through every single case: *escapism*. To alleviate alcohol abuse we have to remove the need to escape. By educating and cultivating the mind and transforming our mental debris into insight, we banish the threat of the sobriety saboteurs: fear, pain, futility and guilt, and disable the need to escape. Once we grasp that life is a journey of infinite possibilities, an adventure playground filled with innumerable opportunities, the need to escape disappears.

2. Inhibiting memory with alcohol and temporary forgetting your problems doesn't solve anything. Continually denying your troublesome issues leads to repression, a mechanism whereby your problems are banished to the realms of the unconscious. Although hidden from sight, they are not dead and buried: they are buried alive and must find a means of expression. Unresolved issues will always return to mount an assault on your life that is both bewildering and

destructive: phobias, severe mood swings, irrationality, paranoia, unpredictability, aggression, neurosis and psychosis. The moral of this story is as follows:

The most effective way to escape your problems is to solve them

---

- Using language effectively is a key variable in the process of radical transformation. Refrain from using language in a way that programs your mind in an inhibiting manner. Negative language leads to corrosive inner dialogue, which, in turn, leads to life-denying behaviour

Nourish your mind with wisdom and inspiration and your external world will transform to reflect this shift

- Addiction is simply habit. By definition, rather than being something we are powerless over, a habit is something we have formulated; a sequence of internal and external events we have devised in response to a specific stimulus. *If we devised it, we have the power to change it.* Supplant your alcohol habit with a vow to immerse yourself in enlightening knowledge and radically transform your life. Habituate this practice and you will undoubtedly reach your true potential.

Drink in life-affirming knowledge, not alcohol

- When a piece of fruit decays and goes toxic, it never returns to its edible state. Likewise, once you have crossed the Abreactive Threshold, you will never return to normal drinking. All subsequent bouts will result in abreaction on a physical, emotional or mental level, or any combination of the three.

- Alcoholism is a Habituated Automatic Response Mechanism (HARM) triggered by one of the four Sobriety Saboteurs. Refrain from HARM-ing yourself, make your destructive cognitive patterns conscious and disperse them. The resulting psychic space can then be filled with inspiration, insight, creativity, joy and wisdom.

- *Will-power* supported by *toward* and *away from motivation* will overcome *won't- power.*

- Don't fight alcoholism, understand your mind.

Section Two Exercises

Exercise 1: Determining whether you have crossed the Abreactive Threshold?

Sit somewhere quiet and contemplate the occasions when you have consumed alcohol lately. Decide whether your experience was normal or abnormal. Abreaction can manifest in innumerable ways, sometimes it is very subtle. Below is a list of examples:

1. **Craving to drink more**
2. **Memory loss**
3. **Irrational behaviour**
4. **Aggression**
5. **Nausea**
6. **Shaking**
7. **Convulsions**
8. **Paranoia**
9. **Deceit**
10. **Neurosis**

This exercise should take very little time. Most people don't need to contemplate their drinking escapades to find the answer. Once you have crossed the Abreactive Threshold, determining whether your reaction to alcohol is normal or abnormal is usually startlingly obvious. If you come to the conclusion that you *have* crossed the Abreactive Threshold, then the rest of this book will reveal a philosophy for life that will propel you into a fourth dimension of existence.

Exercise 2: Motivation

- Take a pen and paper and make an inventory of all things you will move *away from* when quitting alcohol; for example: hurting your family, or embarrassing yourself, etc.

- Repeat the process above, but this time list everything you want to attain, or move *towards*, in sobriety. For example: a new career, or a happy family life.

- When you have finished, read through the lists. Acknowledge the things you want to move away from, then place your attention on the things you want to move towards.

- Expand on the items in your *towards* list. Add some specifics. For example, I want to become a professional author and provide abundantly for my family, doing something I'm passionate about – writing.

- It is not productive to dwell on the things you want to move away from as it often instils guilt. Most people are well-aware of what they want to leave behind. So concentrate on your towards list. Read it every day and imagine yourself achieving the things listed. Let your imagination expand until you totally believe you can achieve your objective. Keep your mind focused and allow the energy evoked to fuel your will-power to reach your optimal potential. This procedure is so powerful that we will explore it further in the forthcoming pages.

Part Three
Turning Wine into Water

Turning Wine into Water

The Alchemist's mind is as fluid as water. His strength lies in his ability to allow his consciousness to flow around the obstacles he encounters and adapt to whatever route proves possible. As a river gathers power by melding with other rivers, so the Alchemist's mind accumulates power by joining with other sources of wisdom and inspiration. A flowing river never stagnates; it is replenished in every given moment. It has but one intention – to flow back to its source where its power is absolute.

The title of this phase of the philosophy is **Turning Wine into Water**, or simply put - stopping drinking. If you feel any resistance to the thought - any doubt that you are capable of stopping, just let me remind you of a simple fact:

> *I drank two bottles of spirits per day, plus anything else I could lay my hands on, including methylated spirits, surgical spirits, aftershave and deodorant spray. On two occasions I lay on my deathbed after consuming a lethal cocktail of pain-killers and alcohol. Not only did I stop drinking, but I radically transformed my life:*
> *If I can do it, so can you – so come on, let's go!*

Chapter 11
Reinstating Choice

Due to the unconscious nature of alcoholism, prior to reading phase two, you probably believed that you were compelled to drink for the rest of your life - the concept of choice seeming absurd. However, having now educated yourself as to the mechanisms of the mind and the essential nature of addiction, you are now an enlightened human being. You have become very aware that you *do* have a choice: continue drinking alcohol; or drink in the wisdom in this book, take control of your life and embrace your true potential – either way, you will have to accept the consequences. Let's remind ourselves of the consequences encountered by people who have chosen before you:

Choice 1 - **Continue drinking - results:** desperation, degradation, fragmentation, embarrassment, paranoia, humiliation, incessant guilt, betrayal, incoherence, strained relationships, aggression, insanity, shakes, sweats, nausea, impotence, loss of vital functions, ruination, insanity and death.

Choice 2 - Abstain and embrace your true potential - results: boundless and limitless opportunities, respect, purposeful living, meaningful relationships, fulfilment, inspiration, serenity, creativity, freedom, abundance, adventure, joy, happiness and wholeness.

Now it's your turn. Do you want to continue on the downward spiral towards destruction, or change wine into water and embrace your boundless potential? The choice is yours. This book is not intent on persuading you to quit drinking; its objective is to inform choice. Choice, unlike hope, leaves no room for failure.

**'Destiny is not a matter of chance,
it is a matter of choice;
it is not a thing to be waited for,
it is a thing to be achieved.'**
William Jennings Bryan

- If you want to look into the eyes of your loved ones and see them glisten with happiness as they acknowledge the radical transformation within you, then read on.
- If you want to manifest your dream life and spend the rest of your days revelling in fulfilling your primary purpose, then read on.
- If you want to create abundance in every area of your life, then read on.
- If you want to experience blissful feelings that are not attainable through the bottle, then read on.

If not then I sincerely hope you are a prototype; the first of millions who is able to resume normal drinking after crossing the Abreactive Threshold. To my knowledge, it's never been achieved: but some of my dearest friends have lost their lives in their misguided attempts.

> **Drink in wisdom instead of alcohol and watch your life radically transform**

Chapter 12

The Road to Freedom –
The Six Stage Cycle of Transition

Elisabeth Kubler-Ross, best-selling author and recipient of more than twenty-five honorary doctorates, identified five stages of transition relating to death and dying. The Cycle of Grief and Loss, as it is called, was initially devised to assist people to undergo a healthy grieving process after bereavement. Subsequently, it has been adapted as a tool to aid transition through all types of loss.

The feeling of loss is commonly reported by people abstaining from alcohol. Not simply the loss of alcohol, but losses pertaining to the underlying issues that give rise to destructive drinking; for example, loss of relationships, loss of identity, loss of childhood, and loss of employment. Consequently, the Cycle of Grief and Loss has become a particularly effective tool for monitoring and measuring progress along the road to freedom.

In addition to the five stages of Loss and Grief devised by Elizabeth Kublar-Ross, there is one additional transitory stage commonly experienced during the early days of Sobriety – the **_Honeymoon Period_** – which generally commences a few months after the acceptance stage. The six stages are as follows:

1. **Denial**
2. **Bargaining**
3. **Anger**
4. **Depression**
5. **Acceptance**
6. **Honeymoon Period**

The Six Transitory Stages

What follows is an overview of the six transitory stages commonly experienced by people undertaking the transition from **Alcoholic to Alchemist**– including myself. The objective of the information is to heighten your awareness as to the things you *may* encounter, rather than things you *will* encounter. Do not *expect* these things to occur, simply be *prepared* for them should they show up and follow the guidelines suggested to deal with them.

DENIAL

Manifests as:

- Fear (fear driven)
- Protecting the habit
- Refusal or inability to face problems
- Delusion
- Adherence to the maladaptive beliefs of the '-ism' – e.g. alcohol is a 'cure all'
- Escapism
- Defence against the truth and reality
- A coping mechanism for survival

Denial is a defence mechanism designed to protect the alcohol habit when it is perceived as a 'best friend' or 'cure-all'. At this stage, people tend to defend the habit because they are frightened to abstain and face reality. Life is perceived as unbearable without alcohol. They are often overwhelmed by feelings of fear, guilt, pain or futility, and misguidedly seek refuge in the very thing that causes them: alcohol. Although people in denial are under the illusion that alcohol still performs some positive function, many have crossed the Abreactive Threshold and experience only destruction and heartache.

BARGAINING: The *what if* or *if only* stage

Common premises:

- 'If only this or that wasn't happening, then I wouldn't drink.'
- 'What if I just have one or two on a Friday night?'
- 'What if I stick to beer only?'
- 'What if I only drink at home?'
- 'It was just a phase I was going through; I'm in control now – what if I just have the one? I'll never go back to the way I was.'

How many times have you heard yourself using these phrases?

People in the bargaining stage have not accepted having crossed the Abreactive Threshold, but they have acknowledged that a problem exists. They know they need to do something about their drinking, but they try to soften the blow by believing they can reduce their alcohol intake rather than completely abstaining. Don't be seduced by the maladaptive strategies of your unconscious mind. One drink will inevitably lead to many; beer will lead to spirits; and drinking at home will lead to losing your house! Don't succumb to bargaining. Control your mind: don't allow your mind to control you.

ANGER

Manifests as:

- 'Why can everybody else drink normally and I can't?'
- Acceptance of having crossed the Abreative Threshold
- Recognition that alcohol no longer provides relief from unresolved issues
- Feeling betrayed
- Looking for a scapegoat to blame

People at this stage commonly become angry at themselves, life events, others, and God. Their anger is often accompanied by feelings of rage, resentment, and confusion. After admitting having an alcohol habit and accepting that bargaining doesn't work, they feel cornered and strike out at those around them. Their fear and frustration often leads to *shadow projection*, a phenomenon whereby they see their own short-comings and character defects situated in other people and use them as scapegoats – 'it's all their fault,' they exclaim. After fruitlessly expending large amounts of energy on directing their anger externally, they turn it in on themselves and it translates to depression.

DEPRESSION

Manifests as:

- Mourning the loss of a perceived ally – loss of a life-style – loss of identity.
- Barrenness – sterility – meaningless – futility.
- Feeling of being deprived.
- Life without alcohol is awful.
- Numbness.

Exhausted from denial; bargaining didn't work; anger has been exhausted; and so a huge void opens up inside and depression descends.

People often vacillate between the latter two stages - anger and depression - not knowing how to break the cycle. If this state of imbalance persists, relapse usually occurs. Anger and depression are signs that your delusion has ended and reality is setting in – **they are indicative of progression** (although they may not feel like at the time!) When you reach these stages it is imperative that you seek help with the unresolved issues that underlie your destructive tendencies. This is a prime opportunity to identify and process the root causes of your destructive drinking and eradicate them. Working through your unresolved issues can be an adventure that is both rewarding and enlightening. Don't miss this opportunity; remember, *the most effective way to escape your problems is to solve them.* Keep looking forward and remember the infinite possibilities that are now just over the horizon:

Progress don't regress!

ACCEPTANCE

- No longer deluded by the belief that alcohol is a magical panacea for all problems.
- Acknowledgement that drinking ends up in persecution and destruction.
- Desires a better quality of life.

Although this stage often brings mental and emotional imbalance, by rising to the challenges it presents, you stand to annul your relationship with the Sobriety Saboteurs and acquire great strength.

The acceptance stage sees reality return. Negative thoughts often infiltrate our minds, giving rise to guilt, fear, pain and futility. Here are some of the thoughts I experienced during this stage:

- *Remember when you did this or that? You should be ashamed of yourself.*
- *All these people paying you compliments; If only they knew what you're really like, they'd hate you.*
- *Life's monotonous and boring, I need to escape.*

This corrosive inner dialogue starts subtly and builds to a crescendo, *if we allow it to.* Our self-esteem can take a pounding as the Sobriety Saboteurs set about annihilating our self-perception. With our defences low, the maladaptive thoughts of the *'-ism'* start to creep in. *Drink will cure this. Drink cures everything.* Hypnotized by this seductive inner voice and laden with feelings of self disdain, our minds begin to vacillate between enslavement and enlightenment: drink, sobriety; drink, sobriety; drink, sobriety.

STOP! STOP! STOP! If you should experience any of these symptoms; if you should find yourself teetering on the edge of uncertainty, STOP and centre yourself: do not be drawn in. Do not slip back into unconscious processing, and regress to your old ways of thinking. You are on the threshold of freedom – a life beyond your wildest dreams is now imminent! AWARENESS is the key to successfully negotiating this stage. STAY ALERT. LIVE LIFE CONSCIOUSLY. *What you're experiencing is not a step backwards, it is an inevitable stage of your growth;* a prime opportunity to show the Sobriety Saboteurs who's in charge and transcend their influence.

Rather than recoiling from the negative offerings of the Sobriety Saboteurs, just allow your inner-dialogue to be. Thoughts in and of themselves are ineffectual; it's only when our awareness is consumed by them that they assume power. It's only when we believe them that they take on life. Instead of owning these corrosive thoughts, simply observe them. Remain detached and stay centred in your higher awareness. From this dissociated perspective, notice that the troublesome thoughts are simply fleeting impulses of energy and information – nothing more, nothing less. Without a power source to sustain them (your awareness), they will abate. Simply watch them arise and dissipate back into the nothingness from where they came. We have sixty thousand thoughts a day and most of them pass unacknowledged. As you remain detached and observe the contents of your mind, repeat the following affirmation to yourself:

'Today I allow my life to unfold from the wisdom and intelligence of my Indwelling Divinity.'

Continual practice of this technique will see the demise of the Sobriety saboteurs. Deprived of the attention that empowers them, they will abate. Subsequently, your inner wisdom will prevail and your mind will return to a state of equanimity. A relaxed mind is a very productive mind, so once equanimity is attained, you're on the road to optimal functioning and manifesting you dreams.

Humanness Returns

Along with the return of challenging thoughts, the acceptance stage also sees the return of our emotions. This can be a disconcerting experience; a time of intense emotional activity in which our feelings are prone to ebb and flow between contrasting polarities: up and down; high and low; sorrow and joy. Again, this is a normal and inevitable stage of your progression: *it tells you that freedom is imminent*. Meet it with gratitude. Like a pendulum swinging to and fro before coming to rest in the centre, our emotions have a tendency to vacillate back and forth before coming to rest in peace.

Emotional imbalance is a sign of your humanness returning. Years of drinking had rendered you emotionally bankrupt: lifeless, detached, and devoid of purpose. Now the energy that breathes life into your experience is returning. Give thanks – you are human again! Feelings are an integral part of the human experience; they colour and enrich our lives.

Embrace your emotions: they are a sign of your humanness returning

> ### Exercise: mastering your emotions
> Whenever your emotions become turbulent, adopt the same procedure used with your thoughts.
> Don't become embroiled in them, simply observe.
> Don't place value judgements on them: good, bad; right, wrong. Just remain detached and just allow them to be.
> Place your awareness on the different sensations in your body. Observe the movement of energy.
> Know that these feelings have resulted from corrosive inner dialogue that depends on your belief in it to survive. Withdraw your belief and they will expire.
> This powerful exercise has been adopted by our wise forefathers since time immemorial.

THE HONEYMOON PERIOD

After accepting having an alcohol habit and negotiating the bumpy period described above, life without drink can be a liberating and exciting experience. Problems and unresolved issues are temporarily forgotten and supplanted by a great sense of release. Provisional control is resumed and the unconscious strategies that drive the alcohol habit lay dormant for a while. This surreal stage is often referred to as the ***honeymoon period***, a time when quitting alcohol appears much easier than ever anticipated.

The honeymoon period can last anything from a few days to a couple of years; but inevitably the trials and tribulations of life do return to challenge us. Remember, we may have stopped drinking, but, as yet, we have not eradicated the catalysts that give rise to our destructive tendencies. The end of the honeymoon period is commonly associated with relapse. People become complacent and the Sobriety Saboteurs weave themselves into the growing disquiet of their minds, ready to mount a psychological ambush.
For years alcohol anaesthetized our turbulent feelings and suppressed our troublesome thoughts. Then we crossed the Abreactive Threshold and they came flooding back to consciousness. Now, drink serves only to heighten our distress. So we quit. After the short but unpleasant business of withdrawal, our problems temporarily abate as we enjoy the novel experience of life without drink.

Pressure begins to build, however, as loved ones and friends sing our praises and take delight in watching our progress. As each day passes, their expectations rise. Though part of us revels in the praise and respect we're receiving, simmering beneath the surface is often doubt and uncertainty. Fear of letting our loved ones down – *what if I relapse? Will I make it? Imagine the devastation if I drank*. As doubt and fear begin to veil the initial excitement evoked through the novel experience of sobriety, the honeymoon period tends to subside.

When the honeymoon period ends it can feel like a major set-back. But, once again, this is an inevitable stage of your ***progress***. It is not natural to stay on a permanent high; that is often a sign of imbalance in which your problems are veiled by denial. The river of life inevitably bounces off the banks of both pleasure and displeasure: flow with it. Alchemists, like the element of fire, consume every obstacle in their way and use their energy as fuel for themselves. Every obstacle encountered can be transformed into life-enhancing energy. For example, when we live life consciously we realise that the underlying fears and doubts experienced during the honeymoon period serve an extremely positive purpose: *they prevent complacency from setting in.* All that is happening when you come down from the honeymoon period is that you are attaining balance and preparing yourself for the next stage of evolution – **the magic is within your grasp now: stay with it!**

Conclusion

Rather than being a linear progression whereby one experiences denial, moves smoothly through to the honeymoon period, and lives happily ever after, these stages are commonly cyclic. People tend to get so far, then regress back to a prior stage or start the whole cycle again. Don't be alarmed should this happen to you: **You are still PROGRESSING.**

The six stage process is sieve-like in nature. Each time a loss cycles through the stages, a little more pain is filtered away and you acquire more strength and wisdom. Remember, *there is no failure, only feedback*; should you veer off course, use your experience as feedback. Refine your future strategies in accordance with the feedback you receive and set course for a life beyond your wildest dreams.

The key to moving through this six stage transition successfully is your attitude. Look at each stage as a logical progression on the road to freedom. Honour your improvement. Though it may be difficult to appreciate it at the time, acknowledge your efforts and know that you are evolving towards your true potential. Move through the stages with a sense of challenge, expectation and excitement. Know that each discovery you make about yourself propels you towards self-mastery. A healthy person who suffers loss eventually accepts it and moves on. Now it's your time to move on and harness the infinite possibilities that life has to offer.

Chapter 13

Withdrawal Symptoms

**'I once dreaded alcohol withdrawal,
until I realised it signified
the end of my association with the thing
that was killing me!'**
Paul Henderson

Alcohol withdrawal is the body's way of re-adjusting to the sudden absence of alcohol after prolonged or heavy drinking. When you imbibe alcohol it stimulates neurotransmitters - ***chemical messengers*** - in your brain. These chemical messengers are known as Gamma-AminoButyric Acid, but because I can't say that even while sober, I will refer to them as GABA!

The function of GABA is to inhibit over-excitation of the brain; put simply, this means it induces relaxation and sleep. When GABA is mixed with alcohol, this effect can increase to such an extent that it results in sedation of many of the critical functions controlled by the brain: motor control, vision, and many other cortical functions. Alcohol greatly enhances the effects of GABA. Prolonged drinking causes the brain to crave more alcohol in order to sustain this quieting effect. As a consequence, when a person cuts off the alcohol supply abruptly, the brain rebels and withdrawal symptoms begin.

The symptoms can range from mild anxiety to severe convulsions, depending on a number of factors. Extent of addiction, length of addiction, the body's ability to tolerate change, and a person's emotional disposition, all contribute to the severity of the experience. Withdrawal symptoms can be divided into two broad categories: emotional and physical.

Emotional symptoms: depression, nervousness, anxiety, shakiness, irritability, excitability, volatility, extreme sensitivity, mood swings, rapid emotional changes, fatigue, bad dreams, and difficulty concentrating.

Physical symptoms: loss of appetite, headaches, sweating, nausea, vomiting, paleness and clamminess, insomnia, rapid heart rate, dilated pupils, tremors (especially of the hands). Severe symptoms include fever, hallucinations, confusion, black-outs, agitation, convulsions, and in rare cases, coma or death.

Although it is important to be educated as to the possible effects of alcohol withdrawal, many organizations and so called 'authorities' on alcoholism paint an almost unbearable picture. No wonder people carry on drinking! It is true that severe withdrawal symptoms are not very pleasant. My own ranged from mild flu-like symptoms to severe convulsions and hallucinations. Reducing my alcohol intake from two bottles a day to nothing at all, was such a shock to my system that my body went into spasm. You, however, have been educated and have foresight. Before quitting, make an appointment with your GP and seek his assistance. Explain that you intend to quit drinking and disclose, very honestly, the amount of alcohol you consume each day; remember, he can't help you if you deceive him. There are a variety of drugs available to aid the withdrawal process and enable you to undergo the experience with relatively little discomfort. A word of warning, however:

Take any drugs exactly as the doctor prescribes; they should be used as an aid for withdrawal, not another means of escape.

Due to the excessive amounts of alcohol I consumed, my doctor had me admitted to a hospital where the withdrawal process could be monitored and assisted by professionals. If your GP makes this suggestion, I would thoroughly recommend it. Being away from the pressures and distractions of everyday life can be a great aid during the withdrawal process.

Below is a list of helpful hints that will help you negotiate this volatile period.

- Relax as much as possible

- Refrain from making major decisions

- Drink plenty of fluids, especially water

- Take supplementary vitamins (in particular, vitamin B and C)

- Watch television or read a book to keep your mind focused

- Visit our website as frequently as possible and take advantage of the useful videos and audio files that offer huge support. (**www.al2al.com**)

- Take any drugs exactly as the doctor prescribes; they should be used as an aid for withdrawal, not another means of escape.

- Read this book and ingest the wisdom within its pages – the words will help to re-programme your mind

However you decide to manage withdrawal symptoms, rest assured *they will be over in a relatively short period of time.* I transformed from a shivering wreck to a fairly healthy human being in less than two weeks, and that was after chronic and prolonged abuse.

Experience has taught me that physical withdrawal is unpleasant but tolerable when assisted by medication or hospitalization (if necessary). The mental and emotional turbulence that persists (after physical withdrawal abates) poses the biggest problem. But rest assured - the remainder of this book is designed to purge your mind of the issues that exacerbate alcoholism and supplant them with insight, inspiration, wisdom and joy – come on, my friends, upwards and onwards!

Part Four
Mind Over Matter

Chapter 14
It's the Thought that Counts!

'The ancestor to every action is a thought.'
Ralph Waldo Emerson

If the ancestor to every action is a thought, then there must be a direct link between the formless world of energy and the physical world of matter. What's more, this link must be an incredibly powerful one. Look around you right now. Every artefact, every building, every book, every action, every circumstance, every relationship – literally EVERYTHING! - transpired from a thought.

Ralph Waldo Emerson wasn't alone in acknowledging the relationship between the formless dominion of the mind and the physical world; it has been recognised since time immemorial. The bible stated it in the following terms *'as within, so without'* and *'first there was the word and the word became flesh.'* This latter statement should not be taken metaphorically, either. Here, *'the word'* refers to the invisible impulses of energy and information we refer to as thought, and the *'flesh'* as the physical manifestation of that thought.

Great scientist and humanist Albert Einstein also acknowledged the powerful connection between the mind and the material world. In his famous equation $E = MC^2$, 'E' equals energy, 'M' equals mass, and 'C^2' equals the speed of light multiplied by itself. Since an equals sign denotes sameness - one side is the same as the other - then what this equation is telling us is that *energy and mass are the same thing in different forms.* Put another way, it tells us that *thought and action are the same thing in different guises.*

Whilst travelling the world attending conventions, I asked thousands of people why they drank. Without exception the answer I received was - *to make me feel better.* I only had to look at the despair and torment on the faces of these people to know that drink no longer fulfilled its intended purpose. The deadness in their eyes told me they had long since stopped living. Alcohol had simply veiled their problems temporarily; but, like the eye of a hurricane, the brief reprieve was followed by a powerful force that swept through their lives leaving a trail of devastation.

What these people sought was a permanent way to feel better. Removing alcohol alone wasn't going to achieve this. Imagine if there was an antidote capable of instantaneously flushing their bodies with happy or calming chemicals, with no side-effects, and free of charge. If such a thing was available, alcohol would surely become redundant. Well, guess what? There is such a thing! An intrinsic energy that is not only capable of transforming the way you feel at will, but also capable of determining your state of health. This magical panacea can be found in the formless domain of your mind: *your thoughts.*

The way in which you interpret and process experience produces either life-enhancing or life- denying chemicals in your body. Your body is a phenomenal pharmacy, capable of producing innumerable chemicals naturally. These chemicals alter the balance of your cells and determine your physical state. Some instil good feeling and well-being whilst others produce disease and negative feeling. Most importantly, both states are invoked by *choice.* Alchemists are adept at changing negative thinking into a mode of thought that produces well-being and inspiration. To determine how easy it is to *choose* the way you feel, try the following short exercise:

Exercise: choosing your emotions

Find a quiet place, somewhere you won't be disturbed. Close your eyes. Focus on your breath for a minute or two and allow any thoughts to pass....

Now, bring to mind a time of difficulty, a time perhaps when you felt sad or angry. Let the pictures pervade your mind. Turn up the brightness and contrast; hear any sounds and conversations and turn up the volume. Turn all your senses inwardly and allow the experience to expand in your mind. Now, monitor how you are feeling: Sad? Angry? Negative?

Next, remind yourself of what you had for breakfast this morning (this question may seem a little out of context, but it is designed to break the state you're experiencing i.e. return you to a neutral state). Now, close your eyes again, if they are not already closed. Follow your breath for a minute, as before, and now bring a happy scene to mind. Again, turn all your senses inwardly and allow the experience to expand in your mind. See what you saw. Turn up the brightness and contrast. Higher the volume. Immerse yourself in the scene for a few minutes. Now, monitor how you are feeling – light? joyous? Happy?

In just a couple of minutes you have controlled the way you feel, simply by changing the focus of your thoughts. Therefore, rather than being powerless over your emotions, as suggested by certain factions, you can choose the way you feel at will. Realizing this is the first step in self-mastery.

> *Feelings are choices that transpire from thoughts;*
> *to change the way you feel,*
> *change the way you think.*

Healing Thoughts

The power of thought has been known to be capable of transforming a diseased cell into a healthy cell since time immemorial; there are innumerable accounts throughout the history of mankind. Up until recently such phenomena have been deemed as miracles - how and why they happen remaining a mystery. Today, however, through the insights of modern-day science, we know that the human body is literally a field of intelligence; furthermore, this field responds to thought. What we once deemed to be miraculous happenings bestowed on a privileged few are now freely available to everyone.

Thoughts have a tremendous influence on our health and well-being. What we believe about ourselves is translated into the chemical activity responsible for our health and our emotional state.

The human body is equipped with a cellular surveillance system; a mechanism whereby our cells literally 'listen' in to the contents of our thoughts and alter our chemical balance accordingly. If we focus on thoughts of fear, anger, guilt, or pain our brains respond by secreting chemicals that give rise to feelings that correspond to them. The same process is evident in people who repeatedly affirm how sick they are? *'I always get flu when winter comes in.'* or *'arthritis runs in the family; I'll be next.'* Have you noticed how such people are prone to suffering? If we constantly allow our energy to flow into the beliefs that give rise to a mindset of illness, then we will initiate the mechanisms that create the chemistry that induces those illnesses.

> ## Where thought goes, energy follows.

The impact of thought on health and well-being is clearly demonstrated through a phenomenon known as the placebo effect. The placebo effect shows us that our body is a network of intelligence that listens to our mental transmissions and alters itself accordingly.

The Placebo Effect

A **placebo** is a medical intervention that uses deception ethically. Patients are set up to believe that they're undergoing authentic treatment for their symptoms, when, in fact, an ineffectual substitute is administered.

A common example is the use of a sugar pill. A patient is given an inert sugar pill in place of an analgesic (painkiller). Having not been informed of the switch, their mind is duped into believing that they're undergoing authentic pain relief treatment. The results are quite astounding. ***Depending on the extent of a person's expectancy, and their will to want to get better,*** i.e. depending on the degree of their *belief* in the process, healing *does* take place. And not just in a psychological sense whereby the person redefines their illness mentally (that is, chooses not to *think* about it) but in a way whereby the body *actually produces its own form of painkiller!*

Research has found that the placebo experiment causes the brain to release endorphins which, by fusing to receptors in the brain, prevent pain and invoke a feeling of well-being: they are the body's own morphine-like painkillers.

If beliefs can instruct the body's internal pharmacy to administer pain-killing drugs, what else can they achieve?

Although the placebo initially concentrated on pain relief, contemporary research is beginning to indicate that it has the capacity to work for any condition. Numerous carefully controlled studies indicate that the placebo can provide relief from postoperative-wound pain, seasickness, headaches, angina, asthma, obesity, blood pressure, ulcers, and many other conditions. In fact, researchers are now convinced that no system of the body is exempt from the placebo effect and that it is operative in virtually every healing encounter. Even more intriguing, the placebo is sometimes more effective than the actual prescribed drug for the condition!

Believe it and Achieve it!

When we begin to understand the underlying mechanisms that give rise to the placebo effect, a whole new world opens up to us. The placebo effect is dependent on belief, and beliefs transpire from thoughts.

When we place our attention on a thought, we energize it and it undergoes a sequence of unfolding to become a feeling. Thoughts that we consider to be true give rise to the feelings we call *beliefs*.

Beliefs are comprised of two components, thought and emotion. The thought is simply an idea we have internalised and consider to be true e.g. *life is a struggle*. This idea is of little consequence until we empower it with energy. When we infuse an idea with the energy of awareness (i.e. when we focus on an idea), it takes on the power to create. Beliefs are powerful: they are the motivating force behind all our actions.

> **'The world we see that seems so insane is the result of a belief system that is not working.**
> **To perceive the world differently, we must be willing to change our belief system,**
> **let the past slip away, expand our sense of now and dissolve the fear into our minds.'**
> William James

We learned earlier that from childhood onwards we internalise ideas about ourselves and the world in general; these ideas come from various sources: parents, siblings, clergymen, teachers, and so on. Some ideas we reject and they have no further influence on our lives; others we accept and hold to be true - the latter form the basis of our belief system.

Beliefs form the foundation of our life's directional guidance system: *they literally determine the course of our lives.* Therefore, if we want to realise our true potential it is of vital importance that we frequently examine and revise our belief system. The beliefs that served us yesterday may no longer be viable today. We need to challenge them and jettison the ones that impede our growth. Limiting beliefs such as *'No one will employ me now I'm 63'* place unnecessary boundaries on our potential, whereas empowering beliefs such as *'I'm a boundless bundle of potential that can manifest anything I want in life'* propel us to success and abundant living.

> **A belief is simply an idea we consider to be true;
> it is neither right nor wrong; good or bad;
> it is either inhibiting or supportive**

I once believed that I was afflicted with an incurable disease and compelled to drink alcohol until I keeled over and died. I didn't realise that I drank alcohol abusively to escape the exaggerated and distorted interpretations of my mind. Today, *I use my mind – my mind does not use me*. I believe that the world is a field of limitless possibilities and I am capable of achieving literally anything. This profound shift in my belief system has produced remarkable results and continues to do so, on a daily basis.

**Whether you believe you will succeed;
or whether you believe you will fail;
on both accounts you will be correct.**

Henry Ford

Mind Over Matter

Scientists now know that the brain is not hardwired as once believed; it is a dynamic organ that grows and shrinks in accordance with the information it receives. *Brain plasticity* is a term that refers to the ability of the brain to wire itself according to incoming information. To be more precise, it wires itself in accordance with how we *interpret* experience.

When we dwell on a thought, we energize it, and our brain connects various neurons (brain cells) together to form a network that supports our mode of thinking. Such networks are called *neural networks.*

A Neural Network represents a build-up of ideas that are repeatedly impressed upon our mind. Before we continue, let's make an important distinction between our mind and our brain. The mind is a formless domain in which thoughts arise, while the brain is a physical organ that supports the way in which the mind thinks. Another way of stating this is as follows: a thought, *the word,* undergoes a sequence of unfolding to become a physical network, *the flesh* – as stated in the bible. What we are talking about here is literally **mind over matter.**

When the formless impulses of energy and information arising in our mind (thoughts), start to take on physical attributes in the brain, our thinking becomes ingrained and rigid: this is the basis of **habituation**. If we continuously impress negative ideas on our brain, it will respond by creating neural networks to support them. Every time we perform an action that reinforces the negative idea, the neural network will become more pronounced. As a consequence, we habituate negative action (form a bad habit).

Once we interrupt our negative thinking patterns, however, the supporting neural networks weaken and disband. Connections between neurons break and make way for new life-enhancing networks. So next time you make statements such as *'that's just the way I am'* and *'I'm useless at this or that'* or *'I can't stop drinking,'* be aware that you are reinforcing the negative habit-forming neural networks that thwart your growth.

The Chemistry

Neural networks are in constant communication with the *hypothalamus* - the chemical producing centre of the brain. The hypothalamus produces chemical messengers called neuropeptides.

Neuropeptides are created in accordance with information derived from the neural networks and therefore correspond directly to the way we think. Once manufactured, the chemical messengers are dispersed through the bloodstream to various parts of our body. The word *emotion* can be defined as *energy in motion* and used to describe that process whereby chemical messengers are dispersed throughout our body to give rise to the way we feel.

Each cell of our body contains receptors that house the incoming neuropeptides. When neuropeptides dock onto a cell, they change the chemical balance of that cell. The messages they carry correspond to our mode of thinking and inform the cell (which is a self-contained unit of intelligence) to change its structure. Changes in our cellular structure translate to changes in the way we feel.

If we constantly flood our body with chemicals that give rise to - let's say, guilt – the cells of our body will generate more receptors to house the guilt producing messenger. In effect, we will become more prone to guilt. If we fixate our awareness on thoughts of fear, the hypothalamus will create the corresponding neuropeptides; in turn, these neuropeptides will inform our cells to evolve more receptor sites to house the fear invoking messenger, rendering us prone to fear - and so on.

When we change the focus of our thoughts, however, and concentrate on - let's say, thoughts of happiness - the cells will reduce their number of 'fear' receptor sites and develop more 'happy' receptors in order to accommodate the new influx of positive messengers.

> **When we dwell on negative thoughts,
> we produce chemicals in our body that
> give rise to negative feelings.**

There is a continuous dialogue going on between our mind and our brains. Our thoughts tell our brains to produce life-affirming or life-denying chemistry in our bodies. When we think positive thoughts, we produce life-affirming chemistry in our bodies.

Studies have shown that when we evoke feelings of gratitude, for instance, the chemicals in our brain that produce dehydroepiandrosterone (DHEA) - a steroid hormone made by the adrenal glands that acts on the body much like testosterone - actually increases in excess of one hundred percent over a very short period of time. The same studies have shown that when we hold feelings of anger, rage, frustration, and jealousy we send signals to our brain that cause it to produce life denying chemistry such as cortisol adrenaline - the stress hormone.

Taking all this information and applying it to alcohol, enables us to expose a major flaw in the philosophy of those people whose objective it is to *feel better* by drinking. As alcohol is a mind altering drug, it changes the way we think, and our thinking has a direct impact on the way we feel. Hence, before the drinkers cross the Abreactive Threshold, alcohol suppresses their troublesome thoughts. As a consequence, the neural networks that support negative thinking disband, causing the hypothalamus to cease making the chemical messengers that evoke negative emotion - so the drinker feels better.

Pre-Abreative Threshold

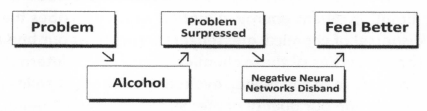

Now, the seductive trap is set - an association between alcohol and good feeling has been made. However, to sustain this feeling, more and more alcohol is needed to suppress the troublesome thoughts. Over time the pressure builds to such an extent that they surge forth from the unconscious to the conscious with devastating force. Once the Abreactive threshold has been compromised in this way, the chemical process in our body is reversed. Rather than suppressing the troublesome thoughts, alcohol amplifies them, causing the hypothalamus to produce negative feelings in the body. The drinker reverts to the bottle to purge himself of the negative feelings, but inadvertently throws fuel on the fire: alcohol now amplifies stinking thinking which gives rise to life-denying chemicals in the body. The whole process then becomes cyclic as negative thoughts curve back on themselves to create negative feelings which eventually become intolerable.

Post Abreactive Threshold

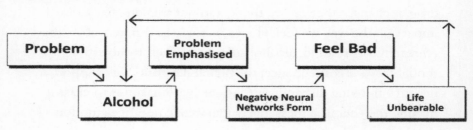

Thoughts energized by awareness lead to emotion. Emotion means *energy in motion* which describes the dispersal of chemical messengers throughout our body. The properties of these chemical messengers determine the nature of the feeling evoked in our body. Feelings determine our quality of life. So to sustain well-being, we must nurture our thoughts carefully.

Trains of thought

Many people exclaim *'but I can't stop the negative thoughts in my head –*
I'm doomed.' Untrue. In fact, by resisting them they increase in both
frequency and potency. Hence the saying, *resistance breeds persistence.*
The answer to their dilemma is to view each thought as a train
passing through a station – *a train of thought.* They may not
control the schedule, but they can choose whether or not to get on
board.

When a negative thought emerges in your mind, allow it to be;
remain dissociated and allow it to pass through the station of your
mind. Conversely, when an inspirational train of thought arrives,
jump on board and allow it to take you on an adventure. Using this
technique ensures that you **live life consciously and *choose* your
destiny.**

Sadly, most people live life unconsciously. They board the same
train day-in, day-out, using a pass stamped "rigid conditioning".
They sleep throughout the journey and end up back where they
started. Their lives are going nowhere.

The few that are wide awake stand on the platform and carefully
observe the trains of thought. When one fuelled by wisdom and
inspiration arrives, they throw caution to the wind and hop on
board. These are the true explorers; unphased by fear. They'll take
many trains and explore the inner landscapes of their minds until
they arrive at their ultimate vision: their dream reality.

Our mind is an ocean of infinite possibilities. There's a never
ending stream of thought from which to choose. You just need to
be selective. ***Control your mind instead of letting your mind
control you.***

Karma

As thoughts unfold to become feelings and beliefs, which are the motivating force that drive our actions, let's now take a look at the closely related phenomenon of *Karma*. Karma is a Sanskrit word that simply means *action*. The law of cause and effect states that all our actions have consequences. Our thoughts, the *cause,* translate into action, which has consequences, the *effect*.

By paying conscious attention to our thoughts, we are able to identify reoccurring cognitive patterns that evoke inappropriate action. Subsequently, we can intervene before the thought unfolds to bring about negative consequences. If we remain oblivious to mental pollution, the *cause* is buried in our unconscious mind. Is not dead and buried, however, it is buried alive. Thoughts are energy and energy must find a means of expression. When unresolved issues are left to fester in our unconscious, they eventually find expression in a multitude of destructive guises: mood swings, aggression, unpredictability - which all have negative consequences. As the consequences of our actions determine the quality of our life, we need to harness our emotional and mental debris and transmute it into fuel for our journey.

The quality of our life is determined by the consequences of our actions, which is the basis of Karma. Our actions, in turn, are driven by our feelings, which transpire as a result of the thoughts we dwell on. So, ultimately, our thoughts are responsible for the quality of our lives.

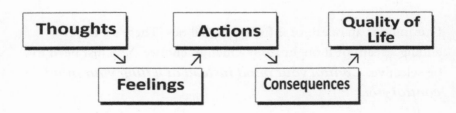

Change the way we think
= change the quality of our life

As alcoholism is located in the mind, not the bottle, this information is particularly pertinent to us. Stinking thinking unfolds to become unbearable feelings, which lead to irresponsible and destructive actions, which have grave consequences. As a result, our lives are reduced to a maelstrom of madness!

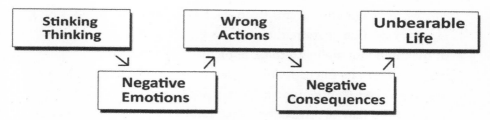

Although putting down the bottle is extremely necessary, it isn't going to solve the problem. Detoxification programs have their place, but they only deal with alcoholism at the chemical level. For sustained success we must tackle the problem at source. Eradicating our destructive thought processes and aspiring for self-mastery is imperative if we want to attain our true potential and embrace the infinite possibilities that life has to offer.

The Law of Attraction and the Power of Thought

Can you imagine having the power to simply focus on something intently and have it manifest? Whether it is money, artefacts, material success, or even attracting a romantic partner, this is the basic principle behind the Law of Attraction.

The law of attraction states that our thoughts are magnetic in nature, drawing to us circumstances that resonate with them. It says that whatever is prominent in our mind will be reflected in our external reality. Some of the greatest minds that have ever graced our planet have known about this law. Albert Einstein phrased it in the following terms.

"Imagination is the preview of life's forthcoming events"

The word imagination stems from the Latin root *imago* which simply means *image*. Imagination, therefore, is the image forming capacity of the mind; our ability to think in pictures. If we use our imagination to its full capacity, we can work wonders with our lives. Every successful entrepreneur has a *vision*, because they are well aware of the Law of Attraction. They hold a clear picture of what they want in the internal dominion of their mind and, sure enough, it manifests - as within, so without!

In theory, this law is simple – focus on what you want and it will manifest. However, rather than focus on what they *do* want in life, most people habitually think about what they *don't* want – and guess what? They attract everything they detest into their lives!
As thoughts create our reality in this way, is it any wonder that our lives have been disastrous? Alcoholism is the epitome of negative thinking: *stinking thinking*. For years we have focused on that which we don't like about our lives. As a consequence, we have inadvertently attracted more of it!

So, from this point forth, all we have to do to radically transform our lives is to think positively. But don't rush off just yet and set about manifesting your dreams; or you may be disappointed. Our ability to maintain a positive focus is impeded by unconscious influences.

Many of our thoughts are unknown to the conscious mind. Although they operate below the threshold of consciousness, they still shape the way we think consciously. They act as filters, ciphering off our positivity and retaining our negativity.

When we wear sunglasses we see the world in a darker light, because the glasses filter out the rays of sunshine. Our negative unconscious thought patterns have a similar effect: they filter our ingenuity and severely restrict our view of what we deem to be possible. For the Law of Attraction to be successful we have to totally believe in the dreams that occupy our imagination. If we have reservations then the corresponding thoughts will negate the process and it will be doomed to failure.

The negative thought processes that mar the attraction process are usually the surreptitious work of the Sobriety Saboteurs.

Fear

Guilt

Psychological pain

Futility

To resume command of our lives and sustain positive thinking, we need to journey inwardly and remove their influence. Think of the conscious mind as a lake and the unconscious as a huge reservoir that feeds it. It's no good sieving the lake to keep it clean if the reservoir is polluted. We must decontaminate the feed if we are to purify and sustain the lakes clarity.

As Alchemists we need to decontaminate our unconscious reservoir in order to keep the lake of our conscious mind clear. By turning our unconscious mental and emotional debris into fuel for ourselves, we will be propelled into a fourth dimension of existence. The next section will assist us with this process.

Summary of main points:

- The formless world of energy becomes physical as thoughts energized by awareness give rise to neural networks. In turn, these neural networks cause the brain to produce chemical messengers (neuropeptides). These chemical messengers are then dispersed throughout the body and change its cellular structure.

- Our cellular structure determines how we feel. If we habitually think guilt or fear thoughts, we will produce guilt and fear chemical messengers that will instruct our cells to produce more of the corresponding receptor sites to support these feelings. Consequently, we become habituated to negative feeling.

- If we think positively, we will produce chemicals that give rise to feelings of well-being and inspiration. Consequently, we become habituated to good feeling.

- The thoughts and feelings we emanate attract circumstances conducive to them: like attracts like.

- To change our lives we have to change our thoughts and initiate a sequence of unfolding that will give rise to the circumstances we desire.

- A belief is simply an idea we hold to be true. It is neither good nor bad, right nor wrong. It is either inhibiting or supportive. If it is the former we can jettison it.

'There is nothing either good or bad, but thinking makes it so.'
Shakespeare (Hamlet)

- Our lives can be orchestrated from beyond the conscious threshold. To take control we need to bring our unconscious patterns into the light of consciousness where we can process and release them.

- When our mind is clear and focused we can manifest anything we desire.

Exercise: To radically change our life, we need to re-evaluate our belief system. Asking ourselves the following questions will aid the process:

- *From where did these beliefs originate?*
- *Are they really my own or did I inherit them?*
- *Were they passed on to me by my parents, my siblings, clergymen or teachers?*
- *Do these beliefs support me currently? If so, in what way? If not, what can I replace it with?*

Take a piece of paper and label four columns as follows:

Belief	Origin of Belief	Empowering or Limiting?	Substitute with

In the first column, write down the nature of the **belief**. In the second write down its **origin** – was it your own or did you inherit it? In the third, acknowledge the **beliefs effects** on you. If it is limiting, then in the fourth column, devise a **new belief** to replace it. Do this for every single belief you can think of.

Successful completion of this exercise will pay large dividends. On completion you would have completely restructured your life's directional system, removing all limitations and paving the way for the life of your dreams.

Chapter 15

Understanding and Transforming the Sobriety Saboteurs

We didn't just wake up one morning and decide to drink destructively. Our alcohol habit transpired as a result of negative, unconscious forces which I call *Sobriety Saboteurs*. The Sobriety Saboteurs are destructive sub-personalities that traverse our unconscious. They act as triggers that ignite the maladaptive beliefs of the '-ism' and give rise to relapse. There are four fundamental Sobriety Saboteurs - guilt, pain, futility and fear - all other manifestations, such as stress, anxiety and the lack of confidence, are derivatives. This chapter teaches us how to reframe our experience of the sobriety saboteurs and use it in a way that enables us to transmute contaminated energy into inspiration, joy, wisdom and creativity, and propel us towards our optimal potential.

GUILT

"A man should never be ashamed to own that he has been in the wrong, which is but saying, in other words, that he is wiser today than he was yesterday."
Alexander Pope

There are two types of guilt: objective and subjective. Objective guilt is a condition caused by violating another person's will or moral code, or breaking the law. Subjective guilt is an awareness of having violated your own moral or ethical standards.

GUILT	Objective	Subjective
Justified	Committed an actual transgression	Inwardly knowing you have compromised your personal ethics / morals
Unjustified (Unfounded)	Blaming yourself for something that wasn't your fault	Believing you are to blame for an imaginary wrong-doing (paranoia)

Guilt can be justified or unfounded. The latter is common amongst people with drink problems. They have a propensity to imagine reasons to feel guilty, with the sole intention of inflicting self-punishment. Their happiness is often sabotaged by corrosive beliefs which instil guilt.

To imagine unfounded reasons to feel guilty is a form of paranoia, a term derived from the Greek *paranous,* which was used to describe a mental illness in which a delusional belief was the sole or most prominent feature. Paranoia is extremely common amongst drinkers. As a result of frequent alcohol induced memory loss, their minds become warped and have a tendency to imagine things that didn't happen. Their superego or conscience then kicks in and becomes intent on convincing them of how *bad* they are for the things that never happened! (A sure sign of this process being active is being unnecessarily hard on yourself).

If you should experience this phenomenon, WAKE UP and STAY ALERT. Recognise it as a destructive ploy of the Sobriety Saboteurs. To counter these attacks, disarm the Sobriety Saboteurs with self love. Self love and self disdain are totally incompatible; they cannot co-exist.

Self condemnation = lack of self-love

To eradicate self-inflicted punishment, go within, commune with your inner child and ply her with love. Remind her of all the good traits and attributes she possesses, and how deserved she is of all the good things in life. Refer to step 6 (page 369) and Inner Child Meditation (page 376).

Undoubtedly, whilst inebriated, especially during black-out, many of us have violated another person in some way: stealing, aggression, violence, character assassination, emotional blackmail, betrayal and manipulation are a few common examples. Although these transgressions need to be acknowledged and redressed, there is no benefit in perpetually condemning ourselves. Self reproach is an example of anger turned inwardly. People with alcohol habits are generally experts at berating themselves - but where does that get them? Ask yourself the following questions:

- How does self-condemnation help rectify the mistakes you have made in the past?
- How does self-reproach transform you into a productive human being?
- How does berating yourself make amends to the person(s) you have harmed or betrayed?

The answer in every instance is *it doesn't.* Self condemnation and self reproach are destructive, futile and often lead to the need to escape via the bottle. In the words of American psychologist Albert Ellis:

**'The more guilt a person tends to feel,
the less chance there is that he will be a happy,
healthy, or law-abiding citizen.
He will become a compulsive wrong-doer.'**

Dr. Albert Ellis

My personal experience of Guilt epitomized these words; it was undoubtedly the biggest obstacle to sobriety that I encountered. Emerging from a drunken stupor was thwart with unbearable feelings of guilt and remorse, often unwarranted and initiated by my overactive imagination. In the case where I had transgressed, the degree of guilt evoked was usually disproportionate to the offence committed - exaggerated out of all proportion. Perceiving myself as a compulsive wrong-doer was a tyrannical form of self punishment – a trait of someone who despises themselves.

I was also filled with paranoia. Unfounded guilt and paranoia are frequently linked. Guilt is often endowed with the delusional qualities of paranoia that cannot be shaken by reason or logic. People with alcohol habits often convince themselves that they are bad in response to some wrong-doing that only took place in their mind. People tell us that we are being hard on ourselves, and rationally we know it, but the corrosive inner-dialogue continues to convince us of our *'badness'*. We have to expel that voice once and for all.

Our first challenge with guilt is to deduce whether it is justified or unfounded. Delusional guilt must be seen for what it is: a spectre - an ingrained mechanism for inflicting unwarranted self punishment. Guilt that is warranted, i.e. guilt that arises from violating another person's will or breaking the law, should be used as a self-correcting feedback system – not an excuse to punish ourselves .

When we acknowledge guilt, we admit to making a mistake. We cannot regress to the past, as in the film Groundhog Day, and correct our actions; but we can vow to learn from our errors. Mistakes, although an integral part of life, are transient: the lessons we learn from them are permanent. By acknowledging our errors and learning from them, we evolve our self-understanding and pave the way for a better quality of life in the future.

Mistakes are transient:
the lessons we learn from them are permanent.

Guilt should be our ally, not our enemy: in fact, we should make it our teacher. When we allow guilt to improve our self awareness, and use its teachings to become better people and improve our quality of life, it has a positive function; it shows us what we need to learn.

'A life spent making mistakes is not only
more honourable, but more useful
than one spent doing nothing.'
George Bernard Shaw

To transform guilt into a productive experience we need to acknowledge the improvement we have made by recognising and owning it. In the words of Albert Einstein:

'A problem cannot be solved from the same level of
thinking as that which created it.'

Acknowledging guilt is an indication that you have attained a higher level of understanding. It shows that you have progressed. Acknowledging a mistake and vowing to utilize the feedback for future improvement is a sure sign that you are adhering to the path of the Alchemist.

Self Forgiveness

During our drinking escapades, when our moral guidance system was out of action and alcoholic amnesia rendered our memory inactive, many of us performed actions we weren't proud of: fought, betrayed, stole, deceived, drove while drunk, and so on. These things are undoubtedly unacceptable - they violate moral and ethical standards. However, becoming the perpetual wrong-doer and permanently berating yourself bears no fruits whatsoever. Rather than helping you to achieve the goal of becoming a respected and useful citizen, condemning yourself simply causes you to sink deeper into a pit of unworthiness. The whole point of retribution is to relieve guilt, not to accentuate it. To help alleviate residual guilt from your drinking days, it is worth reminding yourself of the words of Jesus during his crucifixion.

'Father forgive them for they know not what they do.'

In making this statement, Jesus acknowledges that the people persecuting him had been programmed to act without thinking. They were responding unconsciously. In the same way, you were programmed to act unconsciously during your drinking days. Guilt and retribution are only applicable in situations involving conscious intent to harm. Any harm you inflicted during your drinking days was not consciously intended, it was a side-effect of your psychological disposition at the time - a way of externalizing your internal turmoil. Being an unconscious act it is exempt from blame.

I'm not condoning unacceptable behaviour, and I must emphasize that we need to learn from the feedback we receive from such mistakes; however, to become a productive member of society, you must forgive yourself. By eliciting the lessons imparted by your mistakes, you move forward. The best way to make amends is through productive service to society, and you cannot serve society whilst you're preoccupied with berating yourself!

Futility

A common experience for the newly sober person is a profound sense of futility – a belief that there's nothing worth living for. When the honeymoon period subsides the world is often perceived as a desolate wasteland, bereft of meaning. This is a serious threat to sobriety and shouldn't be taken lightly. Remember, alcoholism is an escape mechanism. When a person finds life boring and meaningless, it becomes unbearable and warrants escape. As a result, the unconscious mechanisms that propel them towards drink are easily re-activated. Research and experience has taught me that futility often gives rise to relapse (escape). Two reasons for this have become highly apparent:

- People have identity crises and no longer know who they are.
- People have not connected with their ultimate purpose; a purpose that fills them with passion and inspiration, commonly called 'Life's Purpose'.

To rise and overcome the challenge of futility, each of us has to develop an awareness of what really interests us. Eliciting our core beliefs and values is an excellent starting point. As we rekindle our relationship with that which is truly meaningful to us, we also resurrect our true identity.

Too often people sculpt their identity and careers from other people's influences and expectations; cultural, societal, and family influences are immensely persuasive. But shaping our identities and moulding our careers in compliance with other people's ideas is a recipe for discontent. We must be true to ourselves and honour our innermost values if we are to realize our optimal potential (see values elicitation exercise on p.231).

Unveiling your Authentic Self

'When you let go of what you are, you become what you might be.'
Lao Tzu

The concept of self is a topic of much debate in psychological circles. However, it is commonly agreed that the messages we internalize from other people during the course of our lives constitutes a large part of what we refer to as '*I*' and '*Me*'.

From birth onwards we internalize messages from significant others: parents, teachers, clergymen, peers, siblings and so on. We are given a name, assigned a number of roles, and placed into certain categories: technician, student, English, father, uncle, slim, heavy, good, bad and so on. From these messages emerges an identity; a *mental construct* of who we *consider* ourselves to be. That part of ourselves we refer to as *I* or *Me*.

For instance, before I embarked on this journey and evolved my understanding of the concept of self, if someone had asked me the question – who are you? I'd have answered: 'Paul Henderson, from Liverpool; English; five foot nine; blue eyes; medium build;

computer technician; uncle; son; brother,' and then listed all my attributes and shortcomings. At this point something startlingly obvious emerges: '*I* am not a constant! '*I* am a collection of labels, roles and beliefs. '*I*' or my *ego* (as the idea of who we think we are is often referred to) is a phantom! If I change my name, my roles, and my beliefs, '*I* still exist. Therefore, my ego cannot be my authentic self.

Deluded into thinking that this fictitious '*I* is our only self, we adhere to the indoctrinated beliefs that it embodies - the negative messages we have internalised over the course of our lives: incompetent, unlovable, deficient, unwanted, bad, powerless, wrong, imperfect, useless, reject or whatever. If left unchallenged these corrosive beliefs will determine our capabilities – what we believe is possible in life. If we blindly subscribe to these beliefs we will never attain our true potential. But remember – they have only transpired as a result of internalising other people's negative messages about us. What qualifications do these people have to make them such experts in our lives? Answer – none. Most people cast aspersions on others as a means of covering up their own character defects and shortcomings (see shadow projection p. 193). When we live life unconsciously we accept them without question and allow them to pollute our self perception. But not anymore! Now you are living life consciously you can choose to jettison this emotional and mental debris and make way for an abundance of self love.

When we become indifferent to the good opinion of others and shed the negative baggage of our past, we open a channel to our Indwelling Divinity and embrace the infinite potential of our authentic self.

Trans-Personality

Did you know that every cell of your body changes within a two year period? Yes, you are out-living the death of your physical body on a constant basis? To deepen the mystery, radio isotope studies have shown us that trillions of atoms that have passed through your body in the last few weeks have also passed through the bodies of every other species on this planet! Yes, that's also correct: you don't even have a permanent licence on your own body; it's part of a much greater whole.

'Every atom belonging to you as well belongs to me.'
Walt Whitman (American poet)

The physical body is akin to a running stream, forever replenishing itself in every moment. We are constantly making new body parts. The skin you have now is not the skin you had six months ago. The skeleton you have now is not the one you had a year ago. In fact, your whole body is different from the one you had only a couple of years ago.

In addition to our physicality changing constantly, our beliefs and feelings are transient too - so how can we claim to have a Self that is constant and authentic? To answer this question we have to transcend the limitations of our conditioning and enter the transpersonal realm of being. Our true self is in this world but not of it.

'We are in this world, but not of it.'
Jesus

Scientists have deduced that our brain is the *executer* of commands but not the *issuer* of them. They have searched every orifice of the brain in a quest to find the phenomenal intelligence that not only has the power to override the brain, but also correlates the trillions of transactions per second needed to keep us alive; to date their search has been to no avail. The only thing we can be certain of is that within each and every one of us there exists a formless intelligence of inconceivable power. This aspect of ourselves was never born and will never die; it is eternal, infinitely wise, and incomprehensively creative.

*

When we break through the constant noise of our internal dialogue and transcend the boundaries of rational thought, we access a part of ourselves that never changes: a field of pure being. This aspect is known by different names in different belief systems: Soul, Atman, Higher Self, Indwelling Divinity, Daemon, Spirit, and Guardian Angel. As it is supremely concentrated in the here and now - the present moment - it is often simply referred to as *presence*.

When we allow life to unfold from this level of our being, there is no challenge too great. Our Indwelling Divinity can provide instantaneous answers to every challenge life beholds. It is a counsellor, psychologist, psychic, philosopher, doctor, artist, genius, guru, avatar, and seer all rolled into one refined being. In addition to being the causal principle behind all of creation, this field of pure intelligence is also the gateway to infinite bliss.

Our Indwelling Divinity is forever present, softly whispering wise words through the silent gaps between our thoughts. We get so immersed in the constant chatter of our internal dialogue, however, that we don't hear it. Instead of bathing in the wise counsel of our essential being, we become embroiled in the chaos of our conditioned consciousness.

The Higher Self is not some alien being that has invaded our personal space - an anomaly that should be treated with reservation, ridicule, or contempt - it is our authentic self. To the detriment of our well-being our conditioning has taught us to discard the internal God. Yet all profound religious and spiritual literature tells us that the kingdom of God is within. Why take counsel from the screwed-up, pseudo-self, we call ego when we have this phenomenal aspect of our being at our disposal? All our wise forefathers and creative geniuses throughout the ages have tapped into this aspect of their being and achieved profound results: insights, foresights, major scientific breakthroughs, novel ideas, and peace. To reconnect with our Indwelling Divinity is to *come home*.

The following steps offer a template to start the process of re-unifying with your essential self:

1. **Establishing Rapport**
   - The first step is to open a line of communication with your Indwelling Divinity and establish rapport. Quiet your internal dialogue by simply observing it; don't get embroiled in your thoughts, simply watch them go by.
   - Next, focus on any question that is pressing at the moment. Listen in silence for the answer.
   - Finally, have an expectation that your relationship with your Higher Self will deepen on a daily basis.

2. **Redefine Your Agreement with Reality**
   We are conditioned as children to discard the true nature of reality in favour of a materialistic world view: if it's not solid, it's not real! As modern-day science tells us, this is nonsense. The underlying principle of life is an all-pervading field of intelligence.

   Our interface with this divine principle is our Higher Self. As our awareness breaks through the confines of our

---

rational mind, we enter a domain of existence where everything is possible: a field of infinite possibilities. In this domain there is no linear time or space. You may think of time as *vertical*. You do not have to wait for your desires to manifest, every possibility already exists. You just have to choose from the infinite possibilities available to you.

3. **Solitude**

Your Higher Self presents itself in silence. Make regular space for solitude and *being* (as opposed to *doing*). Sit quietly with no expectations. Give time and space for your inner wisdom to make itself heard. Listen for the gentle whispers that echo through the peripheries of your mind. Bathe in the embryo of love you find yourself encapsulated in.

4. **Meditation**

Meditation is not a practice that will just prolong your life, make you look younger, and give you the equivalent of eight hours sleep in twenty minutes – although it does accomplish these things – it is a practice that will discipline your mind and silence the internal chatter that constantly detracts from your primary focus. Placing your awareness on your breath is an excellent meditation discipline, or simply focusing on a flickering candle flame. To assist your introduction to meditation, I have provided a series of audio guided meditations that are freely available on our website **www.al2al.com**.

5. **Keeping an Inventory.**

Recording your feelings, thoughts, dreams, insights and foresights, is an excellent way of accentuating your understanding of how your Higher Self and the Universe operate. You can ask your Indwelling Divinity questions, and record whatever insights/answers you receive. If you do this regularly, you will be amazed at the results. Your belief and expectancy will increase. As a consequence, a profound shift in consciousness will take place.

6. **Regular Communication with the Wise Witness Within**
Conduct a regular dialogue with your Indwelling Divinity. Each morning, affirm the following:
'Today, I will allow life to unfold from the wisdom of my Indwelling Divinity.'
Just watch the radical transformation in your life as your Higher Self provides instantaneous solutions to problems. Talk to your Indwelling Divinity as though it was your best friend: ask questions, reveal your fears, and ask for guidance. Most importantly, listen for answers and become aware of the *synchronistic* happenings in your life.

7. **Life Lessons**
Discern the lessons you are encountering and elicit the teachings. Look at life as an adventure in which you have to detect the ways in which the universe speaks to you. Remember, your Higher Self is the interface between you and the Universal Mind. Learn to operate constantly from the level of your Indwelling Divinity. As the workings of your formless essence become increasingly evident, your ultimate path will become increasingly clear.

8. **Dreams**
Your Higher Self will speak to you through dreams. Before going to sleep, your conscious mind, sometimes called the *critical factor*, is quiet; so the channel to your Higher Self is

open and clear. Take advantage of this opportunity and ask your Higher Self a question, or simply hold the question in your mind. Expect an answer during your sleep. On awakening, recall whatever you can of your dream and record it in your journal. Discern the teachings.

9. Mindfulness

Focus on living in the present. Whilst going through your daily business, become aware of that part of you that is experiencing life; that still centre within that is undeterred by events in the material world. Concentrate supremely on the present moment and remember the following saying:

> **'Yesterday is history, tomorrow's a mystery:**
> **so live for today'**

Most problems are created by living in the past, or projecting into the future: the only time we ever have is NOW. By allowing life to unfold from the eternal continuum of the present, you will radically diminish stress and anxiety.

10. Unification: Becoming One with your Higher Self

The objective of all spiritual practices is to *become* one with your Higher Self. So far you have gained rapport and walked alongside your eternal essence. These practices suggest duality; they imply there are two of you. Ironically, the one you have identified with most of your life is fictitious – a mental construct. The only real *you* is your Indwelling Divinity. It's now time to reclaim your rightful heritage and totally surrender to your Higher Self.

Living On Purpose

**'When you are inspired by some great purpose,
some extraordinary project,
all your thoughts break their bonds:
Your mind transcends limitations,
your consciousness expands in every direction,
and you find yourself in a new, great, and
wonderful world.
Dormant forces, faculties and talents become alive,
and you discover yourself to be a greater person by
far than you ever dreamed yourself to be.'**

Pantanjali

When we were young, we were original, inventive and adventurous: anything was possible. We were not afraid to dream our dreams and aspire to achieve great things. Inspiration is something we were - not something we sought. During these magical years we were very aware of our Dharma - a spiritual principle that says we all have a unique purpose in life - a unique gift to bestow on the world. But, as time elapsed, our dreams, aspirations and purpose became distant memories as we were cloned to accept mediocrity and conformity. To be different was deemed a cardinal sin, punishable by true joy and fulfilment!

**'We are all born originals –
why is it so many of us die copies?'**

Edward Young

It is not until the noon of life, commonly called the mid-life crisis - a time when all hell breaks loose as people re-evaluate their outdated values and beliefs - that the lucky ones re-connect with their purpose. Majority of the population just trudge on, disguising their anguish and monotony with addictions: drugs, alcohol, spending, eating, and sex – anything that enables them to escape the futility of their mundane existence. But these *'fixes'* are temporary, illusory, and often destructive. They are misguided attempts to attain the wholeness that can only be achieved by reconnecting to our ultimate reason for living – our life's purpose.

When we discover our dharma, our lives take on a new dimension. Our mission is a desire of the Universe seeking manifestation through us. When we connect with it, the whole universe conspires to help us. Thoughts, solutions, ideas, and creativity permeate our minds; unexpected situations arise; people appear from nowhere to direct us. This all seems to happen automatically, as though some hidden force is orchestrating our destiny from another place - and so it is! These seemingly unexplainable and disconnected happenings are all engineered by the same creative intelligence. The thoughts, ideas, hunches, situations and people that illume our path and guide us forward are all different manifestations of the same intelligence. At the most primordial level of being everything is interconnected and interrelated. Ultimately, we are all one.

'No man is an island entire of itself;
Every man is a piece of the continent,
A part of the main;
If a clod be washed away by the sea,
Europe is the less,
As well as if a promontory were,
As well as a manor of thy friends

> ## Or of thine own were;
> ## Any man's death diminishes me,
> ## because I am involved in mankind.
> ## And therefore never send to know for whom
> ## the bell tolls; it tolls for thee.'
> John Donne

Uncovering Our Purpose

Finding my unique purpose was a gradual process rather than an instant realization. Little by little, over a number of years, it was revealed, evoking an ever-increasing sense of excitement within me. When the mystery finally revealed itself, I experienced the truth of Pantanjali's words above – *my thoughts did indeed break all their bonds: my mind transcended all limitations, and my consciousness expanded in every direction.* What a liberating experience! I had misguidedly searched for feelings of ecstasy and liberation in a bottle for many years, now my body produced them naturally, free of charge, and without any adverse side-effects! I can only describe the whole experience as a homecoming.

As my awareness accentuated above the constricting beliefs of my ego and I allowed every day to unfold from the wisdom and creativity of my Indwelling Divinity, I found myself in a *new, great and wonderful world.* I now realized that my life hadn't simply been a series of random catastrophes designed solely to destroy me; rather, it had been a perfect unfolding of circumstances that enabled me to realise my Dharma.

My purpose, I realized, was to evolve my understanding of the human experience and explore its relationship to the transpersonal aspects of being. I was to disperse my findings by way of books, seminars, workshops and courses. With this wonderful insightful knowledge my whole perspective of life changed dramatically. The trials and tribulations still came and went, but my purpose, like the clear blue skies beyond the thunderous clouds, remained forever present.

Every day became an adventure. Each of the 60,000 thoughts that traversed my mind had the potential to take me on a journey. My mind, I realized, was a field of infinite possibilities.

I experienced two distinct types of thought. Verbally constructed thought – thoughts comprised of words - emerging as a result of internalizing the dialogue of other people, and thoughts broadcast from my Indwelling Divinity. The latter were so easily discernable: they filled me with inspiration and enthusiasm. They set me alight inside. Each inspiring impulse emerging from the depths of my soul generated copious amounts of **enthusiasm**. It is interesting to note the term **en theos,** the root for the word **enthusiasm**, means **in spirit**. Enthusiasm is a sign that we are operating from spirit.

Everything is born in spirit. What we perceive as empty space is actually teeming with intelligence - the intelligence that gives rise to everything in existence: spirit. Within spirit every possibility already exists. The possibility of you being a famous actress; the possibility of you being a renowned author, movie star, or entrepreneur - literally, every scenario already exists – you just have to *choose* from the infinite possibilities.

People who achieve great things don't have exclusive rights on creativity; it is freely available to anyone. The only thing that differentiates them from you is that they have broken their agreement with reality and harnessed their true potential. You are a unique manifestation of the intelligence responsible for all creation – therefore, you are capable of creating anything you desire.

Does our life's purpose have to be some extraordinary mission?

No, not at all; just something that gives you great joy. Steve, my friend whose story appears in the beginning of this book, remained in the same employment for forty-five years - that of refuse collector. He took great pride in cleaning up the garbage on the streets, saying that every time he performed his job he also purged his mind of the mental and emotional debris that blocked his connection to his Indwelling Divinity. Choosing to serve the public in such a humbling way helped him maintain his equilibrium. Steve is a living tribute to the following Zen Proverb:

Before enlightenment; chop wood, carry water.
After enlightenment; chop wood, carry water.

When people attain an enlightened state, they don't necessarily change their roles; they do, however, *perceive what they do in a completely different light*. Mother Theresa described purpose in the following way:

'Do small things with great love'

Whether your purpose involves some great feat or simply accomplishing small things with great love, know that it is the will of God manifesting through you. Whatever it is, it is of great importance. Your talents are unique, bestow them on the world and allow everyone to reap the benefits.

'Hide not your talents, they for use were made.
What's a sundial in the shade?'

Benjamin Franklin

If you want to make a difference in this world, you cannot afford to follow the herd: you must become the shepherd. Rather than following the path people have tread before you, make your own path and leave a trail for others to follow. When your time comes to depart this life, don't let your resting place be in the ground, let it be in the hearts of all those you have touched.

When you were born, you cried and the world rejoiced. Live your life so that when you die, the world cries and you rejoice.

PAIN

'We must embrace pain
and burn it as fuel for our journey.'
Kenji Miyazawa (poet and author)

This section centres on psychological or emotional pain - not physical pain. Although, as with physical pain, psychological pain is a signal from our mind / body system that some pressing issue needs attention.

There are positive aspects to pain that cannot be attained through pleasure. Pain is a highly efficient warning system. Similar to the anti-virus software on your computer, it alerts you of potential problems. If left unattended a computer virus has the capacity to render the whole system dysfunctional, unresolved issues have exactly the same capacity.

> **Unacknowledged pain renders the mind dysfunctional and veils your true potential**

So it's important to take heed of your warning system and act on its alerts. I do not subscribe to the belief that '***there's no gain without pain***' as it suggests that the only way to evolve is through pain and that is simply untrue. However, transmuting pain does often result in forward propulsion.

Pain is an invitation to explore the hidden realms of our minds and resolve the issues that have impeded us for years. This process is rewarding, insightful and extremely liberating. Despite the obvious benefits of processing and jettisoning our mental and emotional baggage, however, our culture teaches us to deny them - misguidedly believing they will dissolve of their own accord when pushed to the peripherals of our mind. This destructive fallacy couldn't be further from the truth. Conscious exclusion of emotional issues leads to repression; the process by which the contents of our conscious mind are banished to the unconscious. Although these issues are forgotten - no longer accessible to the conscious mind - they continue to gather momentum in the unconscious. Repressed material must find a means of expression, and it often does so by assuming a variety of menacing guises: phobias, fears, obsessions, addictions, mood swings, aggression and low self esteem. Sigmund Freud once relayed the following metaphor to relay the adverse effects of such action:

'I once had a student who was extremely troublesome and disruptive. In my quest to alleviate his negative influence I ordered him to leave the classroom and wait in the corridor outside. Without objection he stood up and removed himself. To my dismay, once out of sight, his bad behaviour escalated and he caused a deluge of destruction.'

The moral of the story is as follows:

Banishing problems from memory doesn't cure them;
it simply moves them to a place where
we can no longer see them.
In this hidden place, they gather momentum
and mount an assault on our lives
that often causes conflict, pain and destruction.
Remember, we can't disarm and adversary we cannot see:

Don't hide your problems – solve them.

PAIN - Pay Attention and **Identify** the **Need**
Alcohol is a great anaesthetic capable of temporarily disguising pain; but when the anaesthetic wears off the pain is worse than ever. So anaesthetizing pain with alcohol is futile. In addition, when you use alcohol to quell psychological turbulence, you cannot extract the teachings enveloped in the pain:

Pain is a ploy for your attention
- heed its signals and extract its teachings

Ultimately, pain has the primary objective of informing you of a deficit or lack. *Without exception, all psychological pain transpires from ignoring at least one of your primary needs.* With this in mind, next time pain arises, vow to *Pay Attention* and *Identify* the *Need.* Stamp this acronym in your mind in indelible ink.

P.A.I.N - Pay Attention - Identify Need

As soon as you experience pain, find a quiet place and allow yourself to experience it in its entirety. The healing is in the awareness, in not shrinking from it. In the same way as nature heals a physical wound, all psychological healing comes from awareness. The more we make the source of our pain conscious, the deeper the healing effect. Accepting pain without resistance, and showing courage, endurance, and a willingness to learn are all that's needed. As you monitor the bodily sensations and inner dialogue that accompany it, ask the source of the pain what it needs for healing to take place. Listen carefully to the answers. Sometimes silence has the loudest voice; it is the medium through which your soul speaks. So be still and know the Universe is with you.

The Recoiled Spring Effect

When we feel pain we have a tendency to recoil. Our body constricts and we push everything down. The effect is similar to a recoiled spring in that when we squeeze the ends together it has a natural tendency to push back. If we want to keep it recoiled we have to exert pressure and expend energy. Herein lies the key to transforming pain. Ancient wisdom, such as the Kabbalah, teaches us that a downfall precedes most of the major advances in life. When we experience a painful situation, we often push it down into our unconscious. But like the recoiled spring, this repressed energy will push back. We can either waste vital energy on countering this forward thrust and become exhausted and depleted as a result, or harness it and allow it to propel us forward.

Don't internalize pain, focus it externally and use it to manifest your goals

Summary

- Psychological pain is a signal that some pressing issue needs our attention.
- If left unattended, such issues cause dysfunction.
- Unacknowledged pain veils your true potential.
- Without exception, all psychological pain transpires from ignoring at least one of your primary needs. Pain equals **P**ay **A**ttention and **I**dentify the **N**eed.
- When we resolve painful issues, we free up a vast amount of potential energy that can be used for other activities.
- Don't internalize pain, focus it externally and use it to manifest your goals.

FEAR

'What we seek we shall find; what we flee from flees from us.'
Ralph Waldo Emerson

Undoubtedly, some manifestations of fear are life-sustaining, wise and motivating. Instinctual fear, for example, is an emotional response to a threat - a basic survival mechanism. Without it the human being would have become extinct. However, the type of fear we will be examining here is neither motivating nor wise, it is of the type portrayed by FDR in the following statement:

"The only thing we have to fear is fear itself - nameless, unreasoning, unjustified, terror which

paralyzes needed efforts to convert retreat into advance."
Franklin D. Roosevelt

Most fears are distorted fabrications of the mind and have very little to do with current reality. The mind makes interpretations based on past experience. When a current situation triggers negative or traumatic unconscious material within us, the conscious mind's protective element kicks in and overcompensates by distorting the potential threat or degree of danger that confronts us .

Most incidences of fear are distorted fabrications of the mind

As Franklin Roosevelt points out, *the only thing we have to fear is fear itself.* The stimulus giving rise to fear is very rarely the problem; the way we interpret it is often the great disabler. Fear takes an experience, distorts it out of all proportion, and then uses it to paralyze us.

'Fear makes the wolf bigger than he is.'
German Proverb

Example: Joe's misinterpretation

Joe, fifteen, asks Shirley, a girl he's always adored from a distance, for a date. Shirley declines. Joe is speechless and wants the earth to swallow him up. The corrosive inner dialogue begins: you are ugly; not good enough; boring; who'd want to date you; and so on.
Subsequently, when Joe is attracted to a female, fear intervenes: don't ask her out; it's dangerous; remember last time; it'll only end in tears and rejection.

Epilogue:

Joe refrains from asking women out for the next ten years. His fear of rejection led to a need to escape and he developed a destructive alcohol problem. One day, quite unexpectedly, he bumped into Shirley. She promptly introduced the girl at her side as her partner!

This is a typical example of fear paralysis. Joe's life script, the messages he'd internalized throughout his life, had instilled in him a sense of inferiority. Shirley declining his invitation acted as a stimulus to evoke his inferiority complex. The resulting interpretation, made through the filters of his memory, was totally erroneous – *she didn't dislike him: she was gay!* Joe spent ten years of his life running away from a mere fabrication of his mind! Don't be harnessed by mental and emotional pollution; embrace life, step out of your comfort zone, and claim what is rightfully yours.

A ship anchored in a safe harbour cannot explore the oceans

Fabricated Experience – Artificial Reasoning
The key to understanding fear begins with the observation that it is intimately connected to our thoughts, and the way in which we interpret experience. Fear is often simply fabricated experience supported by artificial reasoning that has no bearing on reality whatsoever.

F.E.A.R. - *Fabricated Experience Artificial Reasoning*
Deep unexpressed fears are often the result of unresolved past issues. Vowing to understand them entails embarking on an insightful inner journey. Whereas unenlightened people see fears as

obstacles to be avoided, the Alchemist sees them as opportunities to transform. As Joe's story epitomizes:

> ## 'Nothing in life is to be feared.
> ## It is only to be understood.'
> **Marie Curie**

All fear can be alleviated with understanding. Take the following example:

Example: Robert's fear of spiders

Robert had a great fear of spiders. Every time he saw one he broke out into a cold sweat and went into panic. When I regressed him during a hypnotherapy session, he found himself in the kitchen of his childhood home. He had a fascination with insects and would catch them and put them into the fridge. During the session he started to sob uncontrollably. When I asked what was happening, he said his mother had caught him putting a spider into the fridge. She promptly pulled him by the ear to the bathroom; threw the spider down the toilet; poured lighter fuel on it; and burnt it. Robert, understandably, experienced trauma. As this episode happened when he was only seven years of age, he had forgotten it – it had been repressed - but the trauma re-presented itself every time he saw a spider. This experience had left him with a strong association between spiders and trauma, so every time he saw a spider he had an abreaction and panicked. Once this was brought into the light of consciousness and explained to him, and the traumatic incident was worked through and resolved, his fear of spiders disappeared. As Marie Curie points out, there was nothing to fear, understanding was all that was needed.

Before we address some common fears and look at the underlying beliefs that give rise to them, let's bear in mind one last, extremely important point: people procrastinate when dealing with fear because they think their fear must subside before they tackle the issue evoking it. If this was the case, many fears would go unchallenged for a lifetime. All the great people in history had one thing in common – they all had courage.

Courage is not the absence of fear; it is a willingness to act despite the presence of fear

*

Following is a short list of common fears along with the underlying beliefs that give rise to them, their manifestations and some suggestions of how to counteract them:

Fear of Abandonment:
Underlying Beliefs:

- Nobody cares about me.

- Nobody wants to know me.

- I'm all alone.

- I'm insignificant and transparent.

- I'm bad, defective or/and unworthy

Manifestations: compensatory behaviour for this fear often manifests as a deep need to be included in everything and an over-eagerness to be part of everything. Whether the pursuit or activity is enjoyable or not is of no real consequence, the objective is to avoid exacerbating feelings of abandonment.

Antidote: Inner child work (see exercise p.374).

Fear of Rejection

Underlying Beliefs:

- I'm a burden
- I'm boring.
- I'm not good enough.
- I'm unattractive

Manifestations: People with a fear of rejection often become insular and unwilling to risk forging friendships and relationships. Many exclaim that they are better off alone, whilst inwardly harbouring a deep desire to connect in meaningful ways with other people.

Starting employment is often particularly problematic, many shy away from it, fearing they won't be accepted by their new colleagues. Others over-compensate by presenting themselves as incredibly popular and interesting, yet their ability to sustain this façade is highly dependent on how others respond.
Antidote: Inner child

Fear of Failure

Underlying Beliefs:

- I'm useless.
- I never get anything right
- I'm stupid
- I'm a disaster waiting to happen

Manifestations: nervousness, severe lack of confidence, stagnancy, and a reluctance to attempt anything.
Antidote: inner child work.

Remember**, there is no failure, only feedback**. When we attempt something and don't achieve the results we expected, we haven't failed – we have achieved a result. What we do with the result is what counts. If we use it to refine our strategies and improve our future efforts then we have transformed a perceived deficit into an asset – which is the essence of alchemy.

The Root Belief of all Fears is Inferiority

Inferiority is the underlying theme running through all the examples of fear outlined above. Over-compensatory behaviour for an inferiority complex often manifests as a need to prove that one is better than others, but this often results in alienation and loneliness. To thoroughly alleviate inferiority you have to recognise that it has emerged as a result of internalizing negative comments from significant people throughout your life. To address the catalyst, you must nourish your inner child with loving nurturance and counteract this negativity. Refer to the Inner Child Exercises (see p.374).

Summary: Core points of this Chapter:

- The concept of self is merely a construct developed from internalizing and subscribing to other people's opinions and influences: it is not a fixed or absolute entity. Remove the labels, roles and beliefs that constitute the *idea of who you think you are* and *you* still exist; therefore, the self construct cannot be your true essence. You are much more than a set of indoctrinated beliefs, assigned roles and labels. You are an inexorable bundle of vibrant energy, composed of the same fabric as the Creative Source of the Universe.

- Our Indwelling Divinity or Higher Self is a formless, eternal, field of phenomenal intelligence, capable of providing instantaneous solutions to any of life's challenges. Allowing life to unfold from this level of being brings liberation and abundance.

- Unwarranted guilt is highly corrosive. Counteract it with self love. Warranted guilt should be used as a self-correcting feedback system.

- Futility does not exist in the external world; it exists only in us. Two primary causes are responsible: loss of **identity** and loss of **purpose**. Re-connect with your true self and discover your life's purpose.

- Embrace pain and burn it as fuel for your journey

- Fear makes the wolf appear bigger! Most fear is fabricated experience supported by artificial reasoning, don't let it paralyse you. Remember, courage is not the absence of fear, it is your willingness to act despite fear.

Exercise: Pain Meditation

Sit comfortably and quietly. Let your body relax. Breathe gently. As you exhale let go of any tension and anxiety, allow past and future to dissipate, and let your plans pale into insignificance. Just be present. Allow your unconscious mind to present any unresolved issues for resolution. Allow the source of the pain to emerge: childhood, relationships, employment or whatever. Focus on the pain. Allow the memories to arise. Feel their energy and become aware of the physical sensations in your body. Awareness is the healing source of all your problems. Don't judge the issue - just observe it; allow your awareness to permeate it. Remain receptive and embrace any lessons. Allow your Higher Self to cradle you throughout. Breathe softly and let the experience expand. Be aware of any aversion or resistance in your mind. Place your awareness on the resistance and just allow it to be. Thank it for its concern and acknowledge that it is only trying to protect you, but know that it has served its purpose and allow it to disperse in its own time. Now notice the thoughts and fears that accompany the pain you are exploring: `it was their fault', 'it will never go away', `I can't stand it', and so on. Let these thoughts rest in your awareness. Let your attention penetrate the problem. Bring your attention to the pain and hold it in gentle repose.

In your own time, allow your awareness to return behind the windows of your eyes. Centre yourself. Feel the gentle pull of gravity on your shoulders. Ground yourself. Then, open your eyes and familiarise yourself with your surroundings.

As we gradually bring to our awareness that which we have previously banished, our mind begins to heal. During this process we must pay careful attention to the sensations that traverse our bodies. We can heighten our awareness and notice the patterns of our breathing, our posture, our back, our chest, our stomach. In all these areas, we can sense expansion or contraction as we release or hold onto our issues.

When you meditate, try to allow whatever arises to move through you until it dissipates - as it surely will. Grief, anger, jealousy, loneliness, and sorrow can all be alleviated with pure attention. Observation can dissolve any issue. Just stay with it. As time elapses, your breathing will soften and you will open to deeper layers of emotion. Let your awareness penetrate these too, until you experience a profound sense of peace.

Exercise: Dreams

Find yourself a comfortable space; a place where you will be free of interruptions. Relax and focus on your breath... notice the rise and fall of your stomach as you inhale and exhale... feel the warmth of your breath... as you exhale, let go of any tension, anxiety and stress.. let it all dissipate into the ether... and breathe in a profound sense of peace... breath out tension... breath in peace (continue this cycle for a couple of minutes).

Now, let this scene come to mind… you awaken from a drunken stupor, your head feels like home to a swarm of bees, buzzing and pounding….. you're slumped on a settee in an unfamiliar room…. someone put you up last night but you can't remember who….. a feeling of nausea rises in your stomach and you break into cold sweats… you race into the kitchen and throw your head over the sink just in time to throw up last night's concoction of poisonous liquids… the stench of vomit fills your nostrils, it wreaks…. Your body starts to shake uncontrollably and suddenly everything goes dark…

…….. you awake disorientated... a friend is standing over you…'what happened?' you ask, sheepishly….. 'I was upstairs and I heard a bang. I rushed down and found you collapsed on the floor, foaming at the mouth and convulsing.' your friend answers…

…. Suddenly, you become aware of the stench of urine hanging in the air….. you look down to find your trousers saturated. …. The embarrassment would have been unbearable only for the fact you feel so ill as not to care… …you're dehydrating so you ask your friend for a glass of water…. when he passes it to you your hands are shaking so much that you are unable to take it off him… he's a true friend, understanding your predicament he puts the glass to your lips…. You gulp down the water with the desperation of a man who has been lost in the desert for months…

…… you're mind begins to drift to your loved ones… they have no idea where you are… their faces drift across your screen of consciousness… their eyes filled with despair as they wander where you are and what you're doing… you become imbued with a deep sense of guilt and remorse… the pain is unbearable… although you are emaciated through lack of food, and your skin has a yellow cast due to damaged liver, you desperately want to escape… you want more alcohol… again, your body begins to convulse and everything goes black…

…… you awake in a strange bed… you can vaguely make out the people surrounding you.. one is a doctor who is talking to your loved ones… one by one you look into their eyes… some are crying openly and need consoling, others are rigid with disbelief… you try to talk to them but you realise they cannot hear you… the doctor pulls the sheet over your head……

You jump up with a start and realise you are in your own bed… you had just experienced a nightmare.. or was it a prophecy of what will happen if you continue your present course?

…. You put your head back on the pillow and drift back to sleep.. another scene materializes… again, you find yourself on the floor of your friends house… an ambulance arrives and you are whisked off to hospital… on the way a wise voice echoes through your mind saying *'you weren't born to be this way - there is an answer'*… this voice has a profound effect on you….

….You are admitted to hospital and given the necessary vitamins and drugs to restore you to good physical health… after a few days your appetite returns and you start to eat again…

...the Sobriety Saboteurs now mount their assault – first, guilt... as you are overwhelmed with a deep sense of remorse the Wise Witness Within speaks once again...

'the best way to escape your problems is to solve them, dear one... up to now you have known no different, you have felt compelled to drink to destruction... you have acted unconsciously and therefore you can relinquish responsibility for your misdeeds and forgive yourself... love yourself, dear one.. know you are worthy of love... think of all the good deeds you have performed for others during the course of your life... think of all the good deeds you intend to carry out in the future... let that sense of goodness expand within you... let it multiply one thousand fold...

Your guilt subsides... you forgive yourself for past transgressions and focus on the good you can do with your life. You vow to take control of your life and accept the consequences from this moment forth...

...Now the second Sobriety Saboteur mounts its assault – pain... your mind is filled with disturbing vestiges of the past: mistreatment, bullying, rejection, abandonment, or some other form of negative experience... you feel the urge to escape arising, but, once again, the Wise Witness Within intervenes....

.... There are positive aspects to pain that cannot be attained through pleasure, dear one. Pain is a highly efficient warning system, similar to the anti-virus software on your computer, it alerts you of potential problems. If left unattended computer viruses have the capacity to render the whole system dysfunctional... unresolved issues have exactly the same capacity... unacknowledged pain renders the mind dysfunctional and limits your true potential.... So take heed of your cognitive warning system and act on its alerts, dear one.... transmuting pain often results in a renewed passion for life. As you disperse polluted energy and transform it back into potential energy, you will be filled with great vitality and a renewed sense of clarity. The pain you are experiencing is an invitation to explore the hidden realms of your mind and resolve issues that have impeded your life for years: the process is

rewarding, insightful and liberating. ...

Something in you shifts... you realise that pain is an invitation to evolve... a chance to discover something about yourself... a chance to transmute polluted energy into potential energy and increase your vitality and passion for life... You vow to embrace pain, understand it, and transmute it....

.....Fear and paranoia now try to disturb your equilibrium... memories of the people you insulted or violated in some way begin to arise.... Your mind spins into a paranoiac frenzy... you fear people are out to get you... other fears arise too... money, how can I pay my bills; I'm in so much debt?.... what will happen when I get out of this hospital and have to face the consequences of my actions?... the Wise Witness intervenes...

... most fears are fabricated distortions of the mind, dear one.... Fear makes the wolf seem bigger... fear stands for Fabricated Experience and Artificial Reasoning... in most instances it is a spectre.... Don't allow a distortion of your mind to promote stasis and render you inert.... Remember you are a good person and deserved of the best life has to offer....nothing in life is to be feared, just understood....

Your fear subsides... you accept that most fear is unwarranted... a negative predisposition of a warped mind... you vow to remedy that...

...... The final Saboteur now tries its hand – futility.... You are filled with thoughts that life is a barren wasteland having no meaning or purpose.... But the Wise Witness Within tells you otherwise...

When you are inspired by some great purpose,
some extraordinary project,
all your thoughts break their bonds:
Your mind transcends limitations,
your consciousness expands in every direction,

and you find yourself in a new, great, and wonderful world.
Dormant forces, faculties and talents become alive,
and your discover yourself to be a greater person by far than you ever
dreamed yourself to be.

Within your heart, dear one, you hold a purpose… a unique gift to offer the world.. whatever the pursuit or activity, you will find yourself to be an expert in it… this is your ultimate purpose in life and it will bring great joy and fulfilment… open your heart, dear one… discover your gift to the world… do what you love and love what you do….

You suddenly find yourself five years into the future. After you left hospital someone gave you a book as a gift… a book entitled **Alcoholic to Alchemist**.. you chose the path of the Alchemist… you've spent the last five years turning the base metals of your mind into your psychological wealth: inspiration, creativity, joy, wisdom... a rebirth has taken place… you adhered to the philosophy rigorously and with great enthusiasm and now you glean the rewards…. You found your purpose in life and pursued it…. You look into the eyes of each member of your family and notice that the despair that once filled them has been supplanted by radiance... the joy of knowing that their treasured family member has returned

Allow the whole scenario to permeate your mind for a while, then when you are ready, open your eyes and readjust to your surroundings.

Also see exercise - Discovering Your Life's Purpose (p.390)

Chapter 16

Cause and Effect

Pro-act don't Re-act

If I had to sum-up the objective of the Alcoholic to Alchemist Philosophy in one sentence it would read as follows:

**To transform a *reactive* person
into a *proactive* person**

The Reactive

To *re-act* means to recycle old behaviour in response to new experiences. When we **re-act,** we don't *progress* - we *regress*, repeatedly reverting to out-dated modes of action. Let's remember, alcoholism is an escape mechanism used to escape a life that is deemed unbearable. If we continue to repeat old behaviour nothing will change.

**"If you keep on doing what you've always done,
you'll keep on getting what you've always got."**
W. L. Bateman

Reactive people are like ships caught in a storm, tossed and buffeted by the tides of life. Without the stabilizing force of a captain they drift aimlessly. Each wave knocks them off balance and they don't have time to recover before the next one arrives to deliver a crushing blow. They are apparently at the mercy of the turbulent *surface* of the ocean; but, as we shall soon see, it is the *undercurrents* which pose the more serious problem.

The word *reactive* implies lack of *conscious* control. Reactive people are driven by unconscious impulses: the *undercurrents.* Although we are powerful beings with the freedom to choose whatever we desire in life, our ability to exercise the faculty of choice is often thwarted by underlying mechanisms which override our conscious intent.

When we **re-act,** dormant forces come alive and render us highly volatile. Like time-bombs, we tick away - ready to explode in response to trivial situations. People inadvertently trigger these underlying forces and we attack them; but they are not to blame. The locus of the problem is situated firmly within ourselves. Our outbursts are triggered by processing the world through the lens of our history.

The Pro-active

When we **pro-act,** we take the helm and set a course for our desired life. With our sails filled with wisdom and insight, we venture out to explore the infinite possibilities the ocean of life has to offer. This wonderful journey starts by fostering an attitude of curiosity and enquiry.

Beneath the Surface

The journey from Alcoholic to Alchemist is contingent on our ability to raise our self awareness and identify the unconscious patterns that sabotage our lives. Many of our current relationships and interactions are negatively influenced by unconscious material. *Have you ever flared up for no apparent reason and wondered what came over you? Or grossly over-reacted to a somewhat trivial situation?* If so - then you have probably experienced one of the primary unconscious processes responsible for major conflict in our lives: **transference,** *countertransference* or *shadow projection*. This section is designed to heighten your awareness of these destructive mechanisms.

'Knowing others is wisdom, knowing yourself is Enlightenment.'
Lao Tzu

Transference

Transference is a Freudian term used to describe how we unconsciously assign feelings and attitudes that we had for significant figures in our early life, to people in our life today. It can be defined as an unconscious phenomenon in which a person projects onto another person the attitudes, feelings, and desires originally linked to early relationships. Simply put, transference is the re-enactment of past relationships in the present. The phenomenon is best explained through true-life examples.

Example 1: John's Transference

John, twenty-eight, had been sober for three years. However, when he turned up for counselling he'd been experiencing angry outbursts that were threatening his sobriety. His last flare-up happened when his partner, Sharon, went into hospital. He had been informed in advance but this notice did little to reassure him. When he received the news, he erupted and smashed some furniture up; his response had frightened Sharon.

When we first spoke, John was full of remorse and totally baffled as to why he'd erupted in this way. This wasn't the first time he had lost control, however; he'd reacted negatively to Sharon's absence on other occasions, but this time the severity of his reaction had escalated to such an extent that he feared losing her.

During his counselling we identified some early experiences which explained his emotionally charged responses. His parents had divorced when he was five years old and shortly after his father had been taken ill and hospitalized. No one had taken time to talk to the small child and explain what was happening. Consequently, John held his mother responsible for his father's absence and illness, believing her leaving was the cause. The psychological pain was so great that his defence systems had banished this experience to the realms of his unconscious. Until he came for counselling, he had no recollection of it whatsoever – it had been repressed.

1

However, repressed material must find a means of expression. If we bury the cause, the effect will simply be delayed. In this case, as with many other cases, the internalized relationship was finding expression externally. When triggered by abandonment threats, John psychologically regressed to that five-year-old child and the relationship he had with his mother represented itself. On this last occasion, Sharon, who had inadvertently triggered these unresolved childhood issues, became a projection - a virtual incarnation - of John's mother. The pent-up negative emotion John's five-year-old inner child held for his mother was transferred onto Sharon, which explains the emotionally charged, irrational response to her leaving. John was unconsciously re-enacting the relationship he had with his mother many years ago. These dynamics were happening at an unconscious level, so neither partner was aware of what was actually happening. As you can imagine, left unattended these unconscious dynamics could have caused mayhem and ended up in divorce.

After gaining these insights and processing the feelings surrounding his parents' break-up and the hospitalization of his father, John explained everything to Sharon. She was very understanding and extremely supportive. Subsequently, John's irrational behaviour subsided and their relationship blossomed.   2

Epilogue:

At the time of writing, John has been sober for eight years, and the couple are currently expecting their second child. John found his therapy so enlightening and rewarding that he decided to train as a psychologist. Today he has a very successful practice in London. *Another tremendous success story!*

Example 2:   Charlie's Transference

Charlene, or Charlie, as she preferred to be called, had a history of alcoholism and violent behaviour. She'd attended a number of anger management classes but these had failed to quell her temper. When I asked her about the violence, she looked dumbfounded – 'I don't know what to say,' she answered, despondently. 'It frightens me; I feel powerless to stop it – I feel possessed!'

After a number of therapy sessions, we identified the trigger for Charlie's irrational outbursts. Rather than being haphazard or unpredictable, there was a pattern to them. Her violent disposition was triggered whenever a male raised his voice or acted in a condescending way towards her.

Whilst exploring her history, the reason became quite apparent. Charlie had a violent father who beat her frequently. She had never spoken about her relationship with him until she came for therapy. Consequently, the experience had been buried deep in her unconscious. Whenever a male acted in a manner she perceived as condescending or threatening, her repressed relationship with her father flared up and found expression though re-enactment with unsuspecting males. Rather than acting objectively to these men, seeing them as real people, she experienced them (unconsciously) as virtual incarnations of her father; hence, the pent up emotion

1

she felt for her father was transferred onto them.

During the subsequent counselling sessions, I helped Charlie to process the pent-up emotions she had for her father. Week after week she broke down and sobbed – something she hadn't done for years. This cathartic release eventually resulted in her anger dissipating and there were no more violent outbursts. In addition, Charlie gained an understanding of why her father beat her; he was subjected to the same rites of passage when he was a child, and was acting out what he had learned from his own parents. On discovering this, Charlie, who hadn't seen her father in years, made contact with him.

2

Epilogue

Charlie is currently five years sober. Her relationship with her once estranged father continues to improve on a daily basis. Charlie is now in the second year of an honours degree in performing arts. *The success stories go on and on!*

Countertransference

The counterpart of transference is a phenomenon known as *countertransference*. When a person becomes the object of transference, it can tap into their own unresolved issues and result in a reaction; this re-action is termed *countertransference* i.e. it is a reaction that *counters* or opposes transference.

None of us are exempt from countertransference; we are all capable of displacing feelings from our past onto other people. During my sessions with Charlie, I became the object of transference. She occasionally, and unconsciously, of course, transferred anger associated with her father onto me. Initially, I felt a re-action to her barrage of abuse; I felt a built up of anger inside of myself in retaliation. As she directed the unresolved pent-up emotions she held for her father towards me, her behaviour started to trigger my own unresolved issues (i.e. activated my countertransference). Under different circumstances these underlying dynamics may have led to a blistering argument, or even violence. Such flare-ups are common in everyday life and often spiral out of control. However, as a trained counsellor, I was very aware of my countertransference and used it to gain insight into the relationship Charlie had with her father.

The way in which to disperse countertransference is to de-personalize the abuse that is directed our way; recognize that, in some way, you remind the perpetrator of a significant person in their past.

Another extremely important point to highlight is that countertransference does not always manifest as a verbal or emotional attack, as the following example shows.

> ## Example: Ron's Countertransference
> *Ron was a psychiatric nurse, specializing in addiction counselling. He was surprised by the strength of his responses to one of his clients. When he was a child, his parents were neglectful and dependent on alcohol. As a teenager he experimented with drugs and alcohol too. From an early age he had learned to fend for himself, cooking and shopping whenever there was money to do so. One of his current clients, a middle-aged man, had been addicted to alcohol for many years. Some of this client's characteristics reminded him of his father. Ron found himself 'taking care' of his client in ways which were professionally inappropriate e.g. worrying about him and giving him advice. On other occasions, he had strong negative feelings towards him. These mixed emotions mirrored the positive and negative feelings he had towards his father.*

Ron's example shows that transference and countertransference can manifest in a variety of ambiguous guises, not just aggression or violence. Here are a few more common examples:

- **Seeing people has helpless, or victims:** This highlights a need to be in control.
- **Inability to confront or disagree:** This may stem from a fear of being disliked, or being seen as incompetent.
- **In competition, or envious:** This may relate to childhood problems with siblings and parents.

To conclude our discussion on transference and countertransference, just remember, if you find yourself acting in ways that impede your ability to relate healthily to others, ways that threaten your cherished relationships, go within and investigate your past. Transference and countertransference are often responsible for disturbing our equilibrium. The subsequent despair can easily lead to a need to escape via the bottle.

Transference and Countertransference are both reactive.
Don't be an effect of past conditioning.
You were endowed with the capacity to achieve great things, be causal and make them happen.

Shadow Projection

"We still attribute to the other fellow all the evil and inferior qualities that we do not like to recognize in ourselves, and therefore have to criticize and attack him, when all that has happened is that an inferior "soul" has emigrated from one person to another. The world is still full of bêtes-noires and scapegoats, just as it formerly teemed with witches and werewolves."

C. J. Jung

Shadow projection is a defence mechanism employed by the ego; a process whereby one's own perceived shortcomings are seen as being situated in other people. In order to maintain its status, the ego disowns anything which threatens its standing in the community; for example, jealousy, anger, laziness, intolerance, self-centredness, selfishness, deceit, and greed (which are all aspects of our *shadow*). Instead of owning these shadow elements, the ego projects them onto other people, turning a personal inferiority into a (perceived) moral deficiency in someone else. The unsuspecting person – the *scapegoat* - is then attacked and criticized.

By disowning our faults and attributing them to other people, we cling onto the infected energy that clouds our judgements and destroys our relationships. Let's not forget,

The external world is a reflection of our state of mind

If we find ourselves casting aspersions onto some unsuspecting person for no reason other than to bolster our false sense of superiority, then it is probable that we are projecting our own flaws onto them. If we are wise, we will use this insight to gain self-knowledge and change the character defects that impede our growth.

Don't project – introspect;
blame is a futile practice.

When we deny our shortcomings and project them onto others, we cocoon ourselves in a shell of darkness. Shadow projections insulate and cripple individuals by forming an ever thickening fog of illusion between them and the real world. When this occurs, their personal world becomes a hostile place to be – consequently, escape is sought; and escape normally leads back to the bottle - so nip it in the bud!

The next time you find yourself criticizing someone, try to connect with the part of your Shadow that is making the critical judgment. For example: '*My partner always wants to be right and she never listens*'. Be very honest with yourself; is there a part of you that always wants to be right? Are you projecting your own defects onto your partner? By employing this practice regularly you will increase your awareness of those parts of yourself that need work. We may not always like the truth, but don't be hard on yourself: *don't treat it as criticism; treat it as feedback.* In this way, the external world becomes an excellent teacher, reflecting back the character defects we need to alleviate in order to reach our true potential.

People who cast aspersions usually define themselves – not others

As well as being mindful of occasions when you are projecting your flaws and defects onto others, there will also be occasions when others project their short-comings onto you. If you are not mindful of this phenomenon, it can be all too easy to internalize their aspersions. Remember, the concept of self, *the idea of who we think we are,* is constructed in accordance with the messages we internalise from other people. Although this is more prevalent during our formative years, if we are of a volatile disposition, these messages can still deeply affect us in adulthood. Therefore, we need to reject the shadow projections of other people and recognise them for what they are: an attempt to purge themselves of *their* flaws and shortcomings at our expense - a deluded way of trying to elevate their status. When we find ourselves the target of unwarranted defamatory remarks, we must realise that the perpetrators are not defining us: they are defining themselves.

> **When people project their character defects onto us and attempt to use us as scapegoats, they define themselves: not us.**

Egoic Consciousness and the Possessive Tendency

Before leaving the subject of cause and effect, let's examine the way in which our Ego is apt to disempower us and render us an *effect* of the competitive society we live in.

At the egoic level of consciousness, we experience ourselves as separate and distinct from others; isolated egos defined by the boundaries of our bodies. From this divided state all conflict is born. The prevailing sense of separateness gives rise to a competitive and possessive culture obsessed with a desire for power, position and prestige; an ethos that breeds conflict of every form: vindictiveness, antagonism, brutality, manipulation, jealousy and so on.

The ego is volatile, demanding, competitive and possessive. In an attempt to elevate its status, it expends vital energy on manipulation, grievances, judgments, comparisons, criticism and other futile energy draining activities. The ego's sense of worth is primarily derived from other people's perceived character defects and shortcomings. By casting aspersions on others, however, we inadvertently emphasize our own insecurities and inferiority. Now, couple this with another psychological phenomenon - the fact that whatever our mind focuses on expands - and the connotations become disturbing:

> **If you are intent on verbally annihilating others
> to inflate your false sense of self,
> then be prepared to dig two graves;
> perceiving your character defects in others
> is self-effacing**

Egoic consciousness is ambiguous. If life unfolds in accordance with your possessive and demanding nature; If people say this or do that; if external circumstances meet with approval; then all is well. If not, then some derisory strategy must be implemented to ensure that *all offenders are punished.*

This mode of operation bears no fruits. The locus of power is constantly placed outside yourself and you are demoted to a mere effect of other people's behaviour and opinions. Each grievance is a declaration of disempowerment. You are being reactive, not proactive. The shift in thinking necessary for contentment and happiness is thus demanded of everyone and everything except yourself. Conducting your life on this basis is futile; you are powerless over other people. Ultimately, the locus of every conceivable problem can be found within yourself. To fully except this is truly liberating.

Eradicating Jealousy

Egoic consciousness and the possessive tendency give rise to perhaps the most corrosive emotion of all: jealousy. Jealousy obliterates all our good qualities. It can make us sick; disturb our sleep, and upset our appetite. Jealousy propels us to attack others, but it serves only to destroy us. So long as we have jealousy we will never shine.

> **Jealousy propels us to attack others, but it only serves to destroy us.**

Jealousy takes away our peace of mind and invites relapse. It cannot be relieved by reading books or attending meditations; we have to make a conscious effort to eradicate it.

Simply put, jealousy is a secondary emotion evoked when we experience hostility towards a rival or someone believed to enjoy an advantage. Most people abhor the feeling and try to cover it up, but camouflaged jealousy is akin to venom: it slowly poisons the mind. A growing sense of inferiority gives rise to an increased tendency to be manipulative, scheming, and possessive. The results are often catastrophic. Jealousy wrecks relationships.

The sad fact is that most of this destruction is unnecessary. In majority of cases the issue in question is often imaginary: a fabrication of a mind infested with inferiority, plagued by paranoia, and swamped by suspicion.

When jealousy arises, don't delude yourself into seeking resolution in the external world: don't blame others – blame is simply an argument against growth. Take a good look within and identify your source of self doubt and insecurity. Jealousy is usually the result of one of the following core beliefs:

- **I'm inferior to....**
- **I'm not worthy of........**
- **I'm not capable of attaining....**
- **I don't possess the necessary resources or attributes**

The clue to the antidote lies in the opening word of these sentences - ***I'm.*** Any sentence starting with the words *I am* or *I'm* appertains to the Ego. The ego is simply a mental construct comprised of labels, roles, and beliefs. As a result, it is highly volatile and easily influenced by the good opinions of others.

Throughout the course of our lives people try to elevate their own status by putting us down and berating us – normally as a result of their own inferiority complexes. Our ego can either reject or accept these opinions. When it accepts them, they transform into corrosive inner dialogue and breed low self-esteem and inferiority within us. Low self-esteem and inferiority are the main ingredients of jealousy. When we believe we are less than others in some way, we feel disempowered. In order to claw back our power we become manipulative, scheming and highly controlling. We try to *fix* the problem externally, but this is simply a waste of time. Others are not to blame. We feel inferior because of the accumulative effect of the negative messages we have internalised (throughout the course of our lives). We have accepted the *good* opinions of others irrespective of their suitability to give them!

Suggestions for Alleviating Jealousy

- **Accept that the issues causing jealousy are in you: not in somebody else.** With the locus of the problem placed firmly within yourself, you have the power to resolve it. Don't fall into the trap of manipulating others to solve the problem. You will end up frustrated and disillusioned. We don't have the power to change others, only ourselves. Every problem can be overcome by changing ourselves.

- **No other person can make you feel any way; you feel the way you do by virtue of how you interpret experience.** Jealousy normally results by virtue of how we *perceive* things, not as a result of how they *truly are*. Honest communication is often a great help. Talking clarifies issues that are open to misinterpretation. When talking to the object of your jealousy i.e. partner or friend, refrain from using blame loaded language: *you made me feel awful; you are up to no good; you don't care for me*. Use language that acknowledges that the locus of the problem is within you: *I* *feel insecure because...; I feel inferior because....* (this usually takes courage but you will feel liberated and lighter).

- **When jealousy arises make it conscious.** Allow the feeling to expand and simply observe the sensations in your body; take a spectator's perspective. Remind yourself that the sensations you're experiencing have resulted from the cumulative effect of past issues that filled you with insecurity and inferiority. Allow the feelings to dissipate and re-evaluate the situation at hand.

- **Challenge the authenticity of your thoughts.** Do they have any credence? Or are they simply fabricated distortions of your mind? Are you jumping to conclusions, catastrophising, or personalising?

- **Direct your awareness to your attributes**, instead of focusing on the situation in question. Recognise the good in you and harness it. Remember the last time you felt full of confidence: hear what you heard, see what you saw, and feel what you felt. Let the experience expand a hundred-fold in your mind. Hear people paying you compliments: *you're so caring, you're so thoughtful, you're so funny etc.* See them in your minds-eye and internalize their positive perspective of you.

- **Develop independence.** Relying on your family, friends or partner for self-esteem is demanding and suffocating. Evoke self esteem intrinsically. Developing autonomy and creating a healthy distance will enhance your relationships. Develop an attitude of trust, relinquish control, and concentrate on your positive attributes.

> ## Evoke Self-Esteem Intrinsically

Summary

- Transference, countertransference, and shadow projection are three unconscious mechanisms that can severely hinder our relationships. Being aware of their manifestations, can prevent their negative influence from creating conflict and turmoil in your cherished relationships.

- Own your character defects and shortcomings and transform them into attributes. Do not disown them by projecting them onto others, that will simply promote stasis.

- Jealousy destroys us. Whenever it descends recognise it as insecurity within yourself. Focus on developing your self-esteem and worth and watch it magically dissipate.

*

Chapter 17

Reframing

In many cases, the way in which a problem is framed or perceived actually constitutes the problem itself: many problems are spectres - distorted interpretations of a negatively conditioned mind.

> ### The way we look at a problem
> ### is often the problem

Our *frame* of reference, or simply - *frame*, is a lens through which we interpret the world; a filtering system comprised of our ingrained beliefs and values. Rather than assigning meaning to events impartially, we make interpretations based on our life's experience.

> ### We do not see things as they are
> ### We see them as we are
> The Talmud

In light of this fact, it is rational to assume that if we redefine our beliefs then our frame of reference must change i.e. we have **reframed**.

Viewing the world through different frames of reference is similar to viewing it through different coloured spectacles: *each lens changes our perspective*. Take the following example from my own experience:

Example: Paul's Alcoholism

In the early days of sobriety, I moped around, contemplating the years I'd wasted through drinking destructively. I was jealous of everything and everybody. Many of my friends had bought houses and nice cars, got married and had children, but alcoholism had deprived me of all these niceties.

In those days, I viewed alcoholism as the problem that had destroyed my life. On many occasions this poverty thinking drove me back to the bottle. Then, in 1996, after a few years sobriety, I had a profound spiritual experience that radically changed my way of thinking.

Rather than viewing my drinking years as a waste of life, I recognised the potential benefits of my unique experiences. The experience I gained from my abusive drinking enabled me to understand, first hand, the depth of the problem facing people with an alcohol habit. Subsequently, I became extremely curious and developed a thirst for literature of a psychological and spiritual nature. In addition, I attended workshops all over the country, took a degree in psychology, and trained for many years in different aspects of therapy. My primary objective was to investigate the causes of people becoming destructive and devise an antidote.

Suddenly, a great sense of purpose was injected back into my life. As I applied all that I'd learned psychologically and spiritually to my own life, I grew from strength-to-strength.

I became enlightened and fulfilled. Every day was a welcome adventure. I documented the techniques I'd used for self development and the benefits I'd received - and my work culminated in the material you are reading right now.

Today I travel the country giving talks and holding seminars; I also travel to write in exotic places which fill me with inspiration. I am now a contented human being who views life as a field of infinite possibilities.

So what changed — what brought about this radical transformation? The answer can be summed up in one word: purpose. I realised that my perception of the past was impeding my life, but this perception was only an interpretation and therefore open to change. I had a choice:

Continue to believe that my drinking destroyed my life, or, re-interpret the experience and view it as the catalyst that defined my future fulfilment.

I chose the latter and viewed my trauma as the springboard that hurtled me into a fourth dimension of existence. The valuable lesson I learned from this experience was as follows:

**The way in which we view a problem is often the only problem.
Redefining the nature of our experience is all that's needed to remove what we perceive to be great obstacles.**

The core belief that gave rise to my initial frame of reference (i.e. my negative outlook), was that there was a critical period in life in which people secure employment, buy a house, find a partner and have children. If you miss this window of opportunity then you are destined to fail and suffer - the opportunity will never re-present itself. The unspoken assumptions here are:

- Life is preordained to follow a rigid curriculum and if you fail to grasp the window of opportunity then you are doomed to a desolate wasteland of despair.

- Getting a job, finding a partner, buying a house, and having children is the only way to gain happiness and contentment

When I revised my beliefs and values and reframed the situation, I realised that happiness and contentment came in a multitude of forms. The way my ultimate happiness eventually manifested was through my connecting with my life's purpose. If I hadn't experienced alcoholism, I probably would never have found my purpose. By reframing my past in this way, I transformed my *perceived* misfortunes into my greatest assets and heeded the words of George Bernard Shaw!

People are always blaming their circumstances for what they are. I don't believe in circumstances. The people who get on in this world are the people who get up and look for the circumstances they want, and if they can't find them, make them

George Bernard Shaw

Exercise: Reframing

- To reframe any given situation, dissociate, step back and become aware of all facets. Take note of what is being said and done. Take the position of observer. Consider the beliefs and values that comprise the frame through which reality is being created. Understand the unspoken assumptions.

- Consider alternative lenses; take different perspectives. Challenge the beliefs that underpin the negative frame. Look through another frame and describe what you see. Change the attributes of the frame to reverse assumed meanings. For example:

   A problem becomes a challenge
   A challenge becomes an opportunity
   A weakness becomes a strength
   An impossibility becomes a probability
   Fear becomes an opportunity to display courage
   Unkindness becomes a lack of understanding
   A deficit becomes your greatest asset

THE HANGED MAN

- Evoke the archetype of the 'Hanged Man.' This character is sometimes depicted in the Tarot deck as Odin, who hung on the living World Tree – Yggdrasil – and received the Runes (ancient alphabets often used for divination). Although he appears to be in a compromising position (upside-down), he oozes serenity and revels in the opportunity to view life from different perspectives.

- Hold counsel with the Wise Witness Within you. Allow other frames to unfold from the wisdom of your Indwelling Divinity. Harness your true potential. Like water, become fluid and flexible and find the easiest route around any obstacle.

Chapter 18

Case Studies

'We may define therapy as a search for value'
Abraham Maslow

Continuing with the themes of enlightenment, self-awareness, and breaking the ties that bind us, this section looks at a variety of case studies which highlight specific emotional difficulties encountered by those who seek counselling for alcohol abuse. I offer them to illustrate the tremendous healing that can take place when people transform their *'base metals'* into *'gold.'*

To reach your true potential it is essential that you have the knowledge and insight to allay your fears, relieve your guilt and dissolve your pain. By studying the following cases, you will assimilate techniques and strategies which will enable you to identify the underlying issues that keep you stuck and resolve them. However, a word of caution: **when dealing with traumatic and volatile issues, it is wise to seek the assistance of a trained professional.** Therapy is a professional relationship aimed at enhancing your quality of life. The more insight you gain into your own private domain, the more you can assist the therapist, and the more liberated you will become. Ultimately, the only expert in your life is you.

> **A therapist will work *with* you – not *for* you**

The psychological and emotional catalysts that give rise to alcohol abuse are generic in nature; they are not specific to alcoholism. The difference being that people who develop alcohol habits, rather than facing and resolving their problems, use alcohol as a means of escaping them. However, as you are now well aware, pouring alcohol onto a troubled mind is akin to throwing petrol onto a fire: it inflames the problem and leads to instability. Emotional and mental turbulence saturated with alcohol leads to unpredictability, irrational behaviour, severe mood swings, paranoia, neurosis, aggression, and depression - not release and closure. Remember, **the best way to escape a problem is to solve it.** In fact, the Alchemist tends to eradicate the word *problem* from his vocabulary entirely and replace it with the word *challenge*. Rather than fleeing from his difficulties, he embraces them, seeing them as golden opportunities to evolve his self understanding and amass wisdom.

In counselling we refer to two types of problem: the *presenting problem* and the *underlying problem*. The presenting problem is the issue that is currently problematic; this problem is often a *symptom* that arises from a deeper issue. The underlying problem is the catalyst that gives rise to the symptom. Another way of stating this is that the underlying issue is the *cause,* and the symptom or current issue is the *effect*.

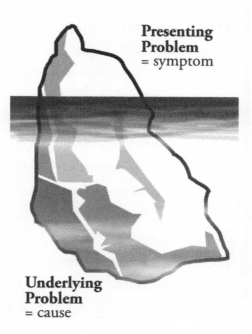

Presenting Problem = symptom

Underlying Problem = cause

Your presenting problem may well be alcoholism, but giving rise to your destructive drinking will invariably be an underlying problem(s): bereavement, futility, relationship difficulties, anger, abuse, low self esteem, and so on. To sustain your sobriety and radically transform your life it is imperative that you resolve the underlying issue(s): removing the symptom (alcohol), is pointless if the issue that gives rise to it, *the cause*, is still active. When you identify, process and release the underlying issues, you build your newfound sobriety on a rock solid foundation.

The following case studies are true, but the names have been changed to protect the identities of the people involved. In every case the presenting problem can be assumed to be alcoholism, *but the underlying issues giving rise to the alcohol habit differ in each case.*

Mathew: Bereavement

Mathew was three months sober and in a highly volatile state. His wife, who he adored, had died four years ago and his drinking had become increasingly problematic ever since. After losing his one hundred-thousand pound a year job, he had a spell in an expensive private treatment centre, but discharged himself after twelve days. Subsequently, he had tried Alcoholics Anonymous (AA), but nothing seemed to work.

Intervention

The Sobriety Saboteur prevalent in Mathew's life was pain (in the guise of bereavement). As I spoke to him, it became apparent that he'd never mourned the death of his beloved wife. He spoke of her in the present tense, making statements such as 'she likes to go walking,' or 'she's always buying clothes,' which indicated his reluctance to accept her death. In addition, he had never visited her grave and her clothes remained in their bedroom just as they had been when she had died.

After a couple of sessions in which I gained rapport with Mathew, listening to him and securing his trust, I challenged him. I suggested that his abusive drinking may have resulted from a need to escape the reality of his wife's death. Instantly, he broke down and acknowledged the truth of this observation. His reaction enabled me to gently break through his defence system and guide him through the five stages of grief given below.

Emotional Responses - The Five Stages of Grief

Earlier in the book, you learned about the five stages of grief in relation to alcoholism. Now we will view them in the context of bereavement. Working through the stages is believed to be the best way of finding a sense of peace and acceptance. The basic five stages are as follows:

1. **Denial** – *'They can't have died'*
2. **Anger** – *'I can't believe they died and left me' or 'why has God taken them'*
3. **Bargaining** – *'If only I had stayed with them, or done this or that, they might not have died'*
4. **Depression** *'What is the point of carrying on?'*
5. **Acceptance** – *'I've lost someone I love, but I know I can move on'*

   (Problems occur when people become stuck in stages 1,2,3, or 4)

Immediately following the death of his wife, Mathew was numbed with shock. This stage is often accompanied by **denial**, a defence system aimed at lessening the intensity of emotions felt by the bereaved. Mathew felt guilty at this point; he said he didn't feel anything. I normalized the process by saying it is not unusual for feelings to be numbed following the death of a loved one; it is a defence mechanism - people often have a delayed reaction. Some people don't deal with their emotions for days, months or even years after the death. On hearing this information, Mathew's guilt began to subside.

A few weeks later, Mathew started to feel **angry**, inwardly raging about being left alone - angry that more could have been done to save his wife. He suppressed these feelings as he felt they were inappropriate and felt guilty about being angry. Again, I normalised the process. I pointed out that he had lost someone very valuable to him and it is normal to feel a sense of injustice. Subsequently, I assisted him to express his anger: shout, ball, cry, whatever form it took.

Prior to his wife's death, Mathew went to church and bargained with God. In return for saving his wife, he would dedicate the rest of his life to good causes. He was now extremely angry that his prayers had been refuted. After the death he castigated himself for not doing more to save his wife **(bargaining)**. I pointed out that his wife had terminal cancer, and he had remained by her side every step of the way – he couldn't possibly do anymore. Here, I used cognitive behavioural therapy to counteract Mathew's distorted thinking and enable him to rationalize the situation. This brought about major cathartic release, and enabled him to leave the burden of unreasonable guilt behind.

Several months following the bereavement, Mathew began to experience a general sense of **depression**, becoming disinterested in life; he began to eat less, lacked concentration and found himself crying at random things. As a result, he found it hard to keep things in proportion. I reframed this experience, informing him that it was an inevitable part of a healthy grieving process. I encouraged him to talk his way through this stage. I also suggested that he concentrate on external pursuits rather than going into himself. He hung onto the phrase *this too shall pass* and started to attend his local gym. Day-by-day he felt a small improvement.

Finally, **Mathew** accepted the death; this doesn't mean he forgot or stopped caring, he accepted death as an inevitable part of living. Subsequently, he re-experienced some feelings of depression and anger, but he was able to acknowledge and process these feelings, and consequently move through them.

At the time of writing, Mathew has been sober for two years and is currently in negotiations with the firm who fired him. After explaining his predicament, his former boss was empathetic and decided to put him forward for a new position. When we last spoke, he told me he had been studying some spiritual literature that helped him immensely. He said that when people experience the loss of a loved one, it is wise to be conversant with the Sanskrit word for *human*, **nara,** which means *that which cannot be destroyed; that which is eternal.* The ancient scriptures declare the following:

> **You are not a mortal being; you are**
> **a child of immortality.**
> **The body is impermanent, the indweller is immortal.**
> **One day you will return to the oneness**
> **from where you came.**

Margaret: Fear

Courage is not the absence of fear;
it is the willingness to act despite of fear.

Margaret was worried that her fourth marriage was deteriorating due to her drinking. Both she and her husband were heavy drinkers. Whereas he changed very little after consuming alcohol, she was increasingly acting in ways that were embarrassing: insulting guests at parties, collapsing, and, more recently, wetting herself. She realised that unless she addressed her problem, she was highly likely to lose her husband; but she did not know what to do, given their lifestyle and circle of friends. Barry, her husband, was a very successful business man - employing fifty-two people. He frequently threw parties at home for potential business clients, and Margaret would play host.

After a couple of counselling sessions, it became apparent that Margaret had very low self esteem. As a child she was continually criticized and berated by her parents; this pattern continued with her peers throughout her adolescence. Subsequently, determined not to let her inferiority complex hold her back in life, she developed a strategy to counteract it. She developed an altered ego that exuded self assurance, dressed immaculately and spoke with an air of confidence. Like an award-winning actress, she played this role to perfection. For many years she kept up this facade and married a string of successful men along the way (a ploy to counteract her inferiority). The same pattern had perpetuated throughout all her marriages; after a few years, the fear of her true self being exposed became so great that she'd walk away.

This time it was different, however. She adored Barry and

wanted to be with him for the rest of her life. Recently, though, the strain of keeping up the pretence had taken its toll. When she felt her childhood legacy impinging on her current life, she would drink it away; saturate it with alcohol and suppress the memories. But it was taking more and more alcohol to keep her stable and she began having black-outs, during which her behaviour became bizarre and unpredictable. Having crossed the Abreactive Threshold, Margaret would never drink normally again. She stood to lose everything.

She remained in therapy for a year, during which time I facilitated the resolution of her childhood issues. Drink was the symptom, childhood issues were the root cause. Through in-depth exploration of her past, she came to understand that her parents were raised by extremely strict parents themselves and had inherited their critical dispositions from them. This enabled her to understand that their criticisms were not personal, they were programmed responses ingrained from their upbringing. To them - it was normal to berate and criticise. Once she discovered this, she was able to forgive them to a certain degree. Subsequently, we worked on her inner child, using the exercises given on page 374.

During the course of counselling, and despite the fear of losing her marriage, Margaret decided to sit down and have a long talk with Barry. She decided rigorous honesty was the only option available to her. After telling him the truth, he responded with understanding, empathy and love. As a result, their marriage went from strength-to-strength. With no need to escape the truth anymore, Margaret's drinking magically stopped! She continues to play host to her husband's potential clients, and they respond better than ever as she reveals the down-to-earth charm of her authentic self. Barry is extremely proud of her.

Peter: Anger

Peter appeared at the alcohol advisory centre, angry and shouting. He had been referred to doctors, psychologists and counsellors. However, as he always turned up for his appointments inebriated and abusive, no one was prepared to help him. His family seemed to think he didn't really want to be helped; he said they saw him as a 'bad sort' and his wife was now in the process of filing for divorce.

I spoke to Peter and told him that no-one could help him whilst he was drinking, but I was prepared to give him all the help he needed if he attended my clinic without having ingested alcohol. Three weeks later he turned up sober and I made an appointment for him.

Whilst exploring his history, Peter told me that he was one of two children. His brother, Billy, was the apple of his parents' eyes; a straight 'A' student with a flair for sport. Peter's parents took a great interest in brother, Billy, often bragging to their friends about his achievements and accomplishments. Every Sunday, they would attend the football match in which Billy was playing; he was captain of the local Sunday league team. Meanwhile, Peter was cast into the shadows, unacknowledged and emotionally abandoned: he felt transparent and neglected.

I empathized with him - acknowledging how awful his situation must have been for a nine-year-old child. Rapport is most important when securing someone's trust and empathy is the key.

After further investigation, it became apparent that the

strategy Peter had developed for eliciting his parents' attention was rebelliousness; he would often do exactly what they told him not to do. However, despite him staying out all night and getting into trouble with the police, his parents still didn't give him the attention he longed for. Eventually, he went to the extreme and reverted to self-harm (cutting himself). However, instead of being given the love and understanding he so desperately craved, he was simply labelled dysfunctional and bad. The more people impressed on him the notion that he was 'BAD', the more he adhered to his reputation. After serving some time in a young offenders' institution, he moved into an apartment of his own. Feeling isolated and incredibly lonely he turned to drink as a means of escaping his pain. His alcohol consumption quickly escalated and his behaviour became irrational and unpredictable. On crossing the Abreactive Threshold, his unresolved issues came flooding back into his mind, fuelled and accentuated by alcohol. At this point he was terrified – desperate to escape at any cost. On one occasion he found himself so desperate for money for drink that he held-up an off-licence with an imitation weapon and received an eight year prison sentence. After four-years, he was released for good behaviour. During his time in prison, he cleaned up his act and started to take an interest in psychology; reading many books from the prison library.

On leaving prison he managed to stay dry for a couple of years, during which time he met his current wife. The first year of their marriage was relatively problem free; Peter received plenty of attention from his wife – a primary need stemming from childhood. However, due to his history, Peter found it difficult to secure work and Susan, his wife, decided to return to her former employment as a tax officer. This had an adverse effect on Peter; her job became time consuming and he no longer received the attention he was used to. The flames of childhood started to ignite and Peter became insecure and jealous. This progressed to such an extent that he started to accuse Susan of having affairs; he even waited outside of her work, drunk and hurling abuse. Eventually, she couldn't take any more and filed for divorce. Peter's drinking escalated out of all proportion at this point and he became menacing and threatening. As a result, Susan had a restriction order placed upon him. Subsequently, Peter started to isolate himself and seek solace via the bottle. It was at this point he became desperate and turned up at the alcohol advisory centre.

It was plainly obvious that Peter wasn't a 'bad sort,' he had an inner child who felt rejected and abandoned. All the transgressions he committed were a result of not being given the attention he needed as a child. His marriage break-up had resulted from transference. When Susan started work, all the pent up emotions and unresolved issues Peter had with his parents had been transferred onto Susan. Unconsciously, he perceived her as the parents who had abandoned him.

Intervention started with Peter expressing his anger at his parents in the controlled environment of my office. Using a process from Gestalt therapy, I placed two empty chairs in front of him and asked him to imagine his parents sitting in them. He then vented his anger and released his pent-up emotion.

After the cathartic release, we explored his parents' childhood. He acknowledged that their family's main focus was on *achievement. They had been indoctrinated with the belief that achievement was of fundamental importance; that one's status depended on it. Peter began to realize that his parents could only do their best with the tools they had been given. Consequently, his anger transformed into understanding. I pointed out to Peter that every time he abused alcohol, he punished his inner child rather than giving him the love and nurture he so desperately needed. After working through the inner child exercise on page 374, Peter broke down crying — at this point I knew I was winning the battle; he hadn't cried in fifteen years. Peter affirmed that he would listen to the needs of his inner child on a daily basis and give him all the attention he needed. He also acknowledged that the verbal abuse he had bestowed on his ex-wife was actually residual anger he held for his parents.*

On completion of counselling, Peter wrote a lengthy letter to Susan, explaining his findings in therapy. She responded extremely well and the couple started meeting for coffee. Today, they are re-married and have two beautiful children. Peter returned to studying psychology and is now a psychiatric nurse. He transformed himself from Alcoholic to Alchemist.

Josie: Fear

Josie, a single parent with three children, was lonely and isolated. Her ex-partner was violent and unpredictable. Six years ago she and the children were moved into a safe-house for protection. After two years of living in very difficult surroundings, they moved to the other end of the country to start a new life. However, with no support network, friends and family, Josie found it increasingly difficult to cope. Initially, a few drinks during the day took the edge off her fear, but recently it had escalated to such an extent that social services had intervened and put her children on the at-risk register. The drinking, she said, was her way of turning an unbearable situation into one she could cope with.

During therapy Josie expressed her fear that her ex-partner was going to turn up on her doorstep and cause trouble, or find out which school the children went to and abduct them.

After questioning her, I deduced that her fear was unwarranted in this instance. When I asked how many times her husband had tried to find them in the six years they'd been separated, she replied 'never.' Subsequently, however, she went on to explain that her previous husband had found and threatened them after they were divorced – so there was a degree of rationality in her thinking. Again, transference was at work; she was transferring the thoughts and feelings from to a previous marriage into the present. This resulted in her hitting the bottle worse than ever.

On further investigation, it turned out that Josie was prone to pick partner after partner who would physically abuse her. The reason soon became very clear. It is very common for a person to choose a partner with some of the traits of a parent with whom they have unresolved issues. They do this unconsciously with a view to resolving the issues they had with the parent. In Josie's case, she had a violent father. Every partner she had chosen had her father's violent disposition. She was recreating the relationship she once had with her father, with her partners in an attempt to resolve the issues she still had with him. With this new information, Josie was able to break this pattern.

We spent the next few months working through the issues she had with her father. During this period, it emerged that he had suffered post traumatic stress after serving in the army. The awful violence he'd witnessed had triggered his violent disposition. Josie concluded that the mistreatment she was subjected to was not personal; her father was acting out the violence he had observed. Though it didn't justify his behaviour, it gave her a much deeper understanding of the situation.

Exploration of her past was followed up with inner child work during which Josie developed self-love. This self love was reflected in her relationship with her children and they were removed from the at-risk register. Her pattern of choosing violent partners ended as a result of processing the catalyst relationship (the one with her father) and today she is happily married to Robert, a placid and understanding man. Josie, like a true Alchemist, used her experience to carve out a career for herself — she is currently manageress of a domestic violence unit.

John: Futility

John, married with three children, had taken early retirement with a view to caring for his terminally ill father, but his dad died suddenly. With his three children at school and his wife in full time employment, he started to feel isolated and lonely. He quickly succumbed to depression and started drinking.

Initially, drink enabled him to escape into a fantasy world in which he could play any role, but as his consumption escalated, his newfound ally turned foe and mounted an assault on his life that left a trail of destruction. He alienated himself from his children, and after four years of destructive behaviour (in which he served a three month prison sentence for drink driving whilst on a drink driving ban), his wife had an affair with a colleague.

John was distraught when he came for counselling, saying he had lost the will to live. The particular Sobriety Saboteur prevalent in his downfall was futility. After taking early retirement and losing his father, he suffered an identity crisis; he didn't know who he was anymore. Life had become meaningless.

After talking about his on-going family problems, I turned the focus of attention to what John truly valued in life: his core values. He told me he had always had a secret ambition to run his own restaurant but the stability of his job and his family commitments persuaded him to opt instead for security. What he truly valued with regard to work turned out to be responsibility, autonomy, adventure, diversity and challenge – his job in telephone sales hadn't inspired him, it had simply paid the bills.

Subsequently, John went to catering college which gave him a meaningful focus in life. He excelled in his studies and became an excellent chef, securing a job in a high class hotel. In the interim, his wife divorced him. Although this was upsetting, therapy had revealed that their marriage had never been in his best interest. Gloria, his wife, had always encouraged him to forfeit his primary interests in the name of duty. Consequently, his creative and adventurous aspirations had all been stifled.

After working in the hotel for three years, John accumulated enough money to open a restaurant in the country. Today he owns five restaurants in different locations. His rise from the ashes secured the admiration of his three daughters, and slowly but surely, they came back into his life. All three of them are now involved in his catering enterprise; each managing one of his restaurants.

Last time I spoke to John, he informed me that he'd found his purpose in life as well as his true identity. John had always had a budding entrepreneur waiting for an opportunity. Stifling this creative element had led to futility and discontentment. The final straw came when he took retirement and his father died. However, as with all Alchemists, John turned his ill fate into his fortune. His new life has been built on his core values, and he's now reaping all the benefits (see values elicitations exercise on page 231).

Dominic - Sexual Identity Crisis

Dominic was raised in the rough suburbs of the city. His elder brother often taunted him. Inwardly, he was a mild and passive person, but he had to don the mask of a streetwise tough guy to deflect the wrath of the local gangs.

He was introduced to alcohol at the age of fourteen and it immediately banished his fears and insecurities. Hence, his drinking escalated very rapidly. With his inhibitions suppressed and his conscience out of action, he became popular for a while with the kids on the street — a role model for all the budding tough guys. Even his elder brother gained a healthy respect for him. But after a few years, drink started to take its toll and his tough exterior began to crack. He was beaten up badly on a few occasions and lost his 'street-cred' as a consequence. He deteriorated rapidly, and was drying out in hospitals and going into rehabs, but he couldn't sustain his sobriety.

When he came into therapy, he was desperate and despised himself. All these years a secret had been eating away at him; a secret which caused him to escape into the bottle repeatedly: Dominic was gay. Coming from a predominately male background where being macho was held in high regard, and living in an area where homophobia was rife, admitting his sexual preference would have been social suicide; so he hid his true identity.

Initially, alcohol assisted him in keeping up his macho facade. With his conscience suppressed he was able to act as a macho male and beat people up, but the guilt was unbearable when the effects of alcohol wore off. Eventually, he crossed the line -

the *Abreactive Threshold* - and all hell broke loose. In a drunken stupor, whilst experiencing alcoholic amnesia, he announced to his brother and the rest of the crew that he was gay. His brother immediately disowned him, and he became the target of vicious ridicule from the other cronies. Ostracized and desperately lonely, Dominic went into steady decline.

When he turned up for counselling he was emaciated and desperate. After spending time in squats, not eating and drinking excessively, he needed medical treatment. I made arrangements for him to go into a rehab and detoxify. Three weeks later, he returned; now the symptom had been removed (alcohol), we had to remove the cause.

During therapy I encouraged Dominic to accept his true identity; to accept his sexual preference and love himself for who he was. I pointed out his attributes. In the face of great adversity, Dominic had devised a strategy to cope with his dilemma. He had been hailed as a hero, tough guy in his local community after developing an altered ego that was admired in his circle. To achieve and sustain this transformation had taken great resilience and inventiveness. However, his energies had been focused in the wrong direction; he was living a lie. I asked him to imagine what he could achieve if these attributes of resilience and inventiveness worked for him, rather than against him.

Inner child work enabled Dominic to love and accept himself for who he truly was. He decided to start a new life in a different neighbourhood. Subsequently, he moved to London. Having secured employment as a hotel receptionist, he entered the gay scene and honoured his sexual preference. Four years ago he *entered into a civil partnership with Ian, and he has been extremely happy and sober ever since.*

Part Five
Moulding the Future

Chapter 19

Values Elicitation:
Laying a Firm Foundation on
Which You Can Build the Rest of Your Life

To embrace your true potential the foundation of your new life must be structured in accordance with the concepts, ideas, notions, attributes and qualities that are of most importance **to *you*** i.e. *your* **core values**. Living in accordance with the expectations of other people or adhering to the indoctrinated standards of society is a recipe for discontentment and stagnation.

> **'Most People are other people.**
> **Their thoughts are someone else's opinions,**
> **Their lives a mimicry,**
> **Their passions a quotation.'**
> Oscar Wilde

This planet is full of unfulfilled clones who trudge drearily from day-to-day doing what society expects of them. Like programmed robots they follow the herd, afraid to step out of the confines of *'normality.'* They stick at jobs they cannot abide, because 'it pays the bills.' They stay in relationships that have long since stagnated because it's safe and all they have ever known. Their dreams and aspirations have been reduced to distant memories. What a sad way to live! But, more importantly for the person with a destructive alcohol habit, these examples of stagnancy, unhappiness, and discontentment warrant escape – need I say anymore?

> ## You are unique. Your needs are unique.
> ## Your talents are unique.

When you were young, you were not afraid to dream and aspire to fulfil your dreams. Just the thought of what you were going to do with your life energized you. Remember the magic of those days; that wonderful feeling of exhilaration brought about by contemplating your aspirations. What happened? In short, you became subject to the hypnosis of society; cloned by the conformists. All your dreams and aspirations simply faded into the abyss. Well it's time to reclaim that youthful exuberance. Come on – wake up! Feel that sense of excitement building again! It's time to inject *vibrancy* and *adventure* back into your life!

 By allowing your life to unfold in accordance with what truly inspires you, you will start to live abundantly instead of merely existing. You will re-ignite that magical zest you had as a child and be propelled into a dimension of existence in which your dreams and aspirations come alive.

The first step on this journey is to re-acquaint yourself with the things you treasure; things that make your heart leap and your pulse race; things that fill you with joy and excitement; things that are deeply meaningful to you. Such *things* are *core values* and they will lay the foundation for a new life; an era in which you will reclaim your rightful heritage as creator and inventor; an era in which you will express your uniqueness and be joyous and free.

The following exercise is designed to help you elicit your core values. Give it the time and commitment it deserves. Don't forget, your core values are the solid foundation on which your new life will be based.

Exercise: Take a pen and paper and circle the top ten things you value in life from the table below. Feel free to add any of your personal values that are not listed.

Adventure	Challenge	Learning	Teaching	Intimacy
Diversity	Creativity	Compassion	Courage	Inventiveness
Open-mindedness	Achievement	Knowledge	Fun	Kindness
Wisdom	Social Network	Success	Commitment	Health
Family	Support	Love	Humility	Honesty
Independence	Self discipline	Peace	Silence	Meditation
Pleasure	Sensitivity	Trust	Recognition	Growth
Fairness	Gratitude	Freedom	Integrity	Influence

Example:

1. Adventure
2. Intimacy
3. Inventiveness
4. Open-mindedness
5. Diversity
6. Silence
7. Meaningful relationships
8. Knowledge
9. Love
10. Freedom

- Now contemplate your list and be sure it contains the things you value more than anything. If necessary make changes; omit or add items. When you have finished, contemplate the list once again, until you are absolutely certain it represents your core values.

- Now revise the list and prioritize your values i.e. number one is your primary value etc.

  (**Note:** if certain values are of equal importance to you and you find it difficult prioritizing, indicate it in your list or skip this step completely).

Example:
1. Love
2. Meaningful relationships
3. Intimacy
4. Freedom
5. Adventure
6. Diversity
7. Open-mindedness
8. Inventiveness
9. Knowledge
10. Silence

- Again, contemplate the list and revise the priority if necessary.

- Once you are absolutely certain that the list reflects and prioritizes your core values, focus on each one and write a paragraph about what it means to you. Make sure you take your time and allow the essence of each value to permeate your being.

Core Value	What it means to me

After finding your core values and writing a paragraph on each, you may wish to consider them in different facets of your life e.g. career, relationships, etc.

Here are some of my core values. I have concentrated on relationships and careers. For each category I have listed three items e.g. meaningful relationships, intimacy, and freedom for the 'relationship' category. I suggest you list as many items as you can. The more time you give to this exercise, the more you will discover the deep meaningful things that truly nourish you. Don't be surprised if it evokes tears, or sends you dancing around the room with joy: *this exercise uncovers the treasures you buried long ago.*

Paul Henderson's Core Values:

Relationships:

1. **Meaningful Relationships**

   Meaningful relationships are important to me because I like to feel a special connection with the people in my life. I like to surround myself with people who inspire and stimulate me; people who breathe life into me. True friendship involves an atmosphere of trust where I can fully express myself without reservation or fear of being judged. Conversely, I thrive in an atmosphere of light-hearted humour and fun. Laughter is extremely healing. A meaningful relationship, to me, is one which fosters understanding, acceptance, empathy, encouragement, support, love and laughter; one that can traverse the full spectrum of emotions with ease, trust and warmth. Perhaps my idea of a meaningful relationship can be summed up by the following words of Aristotle: **'What is a friend but a single soul dwelling in two bodies.'** The primary theme of true friendship, for me, is undoubtedly unity.

[Now I contemplate the above paragraph for 15 minutes, and continue this practice with the following paragraphs]

2. Intimacy

Intimacy is a process whereby two people relinquish all roles and expose their true nature to each other. For me, there are two key variables to intimacy: self-disclosure and vulnerability. An intimate relationship is one in which I am not afraid to be myself and appear vulnerable in front of someone else. Intimacy involves an atmosphere of caring and sharing. An intimate relationship, for me, is an oasis where I have no need to calculate my responses in accordance with the company I keep; I have no need for defences. I can purge myself of embarrassments, delicate issues, and worries without fear of reprisals. Intimacy and liberation from the vicissitudes of life are inextricably linked.

3. Freedom:

All too often the word *relationship* can be supplanted by the word *possession*. For me, freedom is a pre-requisite for a happy relationship. A relationship is not two halves coming together to make a whole, that's dependency - it is two whole people coming together to share a special connection. A person must be free to express themselves for who they truly are; to pursue the things that stimulate and excite them. This is what breathes life into a relationship.

> **Freedom is a mind that is open to everything and attached to nothing.**

By depending on one person as a sole source of happiness, I invite insecurity and jealousy into my life. When my mind is open to everything and attached to nothing, I enjoy the people who enter my life, but I do not tether my happiness to them.

Thus I remain open to the infinite diversity the Universe provides; the multitude of people who enter my life bringing with them the wonderful gift of friendship.

Career

1. Adventure:

> **'Do not go where the path may lead,
> go instead where there is no path
> and leave a trail.'**
>
> Ralph Waldo Emerson

For me, adventure is imperative for a fulfilling career. I am a person who thrives on new challenges. Life is a quest for new, insightful knowledge. I don't want to regurgitate other people's experiences through vicarious means. I want to break the confines of conformity and be a pioneer. To make a difference in this world I have to break away from the herd mentality and become a shepherd. I have to travel the road less travelled. New adventures stimulate me; they inject a deep sense of purpose and excitement into my life. Whether I hit the deck or soar to new heights, it doesn't matter, I feel alive and filled with vitality. The adventurer is fearless, resourceful and creative.

2. Diversity:

The rich tapestry of life is woven from innumerable threads. Each thread contributes to the richness of the pattern. The more fibres that are intricately woven together, the more beauty is revealed in the end product.
Paul Henderson

Like a finely woven tapestry, I want to weave together the infinite possibilities of life to reveal the beauty of my life's purpose. To me, to embrace the infinite diversity that life has to offer means to live abundantly, anything less is a mere existence.

Consistency is the last refuge of the unimaginative.
Oscar Wilde

To date, my curriculum vitae is extremely diverse! I have been a car cleaner, a store man, a milkman, a bum! a student, an actor, a musician, an entertainer, a teacher, an author and an inspirational speaker. But I am still only fifty years old! Like Michelangelo who finished painting the Sistine Chapel in his eighties, the best work of my life lies ahead. I intend to write many more books, become a playwright, write a musical and make a movie – and that's just for starters! I have been given this wonderful opportunity called life, and I intend to embrace *every* gift it presents.

3. Inventiveness:

The power of creative imagination is the midwife of all novel ideas. Within each of us lies a genius awaiting recognition; this genius's workshop is the formless realm of our imagination. Our imagination isn't some psychic playground where we go to drum up unrealistic pleasantries: it is the womb of creation. Look around you right now. Everything you see was once an idea birthed from somebody's imagination. Albert Einstein acknowledged the power of the imagination by making statements such as *'imagination is more important than knowledge,'* and *'the imagination is the preview of life's forthcoming events.'* To be unique is to express your individuality in novel ways. To accumulate knowledge is to regurgitate other people's findings.

The imagination is the image-forming capacity of the mind. And whatever you can conceive in the mind, you can achieve in reality. Being inventive, for me, means to stamp my own unique mark on the world.

Conclusion:

Now that you have identified your core values, it is time to start using them to structure your perfect life and make your world a place of intrigue, fascination and joy. Far too often people identify what they value, and have wonderful ideas of how they would like to utilize and honour them, but that's where it comes to a sudden halt! They stop right there and never put their plans into action. The following section is designed to help you give structure to your ideas, so you can implement them effectively and birth them into reality.

Be S.M.A.R.T. Give Structure to your Goals.

Setting and implementing goals that act as stepping stones to the realization of your life's purpose is a wonderful experience. Not only does it engage your mind and orient it towards your destiny, it breathes life back into the very core of your being. Humans thrive on achievement; it bolsters self worth and radically increases momentum to achieve other goals. Most of all, it purges the mind of any residual negativity and supplants it with inspiration and enthusiasm.

Giving structure to your ideas is imperative. Vague and abstract notions fade away quickly; whereas a concrete plan gives your mind something tangible to grasp on to. When your mind embraces an idea, it acts as a servomechanism to steer you towards its fulfilment.

Before we look at structuring goals, it's important to understand the difference between *objectives, goals and purpose.*

- **Purpose** - relates to our overall vision or primary purpose. For example, my ultimate purpose is to conduct inspirational speeches and write books.

- **Goals** - are the individual tasks, stepping stones that pave the way to our ultimate purpose. For example, I became a teacher of psychology and esoteric material in order to prepare myself to talk and write.

- **Objectives -** are the smaller tasks involved in the realization of your goal. For example, my goal of setting up a training company involved the following objectives: writing courses, advertising, finding venues and attracting students. A goal may have one or many objectives that need to be fulfilled for its successful completion.

One of the best methods for setting goals is the **S.M.A.R.T.** system. S.M.A.R.T refers to the acronym that describes the key variables of meaningful goals:

> Specific - concrete, detailed, well defined
> Measureable - how you know you are progressing
> Achievable - feasible
> Realistic - considering resources
> Time-Bound - a defined time line

Let's look at these characteristics in more detail.

Specific

Specific means that the goal is concrete, detailed, focused and well defined; it highlights the necessary course of action and required outcome. Goals should relay precisely what you intend to happen. To help set specific goals it helps to ask the following questions:

- **WHAT** am I going to do? This is best written using powerful, action verbs such as conduct, devise, build, plan, execute, deliver, etc. Effective language declares your goal action-orientated and focuses on what's most important.

- **WHY** is this important to me? Is your goal in alignment with your core values? Does it breathe excitement into you? Does it carry you in the direction of your ultimate purpose? Does it evolve you as a human being?
- **WHO** do I need to help me accomplish my goal?
- **WHEN** do I want it to be completed?
- **HOW** am I going to implement it?

Measurable

If the objective is measurable, it means you can track the results of your actions. Measuring enables you to identify any glitches at an early stage and readjust your strategy; therefore, it increases efficiency. Most importantly, though, as you witness the fruits of your work, when your results measure up to your expectations and forecasts, you will notice a distinct heightening of your enthusiasm; this powerful motivating force is then fed back into your project and so momentum gathers.

Diagnostic Questions

- How can my accomplishments be measured?
- Does my method of measurement provide a useful source of feedback?

Achievable

Goals need to be achievable. If you over-extend your capabilities and resources, it is very easy to lose interest and deem yourself a failure. Conversely, when you break your goal down into a number of achievable objectives and attain them, you build up momentum and enthusiasm. Whilst being attainable, objectives still need to stretch you, but not so far that you become frustrated and lose motivation.

Diagnostic Questions

- Is the proposed timeframe realistic?
- Do I understand the limitations and constraints?
- Do I have a contingency plan?
- Do I have the necessary resources; if not, how can I secure them?
- Is the project possible?

Realistic

Goals that are achievable may not be realistic; however, realistic does not mean easy. Realistic means that you have the necessary resources to complete the task; whereas achievement is dependent on the demand placed on those resources. Most goals are achievable, but may require a change in your priorities to make them happen.

Diagnostic Questions

- Are you putting an unreasonable demand on your resources to achieve the goal?
- Do you need to revise your priorities to make it happen?
- Do you need to revise your strategy for successful completion?

Time-Bound

Time-bound means setting deadlines. Deadlines create the all important sense of urgency required for the mind to act as a servomechanism. If you don't set a deadline, you will reduce the motivation and urgency required to execute the tasks. Deadlines create the necessary urgency and prompt action.

Diagnostic Questions

- When will this objective be accomplished?

- What is the intended deadline?

**There's a difference between interest and commitment.
When you're interested in doing something, you do it only when
circumstance permits. When you're committed to something,
you accept no excuses, only results.**

To synthesize and assimilate the information presented above, let's
take an example from my own experience. Some years ago I held
the position of computer engineer at a local University. Although I
thrived in the environment and enjoyed the company of my
colleagues, my role had become monotonous and unfulfilling. Being
a person who needs stimulation, diversity and challenge, I became
very agitated and unsettled. As there was no scope for promotion
within the ranks, and my interest in I.T. was waning, I had to make
a decision: leave - or grin and bear it. Although my career needs
were not being met, and the job was not in alignment with my life's
purpose, many of my relationship needs were being fulfilled; my
colleagues were like family and the working environment was a
wonderful social arena. My *'extended family'* and I were able to
intimate, confide, support, encourage and laugh together during the
working day; so I didn't want to leave. With this realization came a
cunning plan!

I decided to set myself a goal. I would pursue another avenue of
work that would fulfil the needs that weren't being met by my *day
job*: challenge, diversity, and adventure. Just for fun, I decided to add
another criteria; whatever I chose to pursue must double my annual
salary within twelve months! Already, I felt the energy and
excitement coursing through my veins. I thrive on challenge and
this was inventive and exciting: a real adventure!

Drawing on my resources, I decided to set up a training company; a
company that would train therapists. Immediately, this felt right –
my heart began to smile and my energy field illuminated. Every day

I immersed myself in knowledge of a psychological and esoteric nature. Training therapists was the perfect way to integrate my primary interest into a career.

Time to structure my goal! The first step was to draft an outline of my intended course of action, as follows:

Outline: my goal is to devise and teach a course in clinical hypnotherapy. The course is to start in September 2006 (it is now January). Whilst devising the course I will seek a professional body to stamp their approval on it, i.e. accredit it. Next, I will approach the venue where I hold meditation classes and negotiate a price for a room in which I will deliver the course. Then I will spread the word via the network of contacts I already have, and advertisements in the local press. In addition, I will expand my website to incorporate my new venture. The name I will use for the training school is the United Kingdom Academy of Integrative Therapy. As this is an umbrella term, it gives me scope to expand into counselling and NLP.

After outlining the objectives of my goal, I made a precise list of activities and deadlines [**Note:** below I have added the corresponding SMART variable]

- Course is to start 16th September 2006 **[specific, time-bound, measurable]**
- Monday night 6 – 9pm **[specific, time-bound]**
- Cost of venue = xxx pounds **[specific, realistic]**
- Cost of advertising: press, prospectus, cards, posters etc. = xxx pounds **[specific]**
- Additional expenses: fuel, office materials, telephone calls etc. **[specific, measurable]**
- Target number of students 12 (minimum) **[realistic, achievable, measurable]**
- Cost per student xxx pounds **[specific, realistic]**

- Course to be accredited by [name of the governing body] **[specific, achievable]**
- Target profit xxx pounds by September 2007 **[specific, measurable, achievable, realistic, time-bound]**
- Anticipated profit by September 2007 xxx pounds **[measurable, specific, achievable, realistic, time bound]**

When I had completed the inventory of the criteria I needed to fulfil, I got cracking straight away. I surfed the net and contacted a reputable professional body that would be ideal to accredit my course; they sent me an information pack. After perusing their criteria, I devised a comprehensive practitioner level Diploma in Clinical Hypnotherapy. A wonderful by-product of this stage was that I learned so much in the process!

On completion, I sent off the prospectus, which included the course curriculum and specific criteria such as cost, venue, and qualifications of the instructors. Six weeks later, to my delight, I received a letter of acceptance from the professional body. This is where measurability is so important. As I could monitor my success by the feedback I was receiving, I knew I was progressing admirably. The letter of acceptance instilled a sense of achievement which fuelled my motivation and sent my enthusiasm levels rocketing. This energy was then ploughed back into my project and utilized to attain further objectives: momentum was building fast and furiously!

Next, I spread the word throughout my network of friends and found there was a great deal of interest. Within a week, I had eight students – another four and my objective had been met, with another five months still to go! Finally, I placed adverts in the local papers and got an excellent response.

Epilogue:

Within a year I had a Foundation Course and Practitioner Level Diploma running in three different locations: thirty seven students in all! I also diversified and delivered transpersonal orientated courses and staged Mind, Body, Spirit fairs. What a year that was! My self-esteem rocketed. I developed a wealth of new friends. I accumulated a vast amount of useful knowledge and I evolved as a person. As for my financial target, well, I far exceeded it: I once lived on a rat infested railway embankment without even my bus fare to my name – now I drove a brand new Mercedes-Benz!

Summary

- Eliciting your core values reveals the solid foundation on which the rest of your life will be built. Complete the Core Values exercise and give it the time it deserves. Contemplate each of your values and allow their essence to permeate your being. Calibrate your life in accordance with them. This important exercise often induces a feeling that you have come to know yourself for the very first time.

- Take the time to structure your ideas on paper. Vague and abstract notions very rarely get off the ground. By using the SMART system to solidify your ideas, you engage the mind in such a way that it will move mountains to manifest them.

Part Six
The True Nature of Reality

Chapter 20

Science and Spirituality Coincide

The findings of contemporary science have profoundly altered our understanding of the true nature of reality. Modern-day physics, in accordance with the great teachings of our wise forefathers, has revealed that beyond the infinite diversity of the material world there lies an all-pervading field of intelligence; a unified field of energy. If we transcend the limitations of our physical senses and lift the veil of material reality, a whole new world is revealed. No longer are we isolated individuals confined to the cell of our bodies, but rather, we are part of an indivisible whole; an intimate web of relationships in which everything and everyone is connected.

Enlightened mystics and seers have always expressed reality in terms of the unification of all things – **a Sacred Singularity.** The Native American Indians expressed it through the digit zero: *the nothingness that contains everything.* They perceived empty space as the womb of creation: the great void from which everything is birthed. Ancient Vedic and Zen philosophy expresses the unity of the primordial essence of all things in the following way (paraphrased from various literature):

As an actor becomes absorbed in his role as Hamlet and forgets he is Mr Jones, so the human being gets so absorbed in his fictitious identity, or ego, that he forgets he's God. God is the single actor playing innumerable roles. Every individual is God, or Atman, the Self of the world. Every life is a role in

which the mind of God is absorbed. By the act of self-abandonment God becomes all beings.

Although it's not necessary to have a deep understanding of science to follow a spiritual path, a basic understanding of how quantum physics supports our wise ancestors' proclamations is extremely useful in enabling us to fully appreciate the true nature of reality and embrace our true potential.

During the first three decades of this century, Albert Einstein, Niels Bohr and Werner Heisenberg, (three genius scientists), observed that the material world no longer resembled a well-oiled machine consisting of innumerable separate objects, but rather, an indivisible whole; a network of relationships that included the human observer in a vital way.

If I were to tell you that everything you perceive as physical, including your *'physical'* body, is actually 99.999% *empty space*, you would probably think I was crazy! But it's true. Furthermore, scientists have recently discovered that the 99.999% we perceive as empty space is actually teeming with intelligence! Even more intriguing is that this intelligence may well be the womb of creation itself.

From this *nothingness* arises a subtle dimension known as the Quantum Field, and from the quantum field the material world emerges. In essence, what we have is an unfolding of pure *beingness or pure consciousness* into various levels of existence. Let's explore this together.

The building blocks of everything material, including our so-called "physical" bodies, are atoms. Our bodies, for instance, consists of cells, which, in turn, are comprised of molecules, and these molecules are made up of atoms. If we continue the process of peeling away the layers that make up what appear to be solid objects, we find that the atom is made up of minute particles that are traversing empty space at phenomenal speeds - now here's where things start to get really interesting. Scientists found that these tiny particles have no solidity whatsoever. Yes, that's correct:

> ## The building blocks of every material object are non-material!
> ## The foundation of the material world is formless!

Everything we *perceive* as physical or solid is actually insubstantial: a vibrating pattern of energy. If our eyes were replaced with sub-atomic lenses we would see the world in a whole new light: a vast sea of energy and information known as the Quantum Field. A *quantum* is the smallest, indivisible unit of something. For example, a photon is a quantum of light; an electron is a quantum of electricity; a graviton is a quantum of gravity. The totality of all quanta (plural), comprises what is now referred to as the Quantum Field.

Quanta have peculiar properties. When we observe them they act as minute solid particles, and when we don't, they become non-material radiations or packets of energy. Chairs, tables, trees, physical bodies, and the book you're reading right now, are all vibrating patterns of energy until we look at them. As soon as we observe them, they freeze into position and appear solid. However, this perceived solidity is an interpretation of our limited senses. In actuality, the entire cosmos is a huge vibrating web of energy.

I know you may be thinking that this is all very interesting but it has absolutely nothing to do with our well-being or attaining our true potential. So let me assure you that this information is life changing;

understanding the true nature of reality and how we interface with it will radically change every aspect of your life. Bear with me a while longer and all will be revealed.

The energy patterns we refer to as our physical bodies are equipped with a mechanism known as perception. It is this faculty of our physiology that magically transforms the energy and information of the Quantum Field into the three dimensional world we call reality – and this is how it happens. When patterns of energy impinge on our nerve receptors, signals are sent to the brain. The brain then interprets this information as the three dimensional world we call reality. What modern physics is telling us is that the material world is actually a construct that takes place in our head. Nothing exists outside of us except waves of energy and information.

**The material world is actually a construct that takes place in our head.
Nothing exists outside of us except waves of energy and information.**

These patterns of energy are magically transformed into material objects when we observe them. ***When we are not looking they are patterns of energy, when we fix our eyes on them they assume solid form!*** As this can be a difficult concept to grasp, let me give you an example to clarify the process.

The air around us is filled with television signals containing sound and video information. We can't see or hear them because they vibrate at a frequency that's way beyond the limited scope of our physical senses. When these signals reach our television sets they are decoded and interpreted into a form we can comprehend i.e. sound and video. The energy and information of the quantum field can be likened to a T.V. signal before it is decoded - patterns of invisible energy and information travelling through empty space. Our system of perception can be compared to the decoding equipment in that it transforms this invisible energy into the three dimensional reality we're experiencing right now. Whereas the television signals are projected onto your TV screen, the information and energy of the Quantum Field is projected onto your internal screen and deemed reality. The experience is similar to putting on a virtual reality headset. When you don the headset, your senses are tricked into thinking you are immersed in another reality, when, in actuality, the source of your entertainment is simply electrical energy that has been processed to give the illusion of a virtual environment. In exactly the same way, our system of perception transforms the energy of the quantum field into the three dimensional virtual environment we call reality. However, unlike the virtual reality headset, our system of perception is an integral part of our physiology; therefore, it cannot be removed - so we find ourselves trapped in the material world (at least in our normal state of consciousness) unable to know the true nature of our reality.

There are two fundamental reasons why this information is of paramount importance to our evolution. Firstly, not only have scientists deduced that every physical object is a vibrating pattern of energy, they have also found that these patterns are interconnected and interrelated; in fact, they have discovered that everything and everybody is part of one indivisible whole.

Radio isotope studies can prove that you have a million atoms in you right now that were once in the body of Napoleon, Jesus, or Socrates. In fact, you can't separate yourself from anything or anybody that has ever existed. In the last few weeks, trillions of atoms have passed through your body that have passed through the body of every other species on this planet! Much like the World Wide Web, you are part of a Universal web of consciousness through which you can communicate, access limitless knowledge, and manifest your every desire.

Secondly, scientists have continuously found that sub-atomic particles or quanta are intelligent in their own right. They are little entities which have the ability to respond to the expectations of whoever is observing them. For example, the results of experiments have been found to differ in accordance with the ***beliefs and expectations*** of the people observing them. On numerous occasions, it has been found that if the people observing an experiment believed it would work - then it did. Conversely, when conducting the same experiment with observers that didn't believe, it failed.

In light of this evidence we can only deduce that our minds have the capacity to communicate directly with the underlying intelligence infused in all matter. Rather than thinking of matter as a benign, inert substance, we need to view it as a vital, organic field of intelligence which responds to thought.

> **The Universe is a living, dynamic organism that responds to our thoughts and expectations. It is by virtue of this interaction that we create our reality**

As the potter's hands mould clay into objects, so your mind moulds the universal intelligence into the events of your future. Remember, Albert Einstein phrased it in the following way: ***Imagination is the preview of life's forthcoming events.***

Whatever we focus on intently in our mind, will actualize. Our energized thoughts and beliefs mould the potential energy of the Universe into our forthcoming experience. In this respect our mind is the womb of creation. There is a Universal law that says **whatever you emanate, you attract**: emanate hostility and you will attract hostility; emanate scarcity thinking and you will attract poverty; emanate abundance and you will attract wealth and prosperity. The choice is yours. Our wise ancient forefathers told us that the external world is a mirror image of a formless, invisible world. Now science is reinforcing their findings.

> ## The external world is a mirror of your state of mind
> ## Change your mind – change your life

What modern-day science is actually telling us is that we live in a field of infinite possibilities. *Every conceivable possibility already exists.* The possibility of you being in the pinnacle of health; the possibility of you being gravely ill; the possibility of you being extremely wealthy, and the possibility of you living in poverty, all exist simultaneously in a this field of never-ending possibilities. To understand this concept, instead of thinking of time as linear – running in a straight line - we must start thinking in terms of *vertical time*.

Scientist no longer speak of *time* in isolation, they speak of the *space-time continuum*. Linear time is a measurement of movement and change through space. When we adhere to the concept of linear time, there is a time lapse between identifying our desires and their manifestation; desires have to be shaped and constructed through the passage of time. In the vertical time paradigm, however, every conceivable possibility already exists. We exist in a realm in which there are an infinite number of parallel realities – a *'Multiverse'* - we just have to figure out how to access the one we desire.

Imagine going into a cosmic superstore filled with every conceivable desire and choosing what you wanted. You had an abundance of money, but when you got to the checkout you were informed that the only valid currency was **the power of intent**. The wise shop assistant advised you to go home, find a quiet place, and imagine manifesting your desire. She told you to imagine it so vividly that you evoked a powerful feeling within. This feeling would be propagated out into the universal intelligence and signposts in the form of people, ideas, solutions, direction, and insights would start to appear and lead to your goal. Although these synchronicities seem to come from different sources, they were all embodiments of the one intelligence which is conspiring to help you. How exciting would that be - if only it were true!

Well, let me inform you - it is true. Alchemists have used this phenomenon to great advantage since time immemorial. The trick in applying it successfully is to learn how to use the power of intent to maximum effect, as we shall see.

Chapter 21

Prayer: The Power of Intent

For thousands of years prayer has been used as a way of communicating with the ultimate intelligence of the universe – God, as it is commonly called. Since time immemorial people have prayed to deities asking for help with difficult or insurmountable situations. But is prayer practical? Is there really a supreme being who listens and responds to our appeals? Or is it simply an impotent act of self-delusion; a means of psychological escape from the trials and tribulations of life?

Prayer and the power of intention are fundamentally one and the same thing; processes in which your mind has a particular focus: a healing, a desire, or an intervention of some kind. I cannot express the importance of this practice in my own personal transformation. I use the power of intention on a daily basis to choose what I desire from the field of infinite possibilities. Narrowing the focus of my mind and one-pointedly attending to the object of my desire, not only brings about a response from the network of intelligence known as God or the Universal Mind, but it also disciplines my mind not to wander. When my mind is supremely focused, I become endowed with great clarity and direction.

The power of intention is effective because *thoughts shape reality*. The scientific implications of the impact of thought on the Universal Mind are inextricably linked to our circumstances. Prayer, or the power of intention, is certainly not an impotent act of self delusion:

it is a highly practical pursuit which brings about amazing results. Whatever we hold intently in our minds i.e. whatever we are praying for, or intending, will show up in the external world, so long as we adhere to certain criteria. If we intend on attracting the perfect partner, or ideal job, for instance, we must believe it with every rudiment of our being; we must also generate powerful feelings that support our beliefs. Alchemists are highly adept at this practice; I've seen people manifest partners, ideal careers, discern solutions to problems, achieve healings and evoke amazing synchronicities time and time again; I've experienced it myself on innumerable occasions. However, remember the criteria; if you practice this process half-heartedly or with an element of disbelief, the effect of your mental transmission and its impact on the Universal Mind will be diluted – if this happens, you may experience difficulties or even no results at all.

The following guide will assist you in optimizing your broadcasting technique, thus maximizing the power of intention. If you wish to radically transform your life and attain the object of your desires, then assimilate and practice the information and techniques below:

1. **Specificity and Clarity:** Be specific and crystal clear as to what you want to achieve:

    Would you like to meet the ideal partner?
    Would you like to increase your income?
    Do you want to find the perfect career?
    Do you want to send healing to someone?
    Are you looking for a solution to a difficult problem?

    Whatever you desire, the power of intention will bring results. Specificity and clarity will increase the accuracy of your results. If you put a vague search string into Google, you will get ambiguous results. In the same way, if your intention is vague and you have no faith in it, the results will bear no fruits.

2.   **Strengthen the connection:** Know you are part of an infinite web of relationships; a mosaic of connections linking everything and everybody. You are not separate from the object of your desire (person, place or thing), you are already connected to it. As a single computer is connected to millions of others of computers via the World Wide Web, you are connected energetically to everything and everyone. To achieve or attain the object of your desire, you simply have to enhance the connection with it telepathically.

3.   **Imagination = image-in-action:** A picture paints a thousand words is a famous statement that holds so much truth. Remember, the word imagination has its roots in the Latin word *imago*, which means image; therefore, imagination is the image-forming capacity of the mind. Imagining a desire, picturing it vividly in your mind, is far more powerful than simply thinking about it. Prayers and intentions are amplified by adding the power of your imagination. Hold an image of your desired object or outcome in mind. Make it vivid. Turn up the contrast and brightness. Associate into it i.e. experience it directly as though it was really happening. If you desire a new job, live out the experience in your mind. Engage all your senses and turn them inwardly. Feel, hear, see, smell and taste your desire. The brain cannot differentiate between imagination and actuality. As you imagine your desire, you will create neural pathways to support its manifestation. The more definition you give to your internal experience, the more success you will achieve.

4. **Believe with every rudiment of your being:** It is crucial to energize your prayers and intentions with the power of belief. If you listen to a radio in your garden on a sunny day and the volume is low, the broadcast will only reach the ears of those in close proximity. Likewise, if your intentions are not amplified by the power of belief, they will not penetrate the web of relationships of the Universal Mind sufficiently to secure the desired result. BELIEVE. BELIEVE. BELIEVE. AND IT WILL HAPPEN!

5. **Relinquish Control:** Once you have broadcast an intention, let go. Entrust the ultimate intelligence of the universe to provide the perfect result. Sometimes our idea of the perfect result is different from that of the Supreme Intelligence of the Universe, so we need to trust wholeheartedly. When we attach to a specific outcome to our desires, we restrict the natural flow of energy between ourselves and the universe. On many occasions I have intended a desire and received an unexpected result. Yet, in every instance, I received something much better than I could have ever anticipated!

6. **Open to Receive:** sometimes an intention may be blocked energetically by an underlying belief. If you find your intentions are not manifesting as you would like them to, ask yourself whether you feel that you are truly worthy and deserving of receiving? If not, then revisit the inner child exercises on p.374. Some people, as a result of negative indoctrination or religious dogma, believe it's inappropriate to have desires; thus they inadvertently repel their desires from an unconscious level. Create the necessary space to receive your desire: jettison the negative indoctrination. KNOW that you are indeed deserving of your desire.

7.   **Synchronicity: accentuate your awareness and look out for the signposts - further evidence linking mind and matter.**

Have you ever experienced a surreal moment in which you anticipated something happening; a feeling of being suspended in another dimension? Time appears to stand still and your awareness heightens to such an extent that you experience a *knowing?* A person, place or thing inexplicably enters your mind. You find yourself deeply intrigued. You are compelled to make the connection. Suddenly, the phone rings or a person turns up in your life and the connection is made without any effort. Or, perhaps, you have a chance encounter with someone on the street and they appear to emanate an iridescent glow, or take on an unusual demeanour. You feel a strong connection; a strange sense of familiarity. Yet you are certain you have never met this person before. Again, the meeting turns out to be highly significant.

What's it all about? How and why does it occur? These mysterious happenings are known as quantum experiences; moments in which the underlying intelligence of the Universe strengthens the connection between a strong need within your psyche and the object of your desire.

Mind and matter are inextricably linked. In reality you have no physical boundaries; you are *entangled* energetically to everything and everyone. The external world is an extension of your internal world, as the following story reveals.

Example: George

George mused over the following question: 'should I uproot my family and take a new position down south?' This question had remained prominent in his mind for a fortnight, but now the deadline loomed and he had to make a decision. His family were happy to make the move but he was apprehensive; worried about leaving a job that had provided him with stability for years.

Later that day, he visited a book shop and randomly opened a book. The following quote by T. S. Elliot jumped out at him:

Only those who will risk going too far can possibly find out how far they can go.

His intuition ignited. Without hesitation he accepted the new position. One year later, his old firm went into liquidation. Five years hence, his new career exceeded all expectations; he now holds the position of managing director!

Such stories are extremely common. Eminent psychiatrist and influential thinker, Carl Jung, believed that such serendipitous happenings constituted a glimpse of the raison d'être of the universe. In accordance with the findings of modern physics, he believed in an underlying web of relationships through which everything and everybody is connected. He coined the term *synchronicity* to describe what he called the *acausal connecting principle* that links mind and matter. According to Jung, such synchronicities occur when a strong need arises in the psyche of an individual.

Synchronicities are not mere coincidences, they are signposts from the omnipresent intelligence of the universe.

Signposts come in many forms: dreams, lines and passages from books, other people, meaningful songs, chance events, the list increases ad infinitum. To recognise signposts you must retain a high level of awareness as they're often revealed in subtle ways. We are continuously receiving signposts but many of them go unacknowledged as we succumb to the hypnosis of life's conditioning. Like radio transmissions, we need to 'tune in' to receive them. Let me relay a personal story that occurred relatively recently:

Example 1: Un*covered* in the *Nick* of Time

During the course of writing this material, I became aware of the importance of the book cover; it had to capture people's attention and invoke intrigue and curiosity. This thought remained at the forefront of my mind for a few days.

After a few days of pondering, I received an email informing me that someone had contacted me via a website that specializes in reuniting old school friends. I hadn't used this website in years, but my details had remained there for people to see. I promptly retrieved the email and found that it was from an old school friend, Nick, who I hadn't seen in thirty five years! After an exchange of texts and emails we decided to meet. When Nick arrived at the agreed place, I noticed he was carrying a huge folder. After he filled me in on the missing years, he asked would I like to see some of his work. When he revealed the contents of his folder, I was amazed at the quality of the art work he had

---

produced. Subsequently, he informed me that, after taking a degree in art, he worked as Graphic Designer. Bingo! The universe had responded to the contents of my psyche: my intention had been answered. Nick had worked for TV, magazines and book publishers – he was a genius when it came to graphic design! I promptly asked him if he would design the book cover for this book and he said he would be honoured to. How amazing; yet another example of the interconnectivity of everything and everybody!

Exercise: Heightening Awareness

From this point forth, ask yourselves the following questions frequently:

- How is my external environment mirroring my internal disposition?
- What subtle happenings appear to be providing me with direction?
- What people, places or things am I unexplainably drawn to?
- What is my gut feeling telling me?

Pay heed to these signposts. Don't dismiss anything as insignificant. As your awareness heightens, you will find that your world is transformed into a wonderful adventure playground!

Chapter 22

The Universal Genie

We have seen how the dialogue between our thoughts and our brain unfolds to create the feelings within us: but the story doesn't end there. The feelings we generate are emitted beyond the confines of our body to permeate the field of energy that links all of creation: the Universal Mind. This amorphous sea of intelligence is a living organism that is highly responsive to our communications.

Our thoughts transpose to feelings, and our feelings transpose into waves of energy that we radiate. These emissions are impressed with information that corresponds directly to the way we think and feel. Subsequently, this information causes quantum changes in the mosaic of consciousness that connects us all. This body of consciousness then responds by creating circumstances conducive to our inner disposition. In effect, the whole world becomes a huge mirror, reflecting back to us that which we project.

Ancient and indigenous people had an excellent understanding of this phenomenon and utilized it to great advantage. The way in which they prayed was somewhat different from the way in which we do it today. They would mentally focus on whatever they hoped to achieve through prayer- for example, a healing, a request for rain, or the provision of food – and allow their internal imagery to expand to such an extent that it became life-like: feeling, hearing, smelling, and tasting the very essence of their desire. They would absorb themselves in their imagination and have a profound belief that their prayers had been granted. Notice I use present tense here *'had been granted'* not *'would be granted.'* Believing their prayers *'would'* be granted negated the process, because *'would'* implies something that will happen in the future, and the future is a psychological concept that never arrives; we only ever have the eternal continuum of the now. When the indigenous people prayed for rain, they would imagine billowing clouds forming in the sky and bursting open to give life to their crops. Turning their senses inwardly, they would feel, hear, see and taste the rain. When they prayed for a healing, they would imagine the sick person in perfect health: feeling and seeing the healing – NOW – in the present moment.

The underlying theory behind their success is that *every possibility already exists in the field of infinite possibilities*: the possibility of drought, the possibility of rain; the possibility of disease, the possibility of perfect health. We just have to choose from these possibilities. *They way in which we choose is determined by the focus of our mind and the extent of the supporting feelings.* For our prayers to be granted, we must believe that they *have* manifested with every rudiment of our being. Innumerable reports of miraculous results have emerged as a result of using this technique: rain in the middle of droughts; healings of the incurable; peace in war torn areas; and crops sprouting in infertile ground; the list is endless.

So what does this information mean to the person on the **Alcoholic to Alchemist** journey? It means *we can create any circumstances we want!* By focusing intently on that which we aspire to achieve and evoking powerful feelings to support it, we radiate a request to the Universal Mind. When we propagate feelings of well-being, the field responds by creating circumstances conducive to well-being. When we broadcast feelings of lack and poverty, the field responds by creating scarcity. Like a faithful servant, it doesn't determine whether your requests are in your best interest or not - it never judges, it simply responds.

The Universal Mind is akin to a genie that grants your every request. Think it; feel it; transmit it; and await the results. Sounds great – infallible! And it is for those who live life consciously. But most of the population of this planet live life unconsciously. Most people are under the spell of social-hypnosis and way out of touch with their feelings.

Every moment of our lives we are generating feelings that produce quantum changes in the Universal matrix of intelligence that surrounds and permeates everything. You might say we are in a constant state of prayer - sending out a continuous string of requests. As most people live life unconsciously, they do not know what information they are emitting. Their feelings are generated from an unconscious level, so they exercise no control over them. As a consequence, the requests they are making to the Universal Genie are often ambiguous or detrimental. Can you imagine having the capacity to wish for anything you desire in life and not knowing it? Furthermore, in your ignorance you inadvertently ask for all those things you *do not* want! In effect, this is exactly what's happening. The underlying principle here is the law of cause and effect, which says that what we give out we get back. As most people live life unconsciously, they inadvertently focus on that which they *do not want* – and guess what? The Universal Genie obliges by granting them their wishes – the negative circumstances show up in abundance. Whatever radio station you're tuned into – that's what you receive.

Putting this information into the context of alcoholism, we come to realise why our lives aren't working. We have deduced that alcoholism is a set of maladaptive beliefs; beliefs which give rise to the stinking thinking that feeds alcoholism. This stinking thinking usually involves concentrating on the things we abhor in life: financial hardship, broken relationships, futility, devastation, powerlessness and so on. As a consequence, the feelings we produce which correspond to these thoughts, cause emanations is the surrounding ether; and these emissions serve as requests to the Universal Genie. Once again, the faithful Genie grants our requests and - hey presto! - our lives become unbearable. The law of cause and effect has transmuted the pollution of our internal domain – stinking thinking – into the chaos in which we are immersed on a daily basis.

To break this cycle of negative attraction, we must LIVE LIFE CONSCIOUSLY. What is needed is self mastery: the ability to choose our thoughts and control our feelings in a manner conducive to optimal living. To do this, however, we must be aware of *will power* and *won't* power? Will power transpires from conscious intent, whilst won't power is the emotive force generated from our unconscious negative programming. Although we may make a conscious decision to change in all earnestness, our will-power is invariably overridden by the power of our unconscious negative programming.

Imagine two radio stations broadcasting conflicting messages simultaneously. One is broadcasting positive messages, the other, negative messages. The positive transmission has only one watt of power, whilst the negative transmission has a thousand watts. Due to this power imbalance, the negative transmission is going to propagate much further and have a far greater influence than the positive transmission. Exactly the same scenario applies to the requests we emit into the field of infinite possibilities. Our conscious intent is broadcast at one watt and will be obliterated by the thousand watts of our unconscious - *unless we derive a method of amplifying our conscious intent.* Fortunately, the ancient and indigenous people left us with a legacy in how we might achieve this.

The key to amplifying our conscious intent to such an extent that it overrides our negative, unconscious programming lies in the power of our imagination. To manifest our desires, we must generate an internal scenario that is so powerful that it penetrates our unconscious. We must bring all our sense-modalities into play, turn them inward, and see, hear, feel, taste and smell our desired outcome. We must believe with every rudiment of our being that our request has already manifested. We must evoke a surge of emotion that pervades every cell bone and tissue of our body to generate a wave emission so powerful that it overcomes any unconscious interference and broadcasts our request loud and clear.

The Nature of Quantum Healing

The power of the mind is demonstrated in its most potent form through the work of the medicineless hospitals in China. These centres avoid traditional medicine and special diets in favour of exercise, love and life energy. As they are learning the art of self-healing, the people who are sick are addressed as **students not patients.** Western-trained doctors play only a minor role and prefer to be called *teachers*. Their main function is to diagnose students when they are admitted and again after a twenty-four hour period.

After diagnosis, students are assigned to a class of about fifty people for a twenty four day treatment. During this period, they spend eight hours a day practicing a healing technique called ChiLel - a practice that provides spiritual nourishment and enlivens the life force in their bodies. Chilel is a synthesis of Qigong and contemporary medical knowledge. Qigong is a practice that involves aligning the breath, physical activity, and awareness, to promote physical, mental and spiritual well being.

During a typical treatment, a student's cancerous tumor is displayed on a screen and monitored by doctors. The teachers then surround the student and emit Chi (the life force). Within a couple of minutes, the cancerous tumour generally dissolves before the doctors' eyes. A few days later the student is checked by the doctors and the healing is usually confirmed.

The hospitals have a success rate of ninety five percent over a range of one hundred and eighty different diseases. The degree of success is not only determined by what happens during treatment, but also by the commitment of the students to practice novel ways of nourishing their bodies after leaving the hospitals. People have miraculously recovered from incurable diseases such as cancer, diabetes, arthritis, and heart disease. Many have outlived their doctors by as much as twenty years!

How does healing occur?

Remember, unlike linear time in which we have to wait for results, the concept of vertical time states that there are an infinite number of parallel realities in which every conceivable scenario already exists. Teachers at the medicineless hospitals initiate an unfolding process in their bodies. As the contents of their imagination transpose into powerful feelings, they generate a field of information which interacts with the forces of creation and causes quantum changes in the matrix of consciousness that envelopes both themselves and the student. The combined effort results in the activation of an alternative (parallel) reality in which the student's cancer does not exist.

Summary

- We choose our desired reality through the power of belief. Whether it is rain in times of drought or a healing, we must believe it has manifested whole-heartedly.

- Although the limitations of our physical senses tell us that we are all individuals with defined boundaries, at the most primordial level of existence, we are all one.

- Our external reality mirrors our inner disposition. *As within, so without*. What we perceive in the mind, we receive from the universe.

- The space between our thoughts is pure potential, containing an infinite number of possibilities.

- The reality you desire already exists – you just have to *choose* it.

Exercise: Mindfulness

Throughout the course of each day, become aware of the feelings you experience. Pay attention to the sensations in your body and become aware of the accompanying thoughts. Ask yourself the following questions:

- Am I concentrating on what I *do* want, or what I *do not* want?
- Are these thoughts conducive to growth?
- Are these thoughts reoccurring?

Part Seven
The Alchemist's Archetypal Journey

Chapter 23

Enslavement to Enlightenment

This chapter contains the Alchemist's journey from enslavement to enlightenment. Each stage is represented by an archetype or a power animal, which, when evoked, will have a profound effect on your unconscious mind. Before we begin, let me clarify what is meant by the terms *'medicine'* and *'archetype'*.

Native American Medicine

To understand the concept of Native American medicine, we must redefine the term *medicine*. In this tradition, medicine can be defined as anything that improves our connection to the underlying principle of life - The Great Spirit - as the Native Americans call it. This includes anything which strengthens our connection to spirit, heals our body, purifies our mind, and brings personal power, strength, and understanding.

According to the Native American tradition, all of nature is connected at an unseen level (note the similarities to the findings of modern-day science). The animals, plants, and rocks all have lessons to impart. Throughout the ages, these messages have helped humanity to survive, providing us with direction, protection, and healing principles.

The animal kingdom is the primary source of these messages. By studying the animals in their natural habitat, we elicit their teachings. The essential nature of each animal embodies a lesson.

For example, the message of the eagle is freedom, vision, focus, power and spirit.

Assimilating the attributes of the animals and applying them to our lives, is a powerful and exciting way to evolve. Animals constantly teach us novel ways to reach our true potential. Each lesson they impart is based on one major idea or concept. When we call upon the power of an animal, we are asking to be endowed with the strength of that creature's essence – or in Native American terms, its *medicine*.

Archetypes

According to eminent Swiss psychiatrist Carl Jung, the psyche consists of various layers, including the *personal* and *collective* unconscious. His theory of the *personal unconscious* is similar to that of Freud's in that it is assumed to be a region of the mind which contains a person's repressed experiences - normally feelings and perceptions appertaining to significant people or events in the person's past. Jung, however, claimed there was a deeper layer of the unconscious, which he named the *collective unconscious*. Unlike the personal unconscious, which is unique to the individual, the collective unconscious is a layer of the mind common to us all.

The collective unconscious houses *archetypes*, which Jung believed to be innate, unconscious, universal patterns of psychic energy. To state it in simple terms, an archetype is a pattern of energy which embodies a particular theme e.g. the hero or the clown; it is an original model or prototype after which other similar things are patterned. For example, Superman and Batman *are the archetypes that have influenced many other hero-type characters which followed - Spiderman, Daredevil, and Iron-man, etc.*

Archetypes are said **to** provide the deep structure for human motivation and meaning. You may view them as imprints hardwired into our psyches which evoke deep feeling and propel us in a certain direction. When we contemplate an archetype and allow its essence to pervade our mind, we assume its attributes and characteristics. For instance, have you ever been to the cinema and become so engrossed in the movie that you have felt yourself become the hero or the lover? This is due to that particular archetype being activated within your unconscious and emerging to dominate your being.

Other examples of archetypes can be seen in the Major Arcana of the Tarot deck (e.g. the Fool, the High Priestess, and the Devil). The Fool archetype embodies the themes of innocence, simplicity, beginnings and faith; it portrays the youthful exuberance we possess when starting out on a new adventure. The fool makes no plans, nor gives thought to possible complications along the way; he takes joy in doing something different and will willingly go where others fear to tread.

The Tarot deck portrays the Fool's Journey through life. Each Major Arcana card represents a stage in the journey and imparts wisdom and guidance that we can assimilate in order to reach our true potential. In the same way, what follows is the Alchemists Archetypal journey through life. Archetypes offer a powerful way of changing our emotional state instantaneously, because they directly impact our unconscious in a profound way.

Read and study the following stages - one stage every day. Initially, go through the journey in chronological order. Thereafter, allow your intuition to guide you to any particular stage that seems significant. After absorbing the reading, seat yourself comfortably and mentally focus on the archetype. Allow its essence to permeate your unconscious mind and contemplate the lessons it relays. For example:

- Is this lesson revealing insights into yourself?
- Is it providing direction?
- Is it highlighting your strengths?
- Is it offering healing?

Allow the answers to emerge from the depths of your unconscious without force. Remain relaxed and open minded and watch as your comprehension of the forces of creation accentuate to produce amazing results in your life.

0 - The Adventurer

Our journey begins with the freedom-loving Adventurer. He represents new beginnings and a heroic quest for self knowledge. The Adventurer is resourceful and creative. He has a different agreement with reality than most, knowing no limitations. He is not afraid to dream his dreams and pursue them with passion. He meets every situation with youthful exuberance. His number is 0, the empty vessel waiting to be filled. The adventurer is not afraid to crash to the floor or soar to the highest heights; he is prepared to take creative risks. His philosophy is that *nothing is beyond the realms of possibility*, as a result, he is wide open to new opportunities.

- In what ways are you bound by rigidity and conformity?
- How can you redefine your agreement with reality?
- In what ways can you tap into your youthful exuberance?
- Remember: a ship anchored in a safe harbour cannot explore the oceans.

---

1 - The Owl

The Alchemist comes to know his hidden aspects though the archetype of the owl. Owl sees and knows the truth. His ability to navigate through the darkest night and bring back nourishment for himself signifies our ability to explore our unconscious (and use our findings to enhance our lives). Owl's message is one of awareness, mindfulness and vision. His ability to see through 360 degrees means nothing goes unnoticed. In Greek mythology, Pallas Athene, the Goddess of wisdom, had an owl sat on her shoulder to light up her blind side.

In what ways are you deceiving yourself?
In what ways are you *allowing* others to deceive you?
Would you like to illuminate your highest path?

Owl medicine enables you to see that which others cannot, which is the true essence of wisdom. When this energy pervades your inner world, your Higher Self is awakened and provides wise counsel on every situation. Your Indwelling Divinity is the light that expels all darkness.

Those with Owl Medicine can see that which is concealed, intuit what is not spoken aloud, and read between the lines. They move swiftly and silently through life's shadows using otherworldly knowledge and wisdom to light up their path. Owl will illumine your blind side making self-deceit impossible.

2- The Magician

Being aware of the illusion is the Magician's greatest attribute. The material world, in essence, is a mass illusion. When we are aware of the illusion, we become free to tap into the underlying intelligence which permeates all things and utilize it for the good of ourselves and all we encounter. The magician's attributes include: power, action, awareness, application, and resourcefulness. He is graceful and confident - able to make things happen with ease. The Magician is in control of his own thoughts, and therefore the ruler of reality. He uses every resource available to him to wield absolute power over all circumstances.

The **Magician** archetype embodies the multiplicity of talents the Universe has bestowed upon you: *originality, creativity, imagination, self-reliance, spontaneity, self-confidence, ingenuity, flexibility, masterfulness, self-control.* This energy will endow you with the **will, skill, optimism** and **initiative** needed to rise to any challenge and successfully implement the changes needed for optimal living. Magician energy will enable you to:

- **Manifest your desires**
- **Transform your belief system**
- **Devise innovative new ideas**
- **Transform a deficit into an asset**
- **Succeed in the face of adversity**
- **Heal yourself**

---

3 - Death

Many of us equate death with an ending, especially the end of life. This archetype, however, pertains to change, exposure, transition, termination, and inevitability. The Death archetype speaks of conclusion; it indicates that major change is needed in a certain area of your life. Every ending gives rise to a new beginning. Death is simply a rebirth which often involves the dissolution of our old perception of self and the emergence of a new one. The Death archetype exposes us to the inevitabilities of life. ***The only thing you can count on in life is death and change.*** No matter how long we've been employed, married, or lived in one location – we are always exposed to change. Life is in constant flux. Death is never the end - it is simply a change of direction.

What traits, attitudes, and patterns have outlived their usefulness?

Become aware of those things that have out-lived their usefulness. Prepare to shed them. Like a harvest, death marks the end of a cycle in which new seeds are sown. A healthy human being undergoes many death and rebirth cycles.

Evolution, by definition, is a natural progression in which the things that no longer serve us expire and make way for a new way of being.

---

4 - The Prophet

On the whole, the archetypal journey of the alchemist is focused on personal responsibility. The underlying persuasion of each archetype places the responsibility of life squarely on the shoulders of the individual. We're in sole charge of our lives, and the **consequences** of our actions determine our direction.

The Prophet archetype is a guiding force. Having the attributes of forbearance and foresight, he is able to foresee the consequences of our current actions. Remember, however, the future isn't set in stone. Life unfolds according to what you are thinking and feeling in the present moment. Change the way you think NOW and the future will take a new direction.

Life is cyclical in nature. W*hat we reap, so we sow;* is the basis of Karma. The Sanskrit word ***Karma*** simply means ***action***, and every action has a consequence. Therefore, our current actions mould our future. Many of us have experienced guilt, paranoia, and fear as a result of inappropriate actions. We are well aware of the subsequent persecution it causes. The prophet archetype urges us to invest more time carefully considering the nature of our thoughts before we act on them. Allow life-denying thoughts to pass, and embrace the life-enhancing ones.

When we concentrate on the Prophet archetype, our attention is focused on our convictions. He urges us to examine our belief systems, how we operate within these beliefs, and how they affect our lives. To accomplish this we must be highly aware of the factors which influence our lives: the *drivers*. We must disentangle our thought processes and identify that which causes us to move in a certain direction. We must be diligent and pursue a course that leads to the highest expression of ourselves. If we take a few minutes each day to consider the effects of our thoughts on our actions, we will initiate a major change in our life.

The Prophet is also endowed with moral insight, and the ability to receive and express divine inspiration. He is master of esoteric knowledge - incredibly well-versed in the ways of spirit. He guides and instructs, acting as a bridge between us and the Universal Mind. He is forever mindful of his responsibility to assist people on their spiritual path. He is aware of the intricate workings of nature, the movement of spiritual matters, and finely tuned to the stirrings of the mind. He is vitally tapped into the flow of ancient knowledge and instinctively understands the connections between nature, philosophy, science and religion.

- Sit quietly and relax
- Allow your awareness to progress to a time in the future
- From this perspective, look back and see what you have achieved
- Pay careful attention to the peaks and troughs.
- Acknowledge your strengths and weaknesses
- How could you have improved your life?
- What resources and attributes do you need to develop to reach your true potential?
- Evoke the Prophet archetype – the inner visionary
- Allow him / her to reveal your highest path
- The Prophet is an inspired teacher, visionary and proclaimer of Universal will.

5 - The Soul Child

Wear a smile and have friends;
wear a scowl and have wrinkles.
George Eliot

Hidden beneath layer upon layer of conditioning, deep within the depths of our psyche, there lies an unblemished, incredibly wise, yet playful aspect of our being; an aspect that is deeply grounded in its spiritual roots. The Soul Child is that aspect of our being that existed prior to conditioning - prior to being infected by the conflicting messages of society.

As infants we internalise messages about ourselves that give rise to a false perception of self; a fragmented and illusory self called the ego. Before this influx of mental pollution, we were pure, whole, and extremely aware of our true nature: immortal, omnipotent, children of the Universe.

When we are grounded in our true nature, all our fears and worries dissipate - what can there possibly be to fear? We were not born; we will not die; weapons cannot harm us: we are invincible! When we truly acknowledge this truth, there is nothing left to do except laugh!

The Soul Child embodies the wonderment you had as a child. When you evoke this archetype, you see the world through the eyes of that child. The Soul Child is alive, vigorous, curious, adventurous, playful and even mischievous! It exudes happiness.
If you're taking life too serious, wrapped up in complexity, evoke the energy of the Soul Child and embrace the simple pleasures in life.

How would your life change if you traded your worries for wonderment?

Playfulness promotes well-being – how can you incorporate playfulness into your daily activities?

As children we learn to detach and dissociate during times of trouble. This often leads to fragmentation as we *lose* parts of ourselves. Healing involves reconnecting with these lost parts. One such estranged facet is the Soul Child. Evoking the *Soul Child involves* trading your stress and anxiety for wonderment. You are an immortal Child of the Universe, endowed with unlimited potential. When you truly acknowledge this, worry, stress and anxiety become redundant.

Find a quiet place, relax, induce an altered state of consciousness, and evoke the **Soul Child.**

6 - The Lovers - Unity

This archetype is often associated with romantic partnerships and passion. Here, however, we will transcend the earthly meaning in favour of the transcendental state of **unity consciousness**.

The lovers' archetype pertains to yoga – or union with God. At the most primordial level of being there is no separation, no individuality, no '*other*': we are all one. True love is a state in which our being is grounded in the Sacred Singularity. When we operate from the level of Source, we assume our rightful heritage as co-creator of the Universe. With our awareness grounded in the intelligence of the ultimate being we are infallible.

The Lovers' archetype also encompasses the dualistic nature of life: good, bad; harmony, disharmony; joy, sorrow, all of which create ambivalence and emotional imbalance in our lives. The antidote to this uncertainty and unrest is 'love'. To be truly '*in love*' is to be grounded in the oneness of the Sacred Singularity. It is interesting to note that the term '*holy*' – '*enmeshed in the whole*' depicts this state. By immersing ourselves in God consciousness we transcend the nuances of life and bathe in a haven of peace and tranquillity.

The gateway to the sanctuary of the Sacred Singularity is silence and meditation. Take time to relax or commune with nature. Allow your inner dialogue to dissipate and let your awareness slip into the silence which prevails. There you will find balance, equanimity, unity, and serenity – there you will be '*in love.*'

> **Imagine the feeling of wholeness transpiring as a result all your sub-personalities being in alignment and working together for your highest good?**
>
> **Are you ready to be filled with the bliss of being?**
>
> Evoke the '*Lovers*' archetype and reconnect with the ground of all being.
> - Sit quietly
> - Take a few deep breathes
> - Don't *do*, just *be*
> - Allow your thoughts to dissipate and slip into the silent gap that prevails
> - Bathe in the bliss of Unity consciousness
>
> Notice how quickly that void and fragmentation is supplanted by a great sense of wholeness. ***Separation can't exist where unity prevails.***

7 - The Charioteer

Chariot battle was a great endeavour which involved coordination, vision, strength, and determination. Imagine trying to control two powerful steeds while negotiating your way through the chaos, commotion, and perilous terrain of the battle field. This will give you some idea why the Charioteer archetype represents focus, drive and control.

The Charioteer is representative of our ability to harness and direct our energy under conditions of extreme duress. When we become besieged by life, charioteer energy enables us to stay in firm control and focus on the task ahead.

Self-discipline is the key. When our internal forces (the steeds) get out of control, we can be hurled into chaos and devastation (the battle), so we must exercise self-restraint. Our level of skill is often reflected in our ability to be patient whilst maintaining the sheer conviction to triumph.

Are you tired of your self-will running riot?

Would you like to resume control of your life?

Are you ready to harness your energies and steer them in the direction of your Life's Purpose?

Are you ready to control your mind, instead of allowing your mind to control you?

8 - Strength

The strength archetype has a deeper meaning than simply brute force. It involves harnessing the attributes of compassion and understanding to sooth the savage beast within. It is the ability to refrain from impulsive action and weigh up the situation; be a cause not an effect. What people think of you is their business, how you respond is yours.

In the Tarot pack, strength is depicted by a lion and a pure maiden. The lion represents our inner beast - that part of ourselves that needs to feed on '*more*'. This beast always needs more - more money, more recognition, more food, more alcohol or more drugs.

The pure maiden represents our Indwelling Divinity, our source of real strength. True strength is to be proactive, not reactive; true strength is to cry when we're upset; true strength is the ability to nurture, calm and exhibit self-love. Strength is allaying the ravenous *more* beast within and centring ourselves.

> Imagine attaining self-mastery – how would your life change?
>
> How would you like to engender respect?
>
> In what ways can you resolve conflicts with wisdom?
>
> Reconsider your definition of strength. The **Strength** archetype invokes a higher level of consciousness and enables us to meet every difficulty with clarity, courage, and confidence.

9 - The Jester

In medieval times there were two types of Jester. One was considered to be unintelligent and became the butt of people's jokes. The other hid his intelligence behind a clown-like persona to great advantage. The latter would use ditties to relay covert and cryptic messages to the public; for example, clandestine news and plots concerning the royalty.

The Jester archetype embodies our ability to be defiant and rebellious in a constructive way; to break out of the confines of conditioning and stop trying to appease people: let the voice of our truth be known and embrace our uniqueness.

The Jester's message is *'lighten up – life is to be enjoyed.'* Applying a potent combination of wisdom, irony and humour to our problems is a great source of healing. The jester invokes joviality, creativity, playfulness, shrewdness, and cleverness in one holistic package. He uses mischief, rebelliousness, comedy, irony and defiance to create an infallible strategy for living.

> **Do you want to break the confines of conformity and make a difference in the world?**
>
> **Do you treat life as a game to *win,* rather than a game to *play?***
>
> The **Jester** archetype is colourful, jovial, light, humorous, creative, intelligent, rebellious, defiant, responsive, and playful. When imbued with this energy, we live life to the full, enjoy the moment, and lighten everyone's world. The **Jester** knows that wit and wisdom are bedfellows. Disguised in his clown-like persona is a great sense of duty – a yearning to reveal the truth and bring about justice.

10 - The Hermit

In the fast-paced, harried world of today, we can learn much from the hermit's habits. His footing is slow but sure. He takes a premeditated, conscious approach to life, knowing that each step is a small imprint that deepens and clarifies his life's path. Everything he does is executed with great awareness - each breath he takes, each word he speaks, every decision he makes, is a deliberate, conscious act.

When we recognize that each of our thoughts and actions is a building block used to erect our lives, we partake in the conscious construction of our own reality. The Hermit used solitude to elicit this lesson. By removing himself from the normal, chaotic stream of societal thought, he is able to listen to the inner stirrings of his own intuition.

Do you feel a need to retreat from the distractions of everyday life?

Do you seek answers to pressing questions?

Do you sense a deeper, more meaningful reality beneath the mask of matter?

When Hermit calls, turn off your mobile, switch off your computer, and retreat to a silent sanctuary. Hermit energy is a directive to be still, contemplative, and meditative. The Hermit encourages us to hold counsel with the *'Wise Witness Within'* in order to deduce the best course of action, or reveal insights into the true nature of being.

11 - The Hanged Man

The term *'Hanged Man'* can be off-putting, and has a tendency to make us uncomfortable. However, if you look at the Tarot card depicting this character, he shows no sign of struggle on his face. In fact, he oozes serenity. The Hanged Man's expression is one of complete composure. He has no expectation, and all actions have been suspended. The Hanged Man is in a state of purposeful contemplation, aligning his mind and body to the natural rhythm and flow of the Universe. The keywords here are yield, suspend, sacrifice, non-action, and submission,

When we evoke the Hanged Man archetype, we become open to new perspectives. We look at our challenges from different angles. From his unique vantage point he counsels us to look at situations in a new way, suspend judgement and enjoy generating new alternatives. The Hanged Man advises us to stop *doing* and simply *be* for a while. When we withhold action and observe the events in life, we allow things to flow more easily. If, on the other hand, we struggle, fight, and insist on control - we are met with restriction and pressure every step of the way.

> # Don't just do something, sit there!

Sacrifice is a facet of the Hanged Man. He instructs us to give up things that do not serve us. By suspending our actions we are able to identify the path of least resistance: our highest path. The hanged man urges us to remain calm in the face of adversity, step back and deduce the best course of action. He is the epitome of calmness and the embodiment of wisdom.

Instead of acting impulsively and erratically – can you simply pause for a moment?

A single problem has numerous solutions – would you like to discover them?

How would simplifying things enhance your life?

- Step back and evoke the Hanged Man Archetype.
- Assume the position of observer and simply watch your thoughts.
- Focus your attention on a situation requiring a solution.
- Look at it through different frames of reference.
- Consider every alternative and widen your options.
- When you have exhausted every possibility, allow the situation to dissolve back into consciousness.
- Allow the solution to arise naturally – without force.
- Now let another challenge arise and repeat the process.
- Refining your mind in this way will reveal your true potential

12 - Temperance

The Temperance archetype is the embodiment of *balance* and *equanimity* which leads to self mastery. When we become spiritually receptive to the energy of Temperance we hear the tranquil essence of our spirit running through us. Temperance is the flowing river of our spirit running through us and cleansing and purifying our energies. Imagine immersing yourself in a crystal clear waterfall which attuned you to the rhythmic flow of the Universe. Exhilarating, isn't it?

Temperance is an indication that subtle shifts are taking place. When we quietly and objectively investigate our life, we begin to see patterns. Temperance encourages us to use these patterns to find balance and restraint. The keyword *chemistry* is included here because Temperance deals with mixing the right ingredients in our lives in order to flow with the path of least resistance. It takes skill and perseverance to attain balance, but once we do the rewards are great. Temperance supports a body at rest, you will not drown - you will float; so long as you cease to struggle.

Temperance also indicates a commitment to sobriety, healing, emotional stability, and self-love. Very often spiritual seekers evoke this energy when growth is needed after experiencing a spiritual drought. When you are run-down, lost, frustrated, or confused, allow the energy of temperance to infuse every corner of your being and lead you from the wilderness.

Would you like to resolve inner conflict?

Imagine feeling balanced and poised?

Our internal world is populated by many different characters. These 'sub-personalities' are often in conflict with each other. The resulting turmoil gives rise to feelings of fragmentation and unrest. Temperance isn't about choosing one or the other; it is about mixing things until you get the perfect blend. The following exercise is designed to bridge internal division and foster wholeness.

- Relax and clear your mind

- Call forward a part of yourself that is in conflict with another part

- Ask it what it wants

- Listen carefully and acknowledge its needs (All conflicting parts have your highest good in mind)

- Now, call the opposing part out and repeat the procedure

- Evoke the energy of temperance

- Allow the archetype to identify ways of blending the contrasting parts and achieving synthesis.

13 - Devil

The idea of the Devil is daunting for most people. In a suppressed society, topics relating to this archetype are not openly discussed as they illicit intense discomfort. However, if we approach it with open-mindedness and maturity, we can glean a mass of insight.

The ego is the Devil incarnate. Ego tells us that we're either superior or inferior. Ego convinces us that we need drugs, alcohol, or food - to feel content. Ego tells us we need a new car to be admired. Ego tells us to subjugate our friends to second best so we can elevate our own status.

When the Devil archetype is active within us, we've got some serious soul-searching to do. We need to hand control of our lives back to our Indwelling Divinity and resume control. The Devil tells us that we are possessed by our competitive and possessive nature, stooping to a level of functioning that is beneath us. We are designed for greatness yet when we stoop to the level of egoic thinking we're blind to our own beauty. An ego-driven mind operates under the illusion that love and success must be obtained through deceit, betrayal, coercion, and manipulation.

The keywords appertaining to the Devil archetype are: ego, loss of control, error, addiction, illusion, disruption, and enslavement. When the Devil strikes we need to counterbalance our energies with the love of our Indwelling Divinity.

Are you being possessive, manipulative, demanding or controlling?

Are you under-mining others in an attempt to improve your status?

Are you experiencing jealousy?

If so, then the Devil archetype is active within you. To disperse this energy, evoke the *strength* and *lovers* archetypes and operate from a higher level of consciousness – one in which individuality and separateness give way to unity and wholeness.

---

14 - Catastrophe

The Catastrophe archetype is about change; usually very sudden and not-so-pleasant change. Change is typically gradual, allowing our minds to accommodate and adapt to the different shifts in our lives. When a sudden cataclysmic change occurs, it is an anomaly of sorts. Such a drastic upheaval means the Universe is trying to awaken us from our somnambulistic state. This wake-up call comes in the form of an event which shakes us out of a mental and emotional fog.

When catastrophe strikes we mustn't slip into victim mentality and the 'poor me' syndrome, instead, recognise it as a wake-up call. Harness the energy the upheaval embodies and use it as fuel to power a shift in a new direction.

Next time catastrophe strikes ask yourself the following questions:

- **In which direction is the Universe ushering me?**
- **How am I deceiving myself?**
- **What do I need to change imminently?**
- **What am I denying / resisting?**

After asking these questions, evoke one of the positive archetypes - for example, the *Magician* - to enable the necessary change.

---

15 – Wolf: The Pathfinder

Wolf is the pathfinder. He ventures out alone in pursuit of knowledge and returns to the clan to share his findings. He is the embodiment of loyalty and the epitome of wild spirit. Wolves are instinctively pack animals, but maintain a very strong individual urge. They are friendly, social, and highly intelligent creatures. Amongst their numerous attributes are strength, confidence and surety.

When we evoke wolf energy, we are settled in our own skin and have no need to prove ourselves to others. We trust our insights and use our keen senses to act on them. Diversity is of the utmost importance. Exploring different paths breathes new life into our day-to-day routine.

When wolf energy comes alive within you, your innate teaching instincts will come to the fore. You will wish to share your knowledge and assist others to deepen their understanding of the forces of nature and the Great Mystery (The Universal Oneness). It is in the sharing of new insights that the collective consciousness of our planet will reach new heights.

Are you ready to be of service to others?

We cannot take anything material from this life. *To make our lives worthwhile we must give them away.*

Instead of our resting place being in the ground, let it be *in the hearts of all those we have encountered.*

Evoke Wolf energy and foster the gifts of contributing, healing, service, sharing, teaching and using your unique gifts and talents for the highest good of others.

---

16 - The Butterfly

The butterfly's essence is that of transformation. It has four stages in its life cycle:

1. **The egg** - a beginning, an awareness that change is needed and that your old way of life no longer works;
2. **The caterpillar** - the stage of identifying which areas of your life warrant change;
3. **The chrysalis** – contemplation and introspection, going within and deciding how you will manifest the needed changes;
4. And finally, **the birth of the butterfly** - action and the spreading of your wings.

Many people recognise a need for change in their lives but are often too frightened to put their feelings and thoughts into action. They get caught up in the chrysalis stage, cocooned in a rigid shell of fear. When this happens, learn from the courage of the butterfly. The world awaiting the butterfly outside the cocoon is totally different from anything it has ever known during the other stages of its life cycle, yet it sheds its shell and takes to the skies without fear or hesitation.

***

Are you ready to embrace the infinite opportunities which exist in a domain yet unexplored (the unknown)?

Evoke the Butterfly archetype. Shed your cocoon of fear, assume a new way of being, and fly into a new world

***

17 - The Universe

Since time immemorial we have elevated our eyes towards the heavens seeking reassurance and guidance. Looking into the vast expanse of space imbues us with awe and wonderment. Just for a moment, imagine yourself floating serenely through the dark velvet heavens, peppered with an infinite array of stars, planets, comets, and meteors. The sheer magnitude of what surrounds you is enthralling.

Now turn your senses inwardly and concentrate on the vastness of your internal universe, peppered with its infinite array of possibilities. Allow the light of your Indwelling Divinity to cast out any shadows and illuminate your highest path.

The Universe archetype embodies the energies of wonderment, diversity, perfection, inspiration, and creativity; its message is one of hope, healing, guidance, cleansing, assurance, ascension, and rejuvenation. This inspiring archetype urges us to transcend our human nature and evoke the higher energies.

Whenever we are lost, confused or frustrated, we should raise our eyes to the Universe and evoke its infinite power. Allow its healing qualities to pervade our being, and bathe in its inspirational essence. The Universe has infinite organizing capabilities, draw on them and use them to determine your path of least resistance. With the universe as your guide, you cannot fail to reach your optimal potential?

> **Are you realizing your dreams?**
>
> **Are you prospering and achieving your heart's desire?**
>
> **Are you living on purpose?**
>
> Then you are an evolved being who has embraced your natural heritage: *master of the Universe*. The **Universe** archetype is evoked by integrating the lessons, attributes, and resources from the preceding stages of this journey. It is a sign that all your constituent parts are aligned and working together to propel you towards your destiny.

18 - The Sacred Singularity

The Sacred Singularity is the last archetype in the journey of the Alchemist. As such, it embodies the completion of a long, sometimes challenging journey. The Sacred Singularity represents all elements coming together in a unifying experience that embodies success, achievement, abundance, fulfillment, enrichment, and satisfaction. Our once fragmented psyche has transformed into an integrated whole. Opposites have merged and synthesized to work as one. The yin-yang principle is at work bringing balance and unity. Our awareness has elevated to the level of enlightenment and cosmic consciousness. We have become the ultimate creator.

Do you feel integrated and whole?

Can you truly savour the present moment?

Do you have an underlying sense of peace and contentment?

Do you recognise everything and everybody as an extension of yourself?

Congratulations, you have achieved the ultimate goal of the **Alchemist's Archetypal Journey:** *unity.*

Part Eight
Ancestral Alchemy
and Affirmations
(Re-programming the Unconscious)

Chapter 24

Formulas from Our Wise Forefathers

To reach our true potential we must purge our mind of negative indoctrination and supplant it with psychological and spiritual nourishment. Remember, alcoholism is a mind-set, a maladaptive set of beliefs, the answer to which is a profound shift in consciousness:

Sobriety is contingent on replenishing and evolving our mind on a daily basis

This chapter contains a collection of writings from some of the greatest thinkers who have ever graced our planet. Absorbing the wisdom and inspiration herein will induce a contemporary way of thinking based on ancient teachings. Sir Isaac Newton once said the following:

> **"If I have seen a little further it is by standing on the shoulders of the giants who have come before me"**

By digesting and integrating the wisdom in this chapter, you too can expand your vision by standing on the shoulders of the inspirational giants who have come before you. Remember, words are the software that re-programme your mind; let the teachings of these masters permeate your unconscious and produce a profound shift in your thinking.

Tao Te Ching (Verse 36)

The Tao Te Ching is a collection of eighty-one verses that provide the basic philosophy for the school of Taoism - an important pillar of Chinese thought. Written by Chinese sage Lao Tzu, the Tao Te Ching is designed to change your life by radically transforming the way you think. Literally translated it means:

Tao – The Way
Te – Strength / Virtue
Ching – Scripture

I have chosen verse thirty-six to contemplate, as it offers wise counsel on processing our issues and avoiding the accumulation of the unconscious debris that pollutes our mind.

Should you want to contain something,

you must deliberately let it expand.

Should you want to weaken something,

you must deliberately let it grow strong.

Should you want to restrain something,

you must deliberately allow it to flourish.

Should you want to take something away,

you must deliberately grant it access.

The lesson here is called wisdom in obscurity.

The gentle outlasts the strong.

The obscure outlasts the obvious

(Lao Tzu - 6th century BC)

This verse imparts an invaluable lesson:

> ## Do not suppress or repress: EXPRESS!

When in the grips of alcoholism, we used drink as a means of suppressing unresolved issues. Even in sobriety many people continue this pattern, camouflaging their troublesome issues to keep up appearances. Without realizing it, they are creating a monster. Suppressed emotions must find expression and they do so in a multitude of negative ways: psychosis, neurosis, phobias, mood swings, fears, and so on. Suppression and repression impede our natural flow of emotive force and asphyxiate life. Rather than diminish problematic issues, they exacerbate them.

Many people claim strength by hiding their mental and emotional debris from public view, but this sham serves only to inflate their ego. Their stature is built on shaky foundations. Beneath the surface, pressure is building and cracks are appearing. If they don't release the pressure soon, the inevitable explosion will cause chaos.

Verse thirty-six urges us re-evaluate these tactics. It encourages us to turn our strategies upside down and practice opposites. By informing us that *the gentle outlasts the strong* and the *obscure outlasts the obvious,* Lao Tzu urges us to express our emotions.

Paradoxically, hiding unresolved issues increases their power and longevity. Like a pan of water on low heat they simmer away in the background, breeding unease and discontentment. As the flotsam of the past gradually pollutes the shores of the present, we find ourselves becoming increasingly irritable, restless, and nervous. Conversely, when we invite our past issues into consciousness we remove their source of heat and quickly extinguish them. Conscious issues can be processed and released, freeing up vital energy for other activities.

Next time you experience an issue that gives rise to emotional discomfort, put the Tao Te Ching to test. Rather than banish it to the realms of your unconscious, deliberately let it permeate your mind. Refrain from judgement, simply observe it and notice how quickly your discomfort subsides.

The Dualistic Nature of Life

> "Man was made for joy and woe
> and when this we rightly know
> Through the world we safely go.
> Joy and woe are woven fine
> A clothing for the soul to bind."
> William Blake

Accepting the polarised nature of life is essential if we want to attain peace. As up cannot exist without down, and hot cannot exist without cold, so joy cannot exist without sorrow, and peace without conflict - each polarity gives rise to its opposite. Our culture, however, teaches us to deny negative experience and pretend all is well - a practice that saps energy and leads to neurosis.

> "Man's task is to become conscious
> of the contents that press upward
> from the unconscious."
>
> Carl Gustav Jung

In essence, negative and positive energy are the same thing in different guises: they both provide fuel to propel us towards our desired future - as the following story relays:

The Archer

An archer and his young son went deep into the forest. On reaching the centre, the archer took out his bow and retrieved an arrow from his pouch. As he steadied himself and took aim at a tree trunk in the distance, his young son looked puzzled and asked why he was drawing the arrow backwards when the target was in front of him. The archer promptly replied 'it is the drawback that gives the arrow the power and momentum to shoot forward with great speed and reach its target.'

The moral of this story is plainly obvious. The inevitable drawbacks in life are a valuable source of power. Each one has the potential to motivate us. Changing our perception of negative experience and realizing that every *drawback* is a golden opportunity to progress is at the heart of alchemy. Transformation is often borne of crisis because the potential energy contained in the *drawback* is sufficiently powerful to propel us forward towards our goals. In reality, there is no such thing as negative experience, just challenges that provide opportunities to evolve.

Freedom

'Freedom is a mind that's open to everything and attached to nothing'
Author Unknown

The following Story is a true account of a very dear friend of mine:

> *Jimmy struggled for years to break free from the clutches of alcohol. Relapse followed sobriety in cycles, until he met Julie - an attractive woman, four years his junior. Very quickly she became the focal point of his life; his reason for staying sober. The first couple of years were a dream; they spent many happy hours laughing and loving. After this initial period, however, Julie decided she needed to widen her horizons. She enrolled at college and started to attend the gym with a few friends twice a week. Jimmy became paranoid; his jealousy escalated very quickly and wreaked havoc. His possessiveness and irrational behaviour led to their break up. The emotional pain was so great that Jimmy sought escape. He was found dead in the bath two months later with toxic levels of alcohol and barbiturates in his bloodstream.*

Jimmy leaves us with a legacy. If we tether our happiness to a possession, be it a person, place or object, we become enslaved to it.

'What we must own comes to possess us.'

By clinging to objects and people as our sole source of happiness, we invite frustration, pain and turmoil. Everything on the physical plane is transient and impermanent. Without exception, every object - including our physical bodies - is in a constant state of flux. Every material object is simply a convergence of a few elementary particles. The numerous manifestations of these particles are continuously recycling from one label and structure to another. Some atoms that comprised my body yesterday are part of your body today. The Daffodil that blossoms today will decompose in a few days time. Delicious food cooked today will become stale and toxic in a couple of days - the decaying process is irreversible. Thoughts change, emotions change, people change: everything changes! Hankering after transitory things is fraught with uncertainty:

> ## Transient things provide transitory happiness.

The situation is comparable to putting your hand in a stream and trying to grasp the water; the more you grasp the less water you retain. However, if you immerse your open hand in the stream and refrain from grasping, you receive a never-ending supply of fresh water. Similarly, when you attain the objects of your desires, enjoy them to the full: drive that beautiful motor car, romance the girl of your dreams, enjoy your new home - but do not tether your happiness to them. In doing so, you impede the natural flow of the Universe. When you are not grasping and clinging you are wide open to receive. Trust in the process of change - release the old and welcome the new.

Connecting to Source

"The spiritual life does not remove us from the world
but leads us deeper into it."

Henri J. M. Nouwen

Spiritual practice is not designed to eclipse our humanness; it is
designed to enhance it. Transcending the physical domain and
bathing in the bliss of the Sacred Singularity is a wise and fruitful
practice, but when we take it to extremes it can become another
form of escapism.

The physical domain is a valuable gift that should not be discarded.
Where else can we experience the richness and diversity that our
humanness provides? Where else can we feel the passion of a lover,
the warmth of a family bond, or the mental stimulation of problem
solving?

Remaining in a transcendental state is somewhat akin to the
experience of King Midas. Everything King Midas touched turned
to gold; therefore, he could never experience the joy of a warm
embrace or a tender kiss. He equated success and happiness with
wealth and in the process sold the treasure of his humanity.
Likewise, if we aspire to remain in a state of transcendence, we sell
the treasure of our humanity. We are not here to deny our
humanness, we are here to refine it and bring it into alignment with
our spiritual essence.

As we experience the transitory nature of life and embrace the rich
experience that the temporary states of joy and sorrow bring, we
slowly become aware of an unchanging truth: the permanence of
our Indwelling Divinity. This aspect of our being is not intended to
shepherd us away from life; conversely, it enables us to embrace life

to the full. To reach our true potential and make an impact on the world we must be connected to Source. Our Higher Self is the gateway.

The room I'm writing in at present has a lamp, a television, a DVD player, a fish tank, and a coffee percolator. Each object has a different appearance and performs a different function, but they all have the same source of power - electricity. When disconnected from their power source the appliances are rendered useless. Likewise, you and I may have a different appearance and different roles in life, but we are both expressions of one unified field of intelligence. When we become fixated with the mental construction of who we *think* we are (our ego) we inadvertently disconnect ourselves from our power source. A light bulb, television set, or coffee percolator cannot carry out their purpose when disconnected from the electricity supply, as we cannot fulfil our purpose when disconnected from our source.

When a drop is separated from the ocean it wields little power; but when re-united with the vastness of its source, it becomes invincible. To embrace your true potential, allow the drop that is you to dissolve back into the ocean that is your Source, and utilize this infallible power to evolve the collective consciousness of our planet.

In the 1960s, psychologist, **John Bowlby**, formulated a theory that emphasised the importance of a secure relationship with our primary caregiver in infancy. This theory can be adapted to reflect the importance of our connection to the universal intelligence.

According to '*attachment theory*', the relationship we have with our primary caregiver in infancy is crucial to our psychological development. The central theme of attachment theory is that mothers who are available and responsive to their infant's needs establish a sense of security within the child. Knowing that the caregiver is dependable, the child will happily explore the surrounding environment and use the caregiver as a secure base to which she can return when distressed. The central tenets are as follows:

- **Safe Haven:** When a child feels threatened or afraid, he or she can return to the comfort of the caregiver to be soothed and reassured.
- **Secure Base:** The caregiver provides a secure base from which the child can explore the world.
- **Proximity Maintenance:** The child strives to remain close to the caregiver, instilling a sense of security and protection.
- **Separation Anxiety:** When separated from the caregiver, the child becomes upset and distressed.

Similarly, a deep, meaningful connection with our Indwelling Divinity is imperative to our psychological and spiritual development. Our true essence provides a secure base from which we can venture out and explore the rich diversity of life. Just as a child suffers separation anxiety when its mother is absent for a period of time, we become lost, confused and frightened when we abandon our roots and become disconnected from our Source. An intimate connection with our Indwelling Divinity instils confidence and assurance within us. Bathing in the light of our Source replenishes and re-energizes us, preparing us to embark on our next fact-finding adventure. Enthusiasm is the sign that our spirit in control. Remember, *en theos*, the root of the word enthusiasm, means 'in spirit'. As we allow life to unfold from the level of our spirit, we embrace the entire array of glorious gifts this world has to offer.

My Mind to Me a Kingdom Is

My mind to me a kingdom is;
Such present joys therein I find,
That it excels all other bliss
That world affords or grows by kind:
Though much I want that most would have,
Yet still my mind forbids to crave.

No princely pomp, no wealthy store,
No force to win the victory,
No wily wit to salve a sore,
No shape to feed a loving eye;
To none of these I yield as thrall;
For why? My mind doth serve for all.

I see how plenty surfeits oft,
And hasty climbers soon do fall;
I see that those which are aloft
Mishap doth threaten most of all;
They get with toil, they keep with fear:
Such cares my mind could never bear.

Content I live, this is my stay;
I seek no more than may suffice;
I press to bear no haughty sway;
Look, what I lack my mind supplies.
Lo! Thus I triumph like a king,
Content with that my mind doth bring.

Some have too much, yet still do crave;
I have little, and seek no more.
They are but poor, though much they have,

And I am rich with little store.
They poor, I rich; they beg, I give;
They lack, I leave; they pine, I live.

I laugh not at another's loss;
I grudge not another's gain;
No worldly waves my mind can toss;
My state at one doth still remain:
I fear no foe, I fawn no friend;
I loathe not life, nor dread my end.

Some weigh their pleasure by their lust,
Their wisdom by their rage of will;
Their treasure is their only trust,
A cloaked craft their store of skill;
But all the pleasure that I find
Is to maintain a quiet mind.

My wealth is health and perfect ease,
My conscious clear my choice defence;
I neither seek by bribes to please,
nor by deceit to breed offence:
Thus do I live; thus will I die;
Would all did so as well as I!

English Poet, Sir Edward Dyer (1543 – 1607)

This poem encapsulates the core essence of sobriety. Sobriety isn't simply abstinence from drink, it's equanimity of mind: balance. The mind may be seen as having three distinct components: *conditioned consciousness, imagination, and pure consciousness.*

Conditioned Consciousness

This is the domain that houses the messages we have internalized from society; it is often chaotic and confusing. Sir Edward describes the plight of those embroiled in conditioned consciousness as those infected with the disease of *more*. If only they had more money; more clothes; more holidays; more jewellery; more status; more power; more, more, more - then, and only then, will they be happy. But what happens? They exert all their efforts on acquiring *more*, often discarding the feelings of other people along the way, only to discover that their acquisitions have changed nothing. Not only are they still discontent, but now they're terrified of losing what they've accumulated! Remember, every desire contains the seed of its opposite. Along with amassing more of what they thought they needed, they inadvertently acquired more worry, more anxiety, and more stress, which often leads to the onset of ill health.

Every desire contains the seed of its opposite

Sir Edward recognised that *'his health was his wealth and perfect ease.'* In *'seeking no more than may suffice'* he kept his mind a crave free zone. Lack of craving suggests he was master of his mind, and this translated into good physical health. Though poor by material standards, his life was rich because his mind was free of the need to possess objects, power and status. *'They are but poor, though much they have, And I am rich with little store. They poor, I rich; they beg, I give. They lack, I leave; they pine, I live.* Many people have exclaimed 'I'm finished; I've lost it all,' after being relieved of certain worldly possessions. Unlike Sir Edward, they obviously hadn't considered the invaluable treasure of the invisible kingdom which dwells within them.

The conditioned mind is neither good nor bad; it is how we use it that determines its effectiveness. Being home to sixty thousand thoughts per day, it's a domain of infinite possibilities – any one thought being potentially life changing. You can choose inspiration or desperation, but the point is **you can choose**. Sir Edward highlighted this point when he wrote *'yet still my mind forbids to crave.'* When you crave anything - be it alcohol, drugs, food or sex - *your mind is controlling you, you are not controlling your mind*. You have given up the faculty of choice. The seductive voices of society incessantly whisper misguided ideas through your mind: *'buy this object, take that substance, or eat this food, and you will attain happiness, power and freedom.'* And you can get sucked in. You can believe them. But they are simply the internalised offerings of the deluded who are intent on spreading the disease of *more*.

Don't be an *EFFECT* of the conditioned masses, be the *CAUSE* of your chosen destiny. Cultivate your mind; it is the domain where you reign supreme.

Imagination – The Creative Realm

When we penetrate the chaos and confusion of conditioned consciousness, we reach the creative domain. This is the dominion of your imagination; that faculty of your being which shapes the potential energy of pure consciousness into life experience.

Your imagination is fed from two sources: conditioned consciousness and pure consciousness. Although conditioned consciousness is often chaotic and confusing, it is also the gateway through which creative ideas from the external world enter our internal domain, some of which are extremely valuable.

Akin to gold prospectors, we should sieve our conditioned consciousness and separate the gold from the silt. When we discover a golden idea, as with a seed, we should plant it in the field of our imagination and allow our awareness to cultivate it. To do this we need to turn our senses inwardly and see, hear, feel, taste, and smell the idea as though it was already manifest. Remember, the brain doesn't differentiate between imagination and actuality. If you imagine squeezing lemon juice on your tongue, you will salivate – even though there is no lemon! The brain will wire itself in accordance with what you are imagining. The physical and the formless domains of mind and matter will unite to support your idea. Subsequently, you will emanate a vibration that will act as a request to the amorphous see of intelligence responsible for all creation, which will respond by birthing your idea into reality.

Pure Consciousness

The other source of input for the imagination is the final level of the mind: pure consciousness. If we quieten our mind to such an extent that we penetrate the conditioned and the creative layers, we enter the realm of *pure consciousness*. This is the blissful domain of our Indwelling Divinity. Here we are *being* not *doing*. Here we are pure *presence*. When the chaos of life gets unbearable, become silent and bathe in this blissful flow of divine consciousness. Absorb the infinite peace and tranquillity of this domain and allow it to rejuvenate, cleanse and purify every atom of your being.

Ideas birthed from this level manifest as intuition or hunches. They set you alight inside because they are divine impulses emanating from the Soul of the Universe. When your mind is chaotic, you block the Universal flow of inspirational ideas, so make time to empty your mind, and become a conduit for inspiration.

Conclusion

As I write these words, I'm sitting on a veranda, overlooking the turquoise ocean on the sundrenched island of Lanzarote. To think my home was once a rat-infested railway embankment. What changed? What really changed? The simple answer is - *my mind*. I realized that if I wanted to attain my true potential, then I had to reclaim the wonderful formless kingdom of my mind. The mind is versatile; it can be used to create or destroy. I can be the ruler or the ruled. When I am the ruler – *'my mind doth serve for all.'* Thank you, Sir Edward, for reminding me of the wonderful gift of a free and versatile mind.

The main lessons I take from this poem are as follows:

- We all have one corner of freedom: our mind. Perhaps we do not always exercise control over external events, but we reign supreme over the inner kingdom of our mind. When the ocean of life becomes turbulent, detach from the external world, retreat inwardly, and bathe in the calm waters of pure consciousness.

- A silent mind is complete and whole, therefore it never lusts or craves. If you want to attain equanimity, then practice silence.

- Our mind is a vast expanse into which an infinite number of seeds of possibility are sown; sieve it frequently and separate the silt from the gold.

- Whatever we crave or lust after, comes to own us. Don't become enslaved, become enlightened: allow life to unfold from the guidance of your Indwelling Divinity.

- Intuition and Hunches are the silent language of the Gods.

A Psalm of Life

Tell me not, in mournful numbers,
Life is but an empty dream!-
For the soul is dead that slumbers,
And things are not what they seem.

Life is real! Life is earnest!
And the grave is not its goal;
Dust thou art, to dust returnest,
Was not spoken to the soul.

Not enjoyment, and not sorrow,
Is our destined end or way;
But to act, that each tomorrow
Find us further than today.

Art is long, and time is fleeting,
And our hearts, though stout and brave,
Still, like muffled drums, are beating
Funeral marches to the grave.

In the world's broad field of battle,
In the bivouac life,
Be not dumb, driven cattle!
Be a hero in the strife!

Trust no future, howe'er pleasant!
Let the dead past bury its dead
Act, - act in the living present!
Heart within, and God o'erhead!

Lives of great men all remind us,
We make our lives sublime,

And, departing, leave behind us,
Footprints on the sands of time.

Footprints, that perhaps another,
Sailing o'er life's solemn main,
A forlorn and shipwrecked brother,
Seeing, shall take heart again.

Let us then be up and doing,
With a heart for any fate;
Still achieving, still pursuing,
Learn to labour and to wait

American poet, Henry Wadsworth Longfellow (1807 – 1882)

This psalm begins by urging us not to become victims of conditioning. The material world is a mass illusion presented by our senses. What truly lies beyond us is an amorphous sea of infinite intelligence. We must stop viewing the world as an inert and benign object over which we have very little power, and know it as a malleable, living organism that responds to our intentions.

When Henry speaks of Life, he is referring to our Indwelling Divinity - the creative intelligence that breathes life into our cloak of matter. Our body is material and transient; it came from dust and to dust it will return - but this does not apply to our soul. You are much more than your body: you are an inexorable bundle of energy on an eternal journey. Death is simply a transitory stage in which the Soul migrates and begins another adventure.

The goal of life is not happiness or sadness: it is to better ourselves. The river of life bounces off the banks of both joy and sorrow and it is unnatural to cling to either of them. Rather, we should embrace our challenges and use them as fuel to propel us forward. Good, bad, happy, and sad all have a lesson to relay. Experience them in their fullness and extract the teachings each has to offer. And always remember that our goal is not to be better than others, it is to be better than we were yesterday.

This poem urges us to be brave. Step out of the confines of conformity and let the world know who we truly are. Refrain from being cloned and express our uniqueness. Each of us is a genius with a unique gift to bestow on the world; one that will help to evolve the collective consciousness of our planet.

Henry reminds us that *yesterday's history, tomorrow's a mystery, so live your life supremely concentrated in the present,* there you will find eternal peace. Most problems arise from regressing to the past or projecting into the future. Allow life to unfold from the wisdom of your Indwelling Divinity and stay firmly planted in the eternal continuum of the now.

Let each and every one us be a pathfinder and pave the way for those who follow. By improving ourselves, we leave footprints on the sands of time that can be used as a map for those behind who have lost their way. Break the bonds of uniformity and conformity and stamp our impression on the world: *become a hero in the strife!* Currently, *in the world's broad field of battle,* alcoholism is raging. At the time of writing, it is estimated that alcohol abuse in England and Wales kills 40,000 people and costs the economy billions of pounds *every year.* This is your chance to shine; opt out of the herd of dumb, driven cattle and become a shepherd. When you leave this life, let your resting place be not in a grave, but in the hearts of all you have touched.

This poem has been such an inspiration to me - thank you Henry Wadsworth Longfellow! Thank you for reminding me that life is a precious gift that should not be squandered. Thank you for reminding me that the material world is in a constant state of flux, but who I truly am is eternal. Thank you for reminding me that my thoughts and feelings mould pure consciousness into the events of my future. Thank you for reminding me that I have the faculty of choice. Thank you for breathing life into me!

Chapter 25

Affirmations

Master Your Mind – Don't Let Your Mind Master You

Every thought we think has the potential to leave an imprint on our unconscious. Self-talk and the continuous stream of messages we internalise from other people, translate to inner dialogue which leaves imprints on our unconscious. Anything that programmes our unconscious mind in such a way is an *affirmation*.

> **An affirmation is a statement which leaves an imprint on our unconscious mind.**

The accumulation of imprints on our unconscious mind forms the infrastructure of our belief system. Beliefs arise from internalising information that we consider to be true. It is important to realize, however, that truth is subjective and transient; what is true for one person may be false for another, and what you held to be true yesterday may be deemed as false today. As a consequence, our belief system needs to be frequently re-evaluated to see if it supports our current view of life. Outdated and maladaptive beliefs are often responsible for dysfunction.

The repetitious bombardment of negativity on our minds often leads to imprints that promote low self-esteem and pessimism. When internalised, negative messages fuse together and give birth to a sub-personality which I refer to as the *internal saboteur* - a confluence of thoughts and feelings intent on self sabotage. However, as speech was the medium through which we originally negatively programmed ourselves, we can reverse engineer the process by using self talk to re-programme our mind. In this way we become better aligned with our true nature.

An affirmation is a positive phrase that is spoken repeatedly until it becomes firmly embedded in our unconscious mind. This practice not only installs new ways of thinking, but it actually changes the structure and functioning of our brain. As the structure of our brain changes, life-enhancing chemicals are released in our body which give rise to feelings of well-being, so our whole disposition changes for the better.

Positive affirmations can be used to challenge and undermine negative beliefs supplanting them with life-enhancing ones. It is a form of 'brainwashing' in which you wash away the mental and emotional debris that constricts your life, leaving only positive energy which propels you forward.

Though affirmations rely on repetition to break through the conscious mind and become embedded in our unconscious, the process can be speeded up by utilizing our imagination as a powerful amplifier. For example, if we affirm: '*I am attracting my perfect romantic partner.*' Imagine her: see the colour of her eyes, imagine the aroma of her perfume, feel the texture of her skin. The more real this mental construct, the greater it will impact your unconscious.

Before we move on to specific affirmations, I want to make one last important point. It is crucial that your desire is affirmed using positive terminology e.g. 'I am healthy' rather than 'I don't want to be sick.' The unconscious mind does not process negatives, so affirming 'I don't want to be sick' translates to 'I want to be sick.'

I don't Want to be Sick

~ Affirmation One ~

I allow every situation to unfold from the wisdom and understanding of my Indwelling Divinity

This affirmation embodies the Taoist concept of Wu Wei. As you breathe without doing, and grow without trying, Wu Wei is the art of **effortless action.** The aim of W*u Wei* is to achieve a state of perfect equilibrium and obtain an infallible form of power. By surrendering the will of your ego to a power within that is capable of spontaneous right action in every instance, your path of least resistance will be revealed and you will attain peace, fulfilment and joy.

Next time you are faced with a testing situation, allow the Wise Witness Within to come forth and dominate your response. Stay centred in your higher essence, surrender your egoic-will to the will of your Higher Self, and remain open to direction.

~ Affirmation Two ~

Today I will use my imagination to create the future I desire

Imagine having the capacity to make a model of anything you wished for in life, and after it was completed it became real! Like Gepetto the toymaker you could make a Pinocchio that becomes *real!* Wouldn't it be wonderful to sculpt your own reality in such a way? Wouldn't it be a crime if you had such ability but never utilized it? - Well, guess what? You do have such a talent!

Your imagination - or ***image-in-action*** - as I call it, is the midwife that births ideas from the formless embryo of your mind into the physical domain. Remember, *'Imagination is the preview of life's forthcoming attractions.'* Whatever you can perceive in your mind, you can achieve in reality. The brain doesn't know the difference between actuality and imagination. If you repeatedly practice some new chords on a guitar, the part of your brain responsible for processing that function will grow and restructure itself to assimilate the new information. If you simply imagine practicing the new chords, your brain will expand and restructure itself in exactly the same way!

The imagination is the psychic workshop in which we mould our future. Investing time each day to sit down, relax and imagine what you want in life, is an excellent way of constructing your ideal life. The subconscious is a servomechanism which automatically steers towards its target. Paint your target vividly on the canvas of your imagination and your unconscious will move mountains to attain it.

A beautiful derivative of this affirmation comes from a very dear friend of mine:

**"I am filled with divine spirit
and its creative energy"**

Ella Quincy

Some things to remember when using *image-in-action or* imagination:

- Make your mental picture as vivid as possible and turn up the brightness and contrast.
- If the image is still, convert it into a movie.
- Add sounds to the scene and turn the volume up.
- Rather than being a passive observer and watching the scene, immerse yourself in it; experience it first-hand utilizing all your sense modalities. Bring it to life!
- Feel your emotions building as the scene becomes more pronounced. Remember, emotions are the power source of your desire.
- Imagine concentric circles of energy pulsating away from you, propagating your request out into the Universal network of intelligence.
- Let go and have complete faith that the Universe will respond.
- Be patient. Time may elapse before your desire manifests.
- Be flexible. The Universe is much wiser than any individual. Sometimes the results we receive are not precisely what we asked for, but they will most certainly be for our highest good.
- Spend at least twenty minutes per day imagining your perfect future. Make it fun and enjoy the process. Be very aware of the power of the practice, and rest in the certainty that your highest path will be revealed.

~ Affirmation Three ~

Today I Will Nurture the Child Within

This affirmation is aimed at breaking the ingrained self punishment mechanisms that sustain low self-esteem. Self condemnation often manifests subtlely in the form of corrosive inner- dialogue. Inadvertently, we find ourselves colluding with the internal saboteurs. The following points are designed to heighten your awareness of the subtle manifestations of the sobriety saboteurs.

- **Do you find yourself apologising frequently for things that are not your fault?**
  If so, you are condemning the inner child and reinforcing patterns of negativity that were thrust upon him in his formative years. You need to reverse this process. By regularly affirming your intention to nurture the child within, you will eradicate the automated patterns of response that feed low self-worth.

  Next time you find yourself apologising for nothing, or trying to please someone who treats you with contempt, let an alarm bell sound off in your mind. Visualize your inner child and tell him how much you love him. As you practice this technique, the neural pathways that promote low self worth will disband and make way for life-affirming ones.

- **Do you find it hard to say no? Are you constantly people pleasing?**
  If you find yourself unwilling (not unable) to say no, or constantly seeking people's approval, then you are still identifying with the negative messages of childhood conditioning. To counteract this negative programming, you

must consciously stop seeking people's approval and learn to say NO. Both these pursuits are symptoms of a person who has very little self-respect.

Each morning visualize your inner child and tell them how much you love, value, and appreciate them. Tell them that they deserve the very best in life and you are going to ensure that they get it. Assure them that they will be treated with the greatest courtesy and respect. Embrace them and feel their warmth. Look into their eyes and watch their radiant smile as they internalise the praise they deserve.

- **Do you constantly allow work to take priority over pleasure and play?**
  Your inner child needs to play. Play is the best antidote for stress, and stress is one of the biggest killers in our society today. In one of his poems, William Wordsworth wrote *'Let child be the father of man'*. This translates to *'let the Soul child lead the way.'*

Within us we have two inner children, the *adaptive (*or *conditioned) child,* and the *free (*or *Soul) child.* The free child is spontaneous, energetic, curious, loving and uninhibited – it's the part of us that thrives on play and pleasure. I prefer to call this the soul child, as it's very close to its spiritual roots.

Secondly, we have the *programmed* or *adaptive* child, which is a highly conditioned part of our psyche. This sub-personality develops as we learn to change our feelings and behaviour in response to the world around us. When operating from the level of the conditioned child we often revert to complying, sulking, aggression, aloofness and avoidance in reaction to external demands.

When the adaptive child cries out for attention, it is often a sign that we need to interject some fun back into our life. We can do this by immersing ourselves in the essence of our Soul Child and bathing in the energy of playfulness.

Life is not a game to win: it's a game to play.

~ Affirmation Four ~

Today I Will Stay on Purpose

The backbone of our sobriety and our evolution as human beings revolves around our ability to stay on purpose. The one common variable evident amongst the most successful, happy and contented people on our planet is purpose.

Each of us is endowed with a unique gift; a purpose designed to enhance the collective consciousness of our planet. It doesn't have to be a major project, it may be a simple activity carried out with much passion and love, but it will be your unique contribution to this world. People who bestow their unique gift onto the world radiate happiness. People who are on purpose are so happy that the need to escape never arises; therefore alcohol is redundant.

At times, however, people become consumed by activities that detract from their purpose and lose the way. When this occurs, discontentment and sterility set in very quickly. If left unattended they can spiral out of control and lead to a need to escape. So, by affirming to stay on purpose each morning, we take out an insurance policy to protect us from regressing to destructive ways.

~ Affirmation Five ~

Today I Will Honour the Higher Purpose of Every Person I Encounter

When we interact with others at the egoic level, we are apt to succumb to conflict, jealousy, and resentment – all of which are threats to our sobriety. The ego feeds off the misfortunes and perceived character defects of others. It is also highly competitive and possessive. These negative traits are based on our sense of separateness – an illusion created by the limitation of our senses. At our most primordial level we are all part of a unified whole.

To alleviate tension, jealousy, conflict and possessiveness and promote harmony, recognise the Indwelling Divinity in all you encounter. Mentally whisper to everyone you meet the Sanskrit word *Namaste*, which means *'the spirit in me honours the spirit in you.'*

Ultimately, **the spirit in me *is* the spirit in you – we are all one**. Whenever you greet a person in this way, you reinforce an unspoken bond. Any residual disdain you are carrying for them will dissolve as you connect with their true essence. Practice this technique regularly and you will be astounded at the results: your relationships will flourish.

Exercise: Connecting with the Indwelling Divinity of all you come in contact with.

Sit in a comfortable, quiet place; somewhere you will not be disturbed. Close your eyes and follow the rhythm and flow of your breath. Continue this process for about five minutes until you are in a trance-like state...... Now, in a heightened state of awareness, recognise that your body is in a constant state of flux. Although it gives the appearance of non-change, it is constantly changing. Just like a flowing stream whose water is replenished in every given moment, your body is renewing itself continuously..... Imagine, as you exhale, you breathe out parts of yourself that will shortly become parts of other people: your body and the bodies of all other species inhabiting our planet are part of a unified whole....

..... If any thoughts arise, observe them. Just like fish that leap and break the mirror surface of a still pond, watch your thoughts leap from your unconscious before dissolving back into the depths of your mind. Be aware of their transient nature....

......As any feelings arise, detach from the thoughts associated with them and concentrate solely on the sensation in your body. Notice how awareness alone disperses the feeling. Watch the feeling dissipate. Observe it return to the great void from where it came; the nothingness that contains everything. Again, be aware of its transience...Your body, your thoughts and your emotions are all transient – all impermanent.....

.....Now, start to become aware of that part of you that is experiencing your thoughts, emotions and sensations; that part of you that is listening to the sounds around you. Notice there is a part of you that is simply observing everything. Become aware of this indwelling presence.... Turn your attention inwardly and feel this powerful presence. Feel its essence penetrating every part of your being. Allow your awareness to dissolve into this pure beingness; this pure presence. Bathe in its light; the light of pure consciousness. Feel it illume every cell, bone and tissue of your body... in this moment, know you are a child of the Universe...

..... Now imagine you are coming into contact with other people... turn up the brightness and contrast in your mind so that the images are vivid... Notice the same luminosity that inspires your being also illumes these people... the quintessential nature of your being is also the very essence of every other living entity you come in contact with... God is the single actor playing innumerable roles. Every individual is God, the Self of the world. Every life is a role in which the mind of God is absorbed. By the act of self-abandonment God has become all beings.....

... From this point forth you will see the Godly nature in everyone you encounter; a luminescence that transcends their character defects and short-comings... Silently, you will whisper to them, Namaste, *the spirit in me honours the spirit in you;* for the same divine principle which animates you also animates them... every other living entity is your Universal brother or sister: know this implicitly... In actuality, there is no *other*; there is only divinity....

...In your own time call your awareness back behind the windows of your eyes so that you are centred once again within your body. Feel the gently pull of gravity on your shoulders. Feel your feet firmly against the floor and ground yourself.... And, when you are ready, open your eyes and familiarise yourself with your surroundings once again.

~ Affirmation Six ~

Silence Sometimes Has the Loudest Voice: Today I Will Spend Some Time in Silence

Constant chattering and compulsive talking often gives rise to an overact mind; a mind that has difficulty being at rest. Do you lie awake at night unable to switch your thoughts off?

Between each of the sixty thousand thoughts we experience on a daily basis, there is a window of silence – a domain of pure knowledge and inspiration. It is here that the creative force of the Universe operates. Inspirational ideas come leaping out of the still waters of your mind, much like fish breaking the mirror surface of a pond. To bathe in this silent sanctuary is to experience utter bliss.

> ## "Be still –
> ## stillness reveals the secrets of eternity"
> Lao Tzu

In the words of entrepreneur and philosopher, William Penn, '*True silence is the rest of the mind; it is to the spirit what sleep is to the body, nourishment and refreshment.*' Make time for silence and coalesce with the God within.

~ Affirmation Seven ~

I Am Creating a New Network of Supportive Relationships on a Daily Basis

When embarking on a life of sobriety and radical transformation, it is necessary to let go of the friends you no longer resonate with; friends who keep you anchored to your old way of life. We need to surround ourselves with supportive people, genuine friends who have our best interest at heart. Affirming to create such a network sends out an impulse of intent that will draw these people to you.

~ Affirmation Eight ~

Today I Will Embrace the Field of Infinite Possibilities

This affirmation is about breaking your agreement with reality and changing your ideas of what is possible. Everything is possible – it's just your beliefs that convince you otherwise! Michelangelo once said "The greater danger for most of us lies not in setting our aim too high and falling short; but in setting our aim too low, and achieving our mark."

Your Indwelling Divinity is the same creative intelligence that gave rise to everything in existence, including all the geniuses of the world. With that intelligence intrinsic to your nature, how could anything be outside your grasp? When we embrace our true essence impossibilities vanish and give rise to unlimited potential, immeasurable growth, and boundless opportunities.

Guidelines for Constructing Affirmations

1. **An affirmation should be concise**; for example *"I am worthy of love."*

2. **Use present tense** e.g. *I am in good health.* Past and future are psychological concepts that never arrive: we only ever have the NOW. An affirmation stated in future tense is always going to be something which *will* happen, rather than something that *has* happened. Consequently, it will always remain just outside of your grasp.

3. **Avoid negative terminology**. Instead of saying *"I am no longer nervous"* say *"I am confident."* Your unconscious mind does not process negatives; therefore *"I am not ill"* translates to *"I am ill."*

4. **Start with a direct declaration of positive change** e.g. *"My earnings have increased"* If you find it difficult *believing* this statement, dilute it slightly by stating *"I am open to receiving more money."*

5. **Belief in your affirmation and the willingness to change are of the utmost importance**. Although one hundred percent belief is desirable, however, it is not necessary. The willingness to orient your mind in the direction of your desire is all that is needed initially.

Part Nine
The Twelve Step Philosophy

Chapter 26

The Alcoholic to Alchemist
Twelve Step Philosophy for Optimal Living

Phase One: Acceptance and Awareness

Step 1:
**Admit having developed a destructive alcohol habit
as a consequence of attempting to
escape the curriculum of life.**

Abandoning our defence systems and moving away from the belligerent denial that has kept us imprisoned is liberating. We no longer have to scheme to get the money to feed the habit. We no longer have to lie and deceive to defend the habit. We no longer have to expend vital energy on suppressing the truth: it is out in the open – what a relief!

Prior to admitting to having an alcohol habit, our minds were constantly preoccupied with *living a lie*. Every day was Groundhog Day; the cyclic repetition of life denying behaviour: lies, deceit, scheming, manipulation and blame – all designed to feed a habit that was destroying us! Although we constantly reassured ourselves that things would get better, they never did. The spiral was unidirectional: downward.

> ## 'Insanity is doing the same thing over and over again and expecting different results'
> Albert Einstein

On accepting step one, we are no longer prepared to delude ourselves. We no longer subscribe to the belief that alcohol is a magical panacea for the dissolution of all problems. We recognise it for what it is: the fuel that ignites mental turbulence and leads to persecution.

Alcohol kills our conscience and renders our memory inactive. Consequently, we lose control of our faculties and become unpredictable menaces. Our normal standards, morals, principles and ethics disappear as Dr Jekyll turns into Mr Hyde, and off we go on a trail of destruction. On emerging from the drunken escapade we are aghast to be told of our antics during black-out. Highly embarrassed and often guilt ridden, we reach for the bottle to obliterate the memory and the whole destructive cycle starts again.

What a shambles! What an utter waste of a life! And people exclaim that they can't give it up! By quitting alcohol the only thing you're giving up is: ***destruction, anguish, despair, embarrassment, guilt, and remorse: life-denying behaviour.***

Accepting step one reveals the willingness to change and a longing to live. Committed to transforming the mental and emotional debris that has warped our minds for years into psychological and spiritual nourishment from which we will grow and flourish, we awaken the Archetypal Alchemist.

By taking this step we acknowledge two fundamental truths:

- Our primary problem is a refusal or inability to embrace the challenges of life.
- A destructive habit has been nurtured as a consequence of repeatedly using alcohol as an escape vehicle.

Here, we acknowledge that abstaining from alcohol alone will not alleviate the problem; *alcohol is a symptom, not the cause.* Just as weeds grow back if we don't remove the roots, so our destructive alcohol habit will return if we don't address the underlying issues that provoke escape. Relapse is a consequence of unresolved issues surfacing and disturbing our equilibrium. The subsequent mental anguish heightens to such an extent that we seek escape and like lemmings throw ourselves back into the abreactive abyss.

Alcohol is an escape vehicle – if we remove the need to escape, the vehicle becomes obsolete

---

Before embarking on this journey we didn't understand the true nature of the habit that was destroying us – but now that has changed. Step one sees our power return. No longer do we blame others for our dilemma; no longer do we subscribe to the belief that we have contracted some unfathomable disease or personality disorder: we place the locus of control firmly within ourselves. With complete abandon, we accept that addiction is not something that has been unwittingly thrust upon us: it is a HABIT. By definition, a habit is something that *we* have taught ourselves to do; taught ourselves to do so expertly, in fact, that it is now second nature. Even our brain has re-wired itself in support. But once we intervene and consciously break the destructive patterns that underlie our alcoholism, the supporting neural networks disband and make way for new, life-enhancing ones. By consciously breaking the chain of automatic responses that disable us, and replacing them with strategies that enable us, we rewire the brain in a way that gives rise to a radical new way of being.

Break the chain,
rewire the brain

Step one declares us powerful beings who became temporarily detached from our power source. The rest of the steps are designed to reconnect us to our power source and bring about the radical shift in consciousness needed to embrace our true potential.

Step 2:
Having crossed the Abreactive Threshold, we need to abandon the idea that alcohol provided a means of escape and supplant it with the following belief:

The most effective way to escape our problems
is to solve them

Step one put the problem into perspective, highlighting the fact that we'd *taught* ourselves to drink with such expertise that we had *habituated* the process. The objective of this exercise had been to escape our problems.

In the formative stages of alcoholism, our mind tricked us into believing that alcohol was the great enabler: calming our fears, instilling us with confidence, and inducing feelings of ecstasy and euphoria. With hindsight, however, we can see that this was just a seductive ploy which hooked us and reeled us in. Alcohol doesn't improve or alleviate our problems; it simply disables our memory and renders our conscience inactive, giving rise to a whole new batch of problems.

Alcohol once acted as a suppressant - a damn holding back a reservoir of unresolved issues - which presented the illusion that our problems had vanished. As our consumption escalated, however, the pressure built to such an extent that this damn cracked and our unresolved issues came bursting from the unconscious to the conscious with the might of a tsunami.

Once our unresolved issues overwhelm the suppressant effects of alcohol and force their way into our conscious mind, alcohol ceases to offer us even temporary relief. Subsequently, all drinking bouts lead to abnormal reactions that manifest in a multitude of menacing guises: severe mood swings, paranoia, neuroses, psychoses, guilt, remorse, nausea, violence, agitation, delusions of grandeur, depression, and so on.

Step two warrants an acceptance of having crossed the Abreactive Threshold. Once the threshold has been crossed, you and alcohol become incompatible for life. *To accept this with complete abandon is the key to your freedom.*

> # Step 3:
> ## Come to accept that the locus of the problem is a mind infected with fear, futility, guilt and pain – the answer to which is a profound shift in consciousness.

Now we have accepted that our alcohol habit does not provide an escape route from the vicissitudes of life, we need to employ a different strategy to deal with our problems. Step three is designed to bring our awareness to the underlying psychological mechanisms which distort our view of reality and give rise to the Sobriety Saboteurs.

Before embarking on this journey, we tried to eradicate alcoholism by removing the symptom, but our efforts were to no avail: *removing alcohol alone is futile.* Our answer lies in eradicating the **cause** not the **effect** - *the* **catalyst** not the **symptom.** To sustain sobriety and embrace our true potential, we must identify the psychological mechanisms that give rise to our destructive drinking.

By identifying and processing the underlying patterns which give rise to the ***stinking thinking*** that fuels ***destructive drinking***, we release the need to escape. Once we eradicate the need to escape, alcohol becomes redundant.

> ## Stinking thinking gives rise to destructive drinking
> ## Change your thinking - end your drinking

The greatest obstacle to the successful implementation of step three is lack of awareness. We need to accentuate our awareness to such an extent that we can discern that which is an actual problem and that which is a negative construction of the mind. Majority of our *perceived* problems exist in our minds only. They may masquerade as some person, place, or thing in the external world, but, in actuality, this is often an elaborate decoy created by our mental filtering systems: the real problem lies within us. A recent survey conducted with my clients found that a staggering ninety-two percent of the problems attributed to abusive drinking were actually phantoms - distorted interpretations of an adversely conditioned mind. These findings reveal unequivocally that our mind is the primary problem. The amnestic effects of alcohol become so alluring because they present the illusion that we are *getting out of our minds* and escaping our problems, but this is simply a delusion born of desperation.

People attempt to *get out of their minds* since that is where most of their problems exist. Step three is about getting *into your mind*, dissolving the catalysts that give rise to abusive drinking, and tapping into the well-spring of inspiration that is buried beneath them.

Don't Blame, Reframe

We exert so much energy on misguidedly trying to solve our problems by attempting to manipulate and control other people and external situations, that we become depleted, frustrated and disillusioned. When others don't conform to our whims and demands we revert to blame and resentment. But blame is simply an argument against growth; it does nothing other than disable us. By placing the locus of control within ourselves, step three is empowering. We may not always exercise control over external events, but we reign supreme over the inner kingdom of our mind. We have the power to change anything we choose in our internal dominion, and since the external world is a direct reflection of our state of mind, self-mastery holds the key to a life beyond our wildest dreams.

As within, so without

Mastering the Mirages of Our Mind

'There is not one big cosmic meaning for all, there is only the meaning we each give to our life, an individual meaning, an individual plot, like an individual novel, a book for each person.'

Anias Nin

All problems transpire from the meaning we assign to external events. Rather than deceiving ourselves into believing that other people, places and things are the cause of our problems, we need to examine the internal mechanisms which distort our view of reality. Firstly, we must recognise that meaning is not a product of the external world – it doesn't exist *out there*: it exists only within us.

All problems transpire from the meaning we assign to life's events. As meaning is subjective - it does not exist in the external world; it exists only within us – then common sense tells us that all our problems must reside within also. Anything that is intrinsic is under our sole jurisdiction; therefore, we have the power to change it.

Each of us has a unique perspective on life. For one person an event may be considered uncomfortable, whilst for another the very same event may be deemed pleasurable. How is this possible?

As light changes appearance when passed through a coloured filter, external events are coloured when passed through the filter of our memory. Consequently, internal representations and external events are often highly incongruent. Our memory doesn't simply duplicate what's *out there* and store it away; it modifies what's *out there* with previous memories and stores a distortion. Let's take a simple example:

> *John and his girlfriend, Jenny, ambled through the park. Jenny veered off to a nearby stream. When John looked around, she was taking delight in playing with a Labrador which was passing by with its owner. John broke out into cold sweats, his heart started to pound rapidly, and he walked briskly in the opposite direction. John was petrified of dogs ever since being badly bitten when he was six years old.*

This example shows that external reality, the dog, was not the problem. It became a problem only when John added his negative memories to the experience. The same event had contrasting meanings for John and Jenny. For Jenny it was pleasurable; for John it was traumatic. This discrepancy proves that problems have a tendency to arise from the internal disposition of a person, rather than being a direct result of external events. John was not afraid of what was *out there*; he was afraid of what was *in here* (within him). Removing the dog wouldn't have alleviated the problem, processing the original trauma held the answer.

The totality of our life's experiences are internalised to form a mental filter through which all subsequent experience is processed. This is often referred to as our *frame of reference*. By virtue of processing the world through our frame of reference, our perception of life often becomes twisted and warped. Old wounds reopen and give rise to emotionally charged responses which breed disharmony. Subsequently, corrosive inner-dialogue unleashes the Sobriety Saboteurs and we misguidedly seek sanctuary in alcohol.

Negative inner dialogue transpires from a mind-set that is preoccupied with the problem, instead of focusing on the solution that is always available

---

Example: Robert - Abandonment

Robert lived a relatively happy life until he was eight years old. During this period his parents started to argue and fight frequently. One day he returned home from school to find his mother had left; he has never seen her again to this day.

Today, Robert's relationship with his wife, Angela, is fraught with problems. He tends to be smothering and reluctant to let her out of his sight. Two weeks ago, she was late home from work due to stock-taking. When she failed to show at the normal time, Robert felt an inferno of fury building up inside and started to pace up and down the hallway. The corrosive inner-dialogue then kicked-in: 'she's having an affair', 'she doesn't care about me.' When Angela finally came through the door, she was met with a barrage of abuse. Robert venomously accused her of abandoning him. Angela was astonished and frightened by the intensity of his reaction.

The underlying process in this example is transference. Robert unconsciously experienced his wife as the mother who'd abandoned him many years ago. He was not disturbed by the current event; he was disturbed by his ***interpretation*** of it. John was traumatized by the meaning he assigned to the event, which was grossly distorted by negative memories. When viewing this innocuous incident through his *frame of reference*, it became a major problem: one that eventually threatened his marriage.

Filtering systems often lead to irrational responses such as these and put severe strain on our cherished relationships. A loved-one or friend inadvertently makes a comment or performs an action that taps into our negative memory bank and we strike out like a viper, leaving the unassuming person (and often ourselves) perplexed and upset. This is a prime example of acting unconsciously: being propelled by psychological mechanisms which lay beyond the conscious threshold. The underlying mechanism in these cases is also the biggest cause of relapse - *resentment*. Many people return to drink because of some indignation felt as a result of some grievance or other, but the object of their grievance is very often an innocent bystander who inadvertently opens up an old wound (as was the case with John's wife above).

The word resentment means to ***re-feel***. When we re-feel old wounds, we hurt and are temporarily knocked off balance. Our pain generally flares up in reaction to something someone says or does, and we erroneously perceive them as the *cause* of our problem. But the true cause of our pain lies buried deep within our psyche; the words or actions of these people are merely triggers. By making other people scapegoats, we remain ignorant and static.

There is another major psychological mechanism at work here too: *projection*. Projection is the unconscious process whereby we project the contents of our psyche onto other people or events and distort them out of all proportion. The process is similar to watching a scary movie and becoming frightened by it. In actuality, what stands before us is a rather harmless blank screen. Fear arises only when scary images are projected onto it. Similarly, many innocuous life situations are transformed into traumas or dramas as we unassumingly superimpose our negative memories over them. As with resentment, this mechanism sees us inadvertently placing the responsibility for our problems with other people. By projecting the shadow elements of our psyche – our character defects, short-comings and negative memories - onto others, the world is perceived as a hostile place. This delusion gives rise to victim mentality as we believe everyone is conspiring to upset or harm us. As a consequence, we become consumed with paranoia and *'poor me, poor me,'* soon turns to *'pour me another.'*

Projection and resentment are prone to present the illusion that others are responsible for the way we feel. How often do you hear yourself saying *'She made me feel like this,'* or *'he made me feel that way?'* But, in reality, no one can take a feeling and put it inside of us, only we can do that. Eric Berne, founder of Transactional Analysis, put it this way:

> **'No-one can make us feel any way.**
> **The way we feel is determined by virtue of**
> **how we process the world.'**

This statement reinforces the fact that feelings are generated by the meaning we assign to external events. As our self-awareness heightens, most problems are exposed as mirages of the mind evoked by distorted interpretations of external events. These psychological apparitions are commonly responsible for the manifestation of the Sobriety Saboteurs. **F**abricated **E**xperience and

350

Artificial **R**easoning – **F.E.A.R** -underlies most instances of guilt, futility and pain.

Fear is a Phantom

caused by

Fabricated **E**xperience & **A**rtificial **R**easoning

Over ninety percent of our perceived problems occur in the dominion of the mind only. The mind is prone to fabricate experience and support it with artificial reasoning. Take the example of Robert above. His fear of losing his wife had materialized as a result of projecting memories of his relationship with his mother onto his current relationship. Consequently, his perception had become severely distorted. The real-life event and his internal representation of it were in stark contrast. Robert's wife had simply been working late, but his mind had **F**abricated the **E**xperience of abandonment and supported it with the **A**rtificial **R**easoning that it had happened before, so it would inevitably happen again.

Most manifestations of the Sobriety Saboteurs are based on this illusory mechanism. As *fear makes the wolf appear bigger,* so our filtering systems create problems out of nothing. Ultimately, what this suggests is that our destructive drinking transpires as a result of running away from something that doesn't exist – a fabrication of the mind! Furthermore, as these imaginary grievances give rise to the way we feel, and most people who abuse alcohol do so in order to *feel better,* then it is imperative that we wake up and resume control of our mind. Remember, feelings arise from the chemical messengers that our dispersed throughout our body and change our cellular structure, and these chemical messengers are derived from our thoughts. Consequently, if our thoughts are constantly corrupted by negative memories, the subsequent feelings are going to be distressful and warrant escape. Step three urges us to intervene and end this facade.

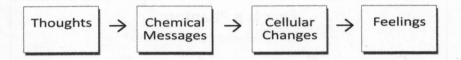

Awareness is the key that will set us free.

Each time you experience a symptomatic manifestation of these mind mirages: mood swings, over-sensitivity, jealousy, neediness, the need to control and so on - **STOP!** Put the following sequence into operation.

Stall: Refrain from reacting

Think: Become aware of the underlying mechanisms that promote conflict: projection, transference, re-sentment

Observe: Allow any bodily sensations to arise; don't respond, don't judge, simply observe. Centre yourself in your higher awareness and watch as the perceived problem magically dissipates.

Proceed: Carry on with your day

Every time you intervene in this way, you interrupt the brain processes that propel you to *re-enact* old destructive patterns. Consequently, the supporting neural networks disband and you gradually resume conscious control of your life. The simple but powerful message of step three is:

Don't blame - *Reframe*

Exercises:

The following exercises are designed to heighten your awareness and encourage you to develop different views of your problems. By taking a different perspective and placing the locus of control within yourself, rather than in some other person, place or thing, you pave the way to the next phase the journey: invoking the shift.

- Meditate on the Owl archetype and absorb its attributes. Owl has 360 degree vision and can see in the dark, making him an expert in surveillance. He is highly alert and quick at identifying potential threats. He sees that which others cannot, which is the true essence of wisdom.

  Develop Owl's skills and watch your life transform. Use Owl energy to go deep into the dark recesses of your unconscious and identify the negative patterns which distort your view of reality. Remain forever vigilante and be prepared to break the chain of conditioned responses that promote disharmony in your life.

- Meditate on the Hanged Man archetype. Although hanging in a compromising position, he oozes serenity. Hanging from a tree, upside-down, he is suspending all action whilst taking a different perspective of the challenges that lay ahead of him. By looking at the world from a different angle, he identifies new options.

  When you are faced with a challenge, temporarily suspend any action while considering alternative explanations. Take different perspectives. Challenge the beliefs which underpin your negative interpretation and review your choices. Look through another frame of reference and describe what you see. In practicing this procedure you will find that very often the meaning you originally derived is reversed, and:

- A problem becomes a challenge
- A challenge becomes an opportunity
- A weakness becomes a strength
- An impossibility becomes a probability
- Fear becomes an opportunity to display courage
- Unkindness becomes a lack of understanding
- A deficit becomes your greatest asset.

When you encounter an authentic problem - one that is not a distorted invention of the mind - meditate on the element of water and apply it to your situation. Allow your mind to become fluid-like and flow around the obstacles you encounter. Like water, allow your mind to adapt to whatever route proves possible. As water develops power by merging with other rivers, allow your mind to merge with other positive influences. With persistence, water can cut its way through the largest of obstacles; an extremely focused mind can do the same. As a flowing river never stagnates, futility never arises when we flow with the infinite possibilities of the Universe. Ultimately, the intention of water is to return to its source: the ocean. You, too, are bound to return to your source and assume your rightful heritage as co-creator of the Universe.

> **Whereas an alcoholic sees**
> **A problem,**
> *The Alchemist sees*
> *An opportunity to evolve*

Summary of Phase One
(Steps One, Two and Three)

Phase one embodies the themes of *Acceptance* and *Awareness*.

- **Step one** asserts that the catalyst of alcoholism is an inability or refusal to meet the curriculum of life. On encountering a problem, we revert to the amnestic effects of alcohol to provide escape.

- **Step two** reminded us that alcohol did not provide an escape route; it simply masked our problems in the short-term. Continually banishing our problems to the realms of the unconscious has grave consequences. Unresolved issues amass in the unconscious until they gather enough force to break down the screen of alcohol that masks them from our conscious awareness. When this critical event occurs we are overwhelmed by a backlog of problems which come flooding from the unconscious to the conscious to disorient us. Again, we reach for the bottle, but this time it is to no avail. Having crossed the Abreactive Threshold, alcohol is ineffective. Adding alcohol to the maelstrom of mental mayhem that now pervades our conscious mind is akin to throwing petrol on a fire. Each time we drink, our problems flare-up and we become dysfunctional, unpredictable entities.

- **Step three** provides education in the psychology behind our problems. In essence, most of our problems arise from distressing circumstances in the past. Negative memories are projected onto current circumstances and they severely impede our perception of life. Believing the whole world is against us, we succumb to victim mentality; but blaming others only breeds stasis. Step three urges us to refrain from blame and take sole responsibility of our lives. It encourages us to be flexible and consider alternative explanations for any given problem. Alchemists transform obstacles into fuel to propel them forward. Whenever we spontaneously erupt or feel a constant irritation gnawing away at us, we need to recognise it as an opportunity to heighten our self-awareness and learn something about ourselves. See it as an opportunity to break free of rigid conditioning. Instead of misguidedly blaming the nearest person, place the locus of control back within yourself and recognise these people as much-needed triggers. Given that they have disturbed our unconscious mind in a way that has caused it to present an unconscious issue for resolution, mentally thank them. They have done us a favour. Remember, we cannot disarm an adversary we cannot see; only when our issues become conscious can we process and release them.

- On mastering the skills and developing the attributes outlined above, you will have laid a firm foundation on which to build the rest of your life. The next phase, *Invoking the Shift*, will expand the teachings of phase one and introduce a transpersonal aspect which will enable you to realize your true potential and grasp the infinite possibilities that life has to offer.

Phase Two: Invoking the Shift
(Steps Four-to-Nine)

Phase two embodies the teachings of the parable of the prodigal son. The symbolism of this tale hides a deep philosophical meaning that has been passed down from generation to generation. Appearing in many cultures, the story portrays the Soul's search to return to its original Source.

And he said, "There was a man who had two sons. And the younger of them said to his father, 'Father, give me the share of property that is coming to me.' And he divided his property between them. Not many days later, the younger son gathered all he had and took a journey into a far country, and there he squandered his property in reckless living. And when he had spent everything, a severe famine arose in that country, and he began to be in need. So he went and hired himself out to one of the citizens of that country, who sent him into his fields to feed pigs. And he was longing to be fed with the pods that the pigs ate, and no one gave him anything.

But when he came to himself, he said, 'How many of my father's hired servants have more than enough bread, but I perish here with hunger! I will arise and go to my father, and I will say to him, "Father, I have sinned against heaven and before you. I am no longer worthy to be called your son. Treat me as one of your hired servants."' And he arose and came to his father. But while he was still a long way off, his father saw him and felt compassion, and ran and embraced him and kissed him. And the son said to him, 'Father, I have sinned against heaven and before you. I am no longer worthy to be called your son.' But the father said to his servants, 'Bring quickly the best robe, and put it on him, and put a ring on his hand, and shoes on his feet. And bring the fattened calf and kill it, and let us eat and celebrate. For this my son was dead, and is alive again; he was lost, and is found.' And they began to celebrate.'   **(Luke 15: 11 – 32)**

This story informs us that our true home is a state of being in which we experience unconditional love, bliss, ecstasy, wholeness, abundance and spiritual nourishment. Our true home has no physical location; it is a state of consciousness in which we are all one.

At our most primordial level, we are all part of a sacred singularity - sometimes called *God* or the *Universe*. Rather than being pious, someone who is truly *holy* has their being grounded in the *whole* or the Source. Only in this undivided state can true richness be found.

Initially, unity-consciousness is our natural state. Like the prodigal son, when we're connected to source, we inherit all the riches of heaven (within). Then we succumb to the hypnosis of social conditioning and misguidedly believe that true wealth is found only in other people, places and the acquisition of things. Our pursuit of these things, however, results in disillusionment: despair, jealousy, greed, insecurity, and conflict. Our initial unified state of mind has been traded for poverty-consciousness. Bereft of meaning and emotionally bankrupt, we seek refuge and a longing to return to our true home transpires. This desire is accomplished through meditation – *being*, not *doing*. In silence, the voice of our Indwelling Divinity is heard with great clarity.

As well as relaying the importance of returning to Source (home) for spiritual nourishment, the other profound message of this parable is **forgiveness.** Although we are apt to feel self-disdain, unworthiness and disgrace for the transgressions we carried out whilst inebriated, the Universe (Father) lovingly awaits our return. The Universe understands that we are not '*bad*' people; we were simply blind and unaware of our errors whilst drunk. Hence, another phrase from the bible becomes apt:

> ## 'Father forgive them
> ## For they know not what they do.'

Rising above our conditioning and embracing our rightful heritage is the essence of phase two. Being part of the Sacred Singularity we are all creators, capable of creating the reality we truly desire. However, to do so we have to enter an altered state of consciousness in which we transcend the hypnosis of social conditioning and reconnect with the power of our Source. Meditation, self-love, and forgiveness, hold the keys. Everything we long for can be found in our true home: ***phase two is your homecoming.***

Step 4:
Aspire to invoke a major shift in consciousness by allowing life to unfold from the wisdom of your Indwelling Divinity.

You are a distinct portion of the essence of God in yourself.
Why, then, are you ignorant of your noble birth?
Why do you not consider whence you came?
Why do you not remember when you are eating, who you are who eat; and whom you feed; do you not know that it is the divine you feed?
The divine you exercise?
You carry a God about with you.

Epictetus

There's a facet of your being which knows the right response to every conceivable situation. Your Indwelling Divinity is a part of the phenomenal intelligence responsible for all creation:

omnipotent, omniscient, and omnipresent. So, *why, then, are we ignorant of our noble birth?* Why do we discard the God within, in favour of a self-seeking, subordinate, pseudo-self?

The simple answer is that life has duped us into identifying with an imposter: our ego. At birth we enrolled into drama school and learned to play the role of Mister or Missus Mortal, a reactive being, programmed to conform to the strict limitations of society. We immersed ourselves in the roll with such fervour that we forgot our true identity.

> **Man has falsely identified himself with the pseudo-soul or ego.**
> **When he transferred his sense of identity to his true being, the immortal Soul, he discovered that all pain is unreal.**
> **He no longer can even imagine the state of suffering.**
> Paramahansa Yogananda

Step four urges us to reacquaint ourselves with the immortal aspect of our being. By allowing life to unfold from our Indwelling Divinity we can be absolutely certain of meeting every situation with confidence, understanding, forbearance and wisdom. This step encourages us to allow our Indwelling Divinity to become our closest advocate, guide and teacher.

**Once you reunify with the immortal essence
that dwells within,
you will optimize your potential
in every area of your life**

Daily Declaration:

At the beginning of every day, make the following declaration:

> **Today, I allow every situation to unfold from the wisdom of my Indwelling Divinity. In doing so, I rest assured that I will meet every situation in a way that enhances my life and the lives of all those I encounter.**

Let this statement be emblazoned in the forefront of your mind throughout the day. This step is about trading conditioned responses for optimal living and this declaration reinforces your intent to succeed. Whenever you encounter a challenging situation, refrain from reverting to conditioned responses and striking out; instead, stay centred in your higher awareness and mentally affirm the following declaration:

'I allow this situation to unfold from the wisdom of my Indwelling Divinity.'

Now reconsider the testing situation. Recall step three and evoke the Hanged Man archetype. Look at the situation from different perspectives and identify your options. In silence, await intuitive direction from your Indwelling Divinity and act accordingly.

> **Intuition is the direction of the Soul**

Continually practicing this process will initiate a shift in consciousness that will propel you into a higher dimension of existence: your life will change beyond recognition. Paradoxically, by relinquishing control to your Indwelling Divinity, you become master of your own destiny.

***

Step 5:
Live Life Consciously

***

This step is comprised of three parts: *awakening, discerning, choosing.*

Part A: Awakening

> *When one realises*
> *one is asleep,*
> *at that moment*
> *one is already half-awake.*
>
> P. D. Ouspensky (1878-1947)

There are two ways to live: consciously and unconsciously – awake or asleep. When we live unconsciously we are entranced by conditioning; oblivious to the reasons why our lives aren't working. We repeat the same routines day-in, day-out; make the same mistakes over and over again; and **re-act** to the same situations time and time again - but we never ask questions. *Why is life this way? What am I doing wrong? What can I change to progress?* We never consciously challenge our actions. We carry on oblivious, regardless of the consequences.

People imprisoned in this mind-set adhere to beliefs that breed stasis: *'life is already mapped out.'* - *'That's just the way it is.'* What a defeatist attitude! Wake up! Life is not preordained: *it's 'just the way it is'* because you haven't changed anything in years! Such people are *effects*, not *causes*. They are constantly buffeted about by the whims of other people. They are REACTORS, not CREATORS. Yet to change a REACTOR into a CREATOR we just have to put 'C' first. If we 'SEE' first the unconscious patterns which drive our repetitive behaviour before acting on them, we resume conscious control of our lives.

Behaviours indicative of reactor mode are: *sulking, blaming, seeking approval, condemning, insulting, bad-mouthing, adopting victim mentality, seeking vengeance, calculating your responses to suit the company you're in, agreeing with the majority just to fit in, unhealthy competitiveness, bullying, and jealousy.* Every time you revert to one of these *effects*, let an alarm sound off in your mind and bring your attention to the fact that you're giving your power away.

To live consciously we must heighten our awareness and catch ourselves in the process of *re-acting*. Every time we interrupt a conditioned response, we break a shackle that binds us and move one step closer to our true potential.

Heightening our awareness can be aided by reverting to step three and becoming aware of the covert operations of our filtering systems. Instead of responding robotically and slipping back into somnambulism, STOP - Stall, Think, Observe and Proceed. Don't shrink from your feelings, allow them to expand. Observe the sensations in your body and allow them to peak. Remember the wisdom of the Tao Te Ching:

> **Should you want to contain something, you must deliberately let it expand.**
> **Should you want to weaken something, you must deliberately let it grow strong.**

In not resisting negative feelings, you weaken and disperse them. In fighting them, you strengthen them. When your feelings have dissolved, revert to step four and ask your Indwelling Divinity for the correct response to the situation. Remember, *every time you interrupt a negative pattern of behaviour, you dissolve the neural networks which support it.* Consequently, you initiate the following four stages of transformation.

The Four stages of Competence:

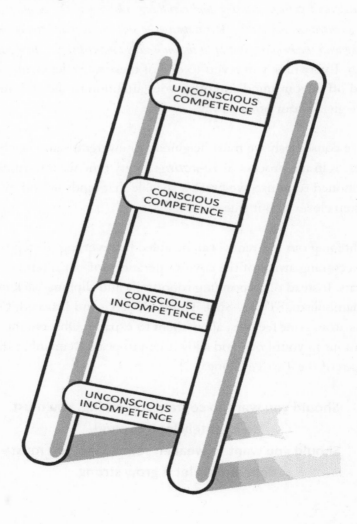

Unconscious incompetence.

When operating at the level of unconscious incompetence, we are totally unaware of our short-comings. We operate in a somnambulistic state: sleep-walking through life, totally oblivious to the underlying mechanisms that wreak havoc in our lives.

Conscious Incompetence

On reaching stage two our awareness has heightened. We've identified the underlying reasons as to why our lives aren't working, but we still haven't developed new strategies to implement the needed change, i.e. we are still incompetent.

Conscious Competence

At stage three, we have not only identified the reasons why we act in preordained ways, we have devised and implemented new strategies to change our behaviour. At present, however, we have to exert conscious effort in executing the new behaviour - it does not come easy. It requires a lot of energy and conscious thought.

Unconscious Incompetence

On reaching the final stage, we have practiced the new strategies to such an extent that they are now second-nature. Each time we are faced with the old trigger, our new way of responding kicks in without any conscious deliberation. When this occurs we have transformed a negative habit into an extremely positive one.

The four stages of competence can be used to measure the degree of progress in any troublesome area of your life. Let's look at an example:

Example :

Every time John faced a problem he drank to destruction. This bizarre behaviour continued for many years and often led to him being locked up. He was oblivious to the reasons why he succumbed to his destructive tendencies. **[unconscious incompetence]**.

After reviewing the situation with a counsellor, he identified that the reason for his abusive drinking was to obliterate his problems. Now he'd developed awareness of the catalyst, but his behaviour had not changed. He still drank to destruction whenever confronted with a problem **[conscious incompetence]**.

Through the Alcoholic to Alchemist Twelve Step Philosophy for Optimal Living, he finally accepted that alcohol did not provide an escape route from his problems. As a consequence, he refrained from drinking. Initially, it wasn't easy; he had to exert conscious effort in implementing his new strategy **[conscious competence]**.

Persistence prevailed bringing gradual improvement. After John repeatedly refused to drink his problems away and set about solving them, his desire to drink diminished. Subsequently, abstinence became second nature. On encountering a problem, rather than seeing it as an obstacle, he saw it as an opportunity to evolve. After examining a problem from different points of view, considering his options, and consulting his Indwelling Divinity, he took great delight in solving the problem – this entire process was carried out without any conscious deliberation i.e. it had been habituated. **[unconscious competence]**.

Live Life: Don't Let Life Live You

Part B: Discernment

To further heighten your awareness and foster the attributes of serenity, acceptance, courage and wisdom, refer to the words of the following prayer:

I ask my Indwelling Divinity to grant me
The serenity to accept the things I cannot change;
The courage to change the things I can; and
The wisdom to know the difference

Recite this prayer frequently. Commit it to memory. Whenever you're faced with an ambiguous or threatening situation, one that fills you with confusion or fear, contemplate the words, slip into a serene state of mind, and deduce whether you have control over the situation or not.

If the answer is *no* then ask for the serenity to simply accept it. Why fret over something you cannot change? Equanimity of mind is maintained in simple acceptance.

If the answer is *yes* but you find yourself apprehensive to take action, then ask for courage. Remember, *courage isn't the absence of fear; it's the ability to act despite fear.*

If you are unable to ascertain whether you have control or not, ask for *clarity*. Again, use step four and hand the situation over to your Indwelling Divinity. This way you are certain of attaining the wisdom to discern the right course of action.

Part C: Escaping into the magic

The final part of step five encourages you to go into the magical kingdom of your mind and ponder the limitless possibilities available to you. Living life consciously involves *choosing* what you desire and manifesting it.

Your mind is a vast emporium of potential. Sixty thousand thoughts traverse it every single day and any one of them has the capacity to take you on an incredible journey. Select your thoughts carefully; discard the negative and harness the inspirational. When you have chosen an inspirational idea, incubate it in the embryo of your imagination. Feed it with concentration and allow it to become alive in your mind. Enlarge the internal pictures and turn up the sounds until the experience becomes life-like. Immerse yourself in the scene. Feel the wonderful feelings evoked. Watch the scenario grow and grow until it is finally birthed into reality. And don't hold back, remember:

> **The greater danger for most of us lies not in setting our aim too high and falling short;   but in setting our aim too low, and achieving our mark."**
> Michelangelo

Set your bar as high as possible and live life in the knowledge that you are capable of clearing it with room to spare. To live life consciously is to know no limits!

Your imagination is the gateway to Cosmic Consciousness; therefore, it is your greatest source of inspiration. Whenever you enter the realm of your imagination you become a conduit for the Universal Mind and activate the genius within. As a result, the chemicals released into your body will evoke feelings of elation and bliss - and they are free of charge, with no adverse side effects! Escape into the creative dominion of your imagination every day. Make it a habit. As your agreement with reality changes, you will actualize a life beyond your wildest dreams.

Step 6:
Develop and sustain self-love through regular communion with your inner child.

In every real man a child is hidden that wants to play.
Friedrich Nietzsche

The *inner child* is a concept used in psychology to denote the child-like aspect our psyche; a sub-personality embodying the residual effects of childhood. Alcoholism and the symptoms that accompany it: depression, strained relationships, severe mood swings, emptiness and low self-esteem, often arise as a result of neglecting our inner child.

The adverse effects of deep rooted childhood experiences lay dormant in our psyche until triggered by current stimuli. When ignited, they evoke strong, irrational responses that knock us off balance. Afterwards, we often exclaim, *'I don't know what came over me then!'*, *'I'm not myself today'*, or *'I was like a man possessed.'* These spontaneous, irrational outbursts are often indicative of a wounded inner child rebelling. The powerful practice of inner child therapy can eradicate the underlying issues that give rise to these eruptions and promote harmony in our relationships.

> ## Like a forgotten fire, a childhood can always flare up again within us.
> Gaston Bachelard

The inner child is the intrinsic embodiment of all our fears, worries, anxieties, and guilt; it is our epicentre of sensitivity. Vulnerability and over-sensitivity are signs that our inner child feels threatened and requires our attention. Ignoring these pleas leads to fragmentation and an underlying sense of dissociation; we feel somewhat distant and detached. But when we listen and act upon these pleas our lives are transformed in miraculous ways.

The feelings of our inner child are not contrived or distorted; they are authentic and need to be acknowledged. Suppressing these feelings puts a constant drain on our vital resources and gives rise to depletion and depression. More importantly, detaching from this authentic source of emotion is a sure way to become lost, confused and totally out of touch with ourselves.

Inner-child therapy helps us de-fuse the explosive source of our destructive tendencies. The unconscious mind presents unresolved issues for resolution via the inner child complex. This can be a highly emotional and disruptive experience, but do not shy away from it; it is a much needed positive development.

Remember, our childhood relationships are not dead and buried; they are buried alive - active in our unconscious. We cannot process and release them until they surface, and turbulent emotions are often indicative of them surfacing. So embrace this turbulence and acknowledge that it is your authentic self trying to break through your rigid defence systems.

The effects of internalised relationships are so important that there is a whole strand of psychology - *Object Relations Theory* - dedicated to them. During childhood we internalise versions of significant people in our lives: parents, peers, teachers, siblings and clergymen, etcetera. Object Relations Theory refers to these introjects as *objects*. The term Object Relations, therefore, refers to the relationships between these internal representations of real-life people and our inner child.

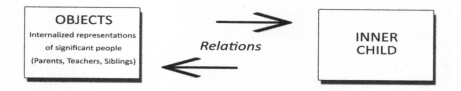

The term transference is used to describe the process of re-enacting these internal relationships with real people in our lives currently: our internalised relationships are mirrored in the external world. Via this mechanism, issues we had with people in our past are *transferred* to people in our lives today and our problems perpetuate. As this is an unconscious phenomenon, it often goes unrecognised and causes mayhem. Let's clarify the process with an example:

Example: Josie's Transference

Josie was beaten by her violent father as a child. Subsequently, she'd chosen partners who also administered violent beatings. A pattern emerged whereby Josie would end one violent relationship and enter another.

When she came for therapy, I explained to her that we internalise versions of significant people in our lives and the relationships we had with them are on-going in our unconscious mind. **The** *internal relationship between her and her father was being re-enacted externally. She chose partners of a violent disposition in order to solve the issues she had with her father, but she didn't know it because it was all happening unconsciously. In effect, she was giving her real-life partners the role of her father. However, trying to resolve the issues she had with her father via her current partners simply didn't work. What she needed to do, was work through the catalyst relationship (i.e. the one with her father).*

After processing and releasing the issues she had with her father in therapy, the destructive pattern of choosing violent partners magically disappeared. She no longer had an unconscious need to resolve issues involving violent men.

This example shows that the content of our psyche is often reflected externally. *When we harbour dysfunctional relationships within, we tend to attract dysfunctional relationships without.* Listening to the anguish of our inner child is imperative if we want to eradicate this destructive phenomenon.

The importance of childhood experience on our psychological development is further emphasised in Attachment Theory (see p. 311). Through longitudinal studies, John Bowlby *et al,* found that the quality of our early relationships shaped our capacity to enter into successful relationships throughout the rest of our lives. They found that children who had caregivers who responded to their needs and acted as a secure base from which they could explore their surroundings, were able to successfully integrate and form intimate relationships throughout the rest of their lives. Having received love and affection in their formative months, these children developed an internal representation of themselves as being worthy of love and affection. Consequently, they developed self-worth and self-esteem.

Conversely, children who didn't have a secure base, found it difficult to integrate. Having not received love and affection as infants, they formed an internal representation of themselves as being unworthy and so developed low self-esteem. So, undoubtedly, the effects of childhood influence on our psychological development are immense. The nature of our experiences in our formative years sets a template for the rest of our life.

'But what if we didn't have a good childhood – are we doomed?' I hear you cry. The answer is a resounding NO. Your primary caregivers - parents, foster parents, or whoever cared for you in childhood - may not have acquired the necessary skills to administer love and affection, but you do have such a person in your life now: You!

The child within never ages; therefore, with the help of the nurturing aspect of yourself, it is never too late to have a happy childhood. Remember, *as within, so without*. As you develop a loving relationship between your inner child and your inner parent, the effects will be far reaching and reflected externally. Your ability to form intimate, meaningful relationships will be greatly enhanced, as your self-esteem, self-respect and self-love begins to soar.

Three important points to note:

- If your primary caregiver did not possess the necessary attributes to administer love and affection, do not interpret it as a lack of love. This is very rarely the case. Their disposition is often a legacy *from their own up-bringing*; they feel the love but find it difficult to express.

- If you had a particularly difficult childhood, I would thoroughly recommend that you carry out the following exercises with the aid of a trained professional. Ideally, one of our licensed therapists (see **www.al2al.com**).

- As these exercises can be highly emotional, a period of approximately six months sobriety is recommended before you attempt them.

Inner Child Exercises

Before being buried beneath layer upon layer of conditioning, our inner children were playful, spontaneous, creative, and intuitive. The following exercises are designed to uncover that spring of vitality and let it embellish our lives once again.

Exercise one: a dialogue between your inner child and inner parent.

Note: this exercise is greatly enhanced if you have a childhood photograph of yourself to which you can relate throughout.

- *Whenever you are feeling upset, sit down and let your inner child relay its feelings to you. With your non-dominant hand, allow your inner child to transcribe its feelings onto paper. Don't edit the words to make them appear more adult-like, write them down exactly how they are expressed.*

- *Now allow your inner parent to come to the fore and contemplate the written requests of your inner child. Allow any evoked emotion to arise and expand. Do not judge the emotion: good, bad – right, wrong, just allow it to be, and observe the sensations in your body.*

- *Still in parent mode, with your dominant hand, write down a response to your inner child. Look at the child's photograph. Really impress upon them how much you care: how much you love them. Tell them exactly how you are going to fulfill their requests. Respond with as much love and encouragement as you can possibly muster.*

This is an excellent exercise to do whenever you are feeling discontented or confused. It is often at these times that your Inner Child is feeling ignored or criticized. The benefits are invaluable. Equanimity is attained by countering the negative feelings of the inner child with the loving, parental part of your psyche. The more you activate the nurturing part of your psyche, the more self-esteem and self-love you generate. As your self reliance grows, your neediness will diminish and reduce the demands you place on others. Emotionally nourishing yourself in this way will also enable you to give freely to others and greatly enhance your relationships.

Exercise two: Inner Child Meditation

Note: it helps to either record this meditation, leaving pauses at appropriate times to assimilate and process pertinent information, or have someone read it to you. Alternatively, there is a recording on our website.

Find a quiet place where you won't be disturbed. Relax and concentrate on your breath... Notice the gentle rise and fall of your breath... notice how this is reflected in the rise and fall of your stomach as it inflates and deflates... As you breathe out, let go of any tension, anxiety and stress... as you breathe in, inhale a sense of lightness and peace. Repeat this procedure for five minutes — in, out. Allow yourself to attune to the rhythm and flow of your breath.... Become one with it... slip into the space between your thoughts... and sink into a beautiful, deep state of relaxation.

Now, allow the following scene to come mind... You are in a ward of a maternity hospital... a nurse passes you a beautiful newborn baby.... Embrace the child and look deeply into its sparkling eyes. ..... Feel the child's warmth as you cradle them. Rock them gently back and forth.... notice how their eyes are filled with wonderment and they're eager to embrace the adventure of life .. this infant is special: extremely special... Become aware of this specialness. The child's eyes emanate a deep need for nurturing love... look into their clear, sparkling eyes and vow to fulfil this need...whisper into the baby's ear 'I love you', repeat this phrase over and over again... **'I love you.... I love you.... I love you'**...

.....This child is a bundle of pure goodness — a reflection of the pure goodness within you.... YOU ARE PURE GOODNESS.... Feel this goodness building up within you, NOW ....let it pervade every corner of your being... look deeply into the baby's eyes and see this goodness shining back at you.... Allow it to expand.. feel the goodness within you multiply - one hundred fold ... one thousand fold.... Feel yourself becoming a beacon of love, an emanation of goodness that illuminates all you come in contact with... notice how people respond to you as you emit this light... it brings out the best in them... they smile and are totally at ease with you... on noticing this, your self-worth heightens: rising, rising, rising.. feel your worthiness expand, and know that you are deserved of the best life has to offer.....

......become aware that the bundle of joy you cradle in your arms harbours a longing..... a longing to bestow a special gift onto the world... a treasure they hold in their heart: their life's purpose... this tiny bundle of love is a genius in one particular area.... their greatest joy will be to give this gift to their earthly brothers and sisters ... tell the child you will support and encourage them in their quest to fulfil their purpose... you will help them find that which they love to do and immerse them in it.....

...... Now, let the years elapse and notice how the child has blossomed into a joyous, creative infant.... notice how they play freely, enjoying the present moment to the full... play with them, NOW.... join in the fun... let go of any inhibitions and

become that fun loving child... let the scene expand in your mind..... make the colours brighter and more vivid... turn up the sound... immerse yourself in the scene... feel those glorious feelings traversing your being. ... bathe yourself in the energy of playfulness... allow yourself to be cleansed and purified by it... remind yourself that life is not a game to win: it is a game to play... allow yourself the luxury of playing frequently....and laugh at the challenges life beholds...

......Let the years progress once again... the child is now a teenager... listen to their values... ask them what they value most..... listen to their answers intently... make it obvious how much you support their aspirations.... What is it they need: love, affection, creative licence, meaningful relationships, abundance, recognition, success, or affluence? Make a mental note of their requests and write them down straight after this session..... Remember:

It is the child in man that is the source of his uniqueness and creativeness, and the playground is the optimal milieu for the unfolding of his capacities and talents.

Eric Hoffer

Life's playground is the optimal environment for the unfolding of the child's capacities and talents... look at the teenager again and feel a great sense of pride at the way they're progressing... note how their progress is down to the love and nurturance you have bestowed on them... every child has an innate need to be loved and cared for, and you have made an excellent job of fulfilling this primary need... look at the youth again..

.... for a brief instance you thought you saw yourself... look again.... you did see yourself... you are observing a long lost part of yourself.. welcome them back...they have now come home....they extend their arms towards you....you look deeply into their eyes, holding your gaze for what seems a lifetime... you extend your arms towards them.... you slowly move towards each other and embrace lovingly... as you do, you blend into one and become imbued with a sense of wholeness... the child has took their rightful place within you, once again..... from this moment forth, vow to commune with them on a daily basis, ask them what they want or need.... make sure to grant them their wishes.... as you do, watch them thrive... watch them evolve into a wonderful human being... one who will make a difference in this world..

.... allow the scene to dissolve now... call your awareness back behind the windows of your eyes, so you are centred in your body... feel the gentle pull of gravity on your shoulders and your feet firmly against the floor.... in your own time open your eyes and familiarise yourself with the surroundings.

On completion of this meditation, write down the wants and needs of your inner child and vow to honour them.

Step 7:

Make an inventory of all the kind and caring acts you've carried out throughout the course of your life - and/or – make an inventory of all the future kind and caring acts you intend to carry out.

As a result of the transgressions we carried out whilst inebriated, most of us developed a propensity to treat ourselves with disdain. Being inherently decent, moral and caring human beings, we find it difficult to accept the wrong-doings we carried out whilst intoxicated and become intent on self-punishment.

Step six began the process of reverse engineering these negative strategies. By nurturing the child within, we develop an internal representation of ourselves as being worthy of love and affection. Consequently, our self- love and self-esteem rise.

Step seven is a logical progression from inner child work in that it is designed to sustain and heighten our self-love and esteem. By reviewing all the good deeds we've performed throughout life, we cultivate an attitude of forgiveness and create a space for love to enter. We are essentially good people who have forgotten our positive attributes. Step seven rekindles our positive memories and gives rise to a shift in consciousness which fosters an extremely positive self-perception.

Exercise:

- Take a paper and pen and list all the kind and helpful acts you've carried out throughout life. Make a thorough inventory, listing as many as possible. Next to each inventory item, make a note of the attributes displayed: love, thoughtfulness, empathy, kindness, consideration, etc.

- When it's complete, sit down in a quiet place and contemplate each one. Allow any associated emotions to arise and expand. Immerse yourself in that wonderful feeling of pride that emerges as a result of your accomplishments. Feel your self-worth growing by the minute. Harness that feeling and let it grow...ten-fold; a hundred-fold; a thousand-fold. Shower your inner child with compliments for all the good work they have carried out throughout life. Watch their ever-widening smile as they receive the praise they've always longed for.

- When you have finished, set your sights on the future. Make a list of all the forthcoming kind acts you intend to carry out. Be very specific: to whom do you intend to be kind? In what ways will your kindness manifest? How will your thoughtfulness enhance the recipient's life?

- Again, find a quiet place and contemplate each one. Let the scenarios expand in your mind until you truly acknowledge the inherent goodness within you.

Note: if you have difficulty in remembering the good you have carried out in the past, go straight to the second part of the exercise and list all the good you *intend* to do.

Give this exercise the time it deserves. Repeat it periodically. The more you dwell on the goodness within you, the more you will deflect the wrath of Sobriety Saboteurs. Consequently, you will increase your capacity for self-love and attract the love of others.

Step 8:
Forgive and be Free

The moving finger writes; and, having writ,
Moves on: nor all the piety nor wit
Shall lure it back to half a line,
Nor all thy tears wash out a word of it.
Omar Khayam (1048 – 1122)

The wise words of philosopher, astronomer and poet, Omar Khayam, remind us of the futility of holding past events responsible for our current circumstances. The moving finger, in this context, may be seen as us. As time elapses and events unfold, we inevitably make mistakes and suffer injustices, but no amount of blame or guilt can turn back the passage of time in order to rectify them.

One of life's greatest myths is the belief that the past is responsible for our present misfortunes. This is a defeatist's attitude. Without doubt, the past does influence our psychological development, but as we gain awareness and insight into ourselves, we come to realize that the past cannot be credited for our present shortcomings without our consent.

Granted, we can *choose* to bond ourselves to the wounds and injustices of the past and allow bitterness and resentment to erode our minds and destroy our lives; or we can choose to turn our anger inwardly, severely berate ourselves for past transgressions, and sink into a morass of melancholy. Either way, guilt, bitterness, or resentment will surely lead to our demise.

There is another option available, however. We can choose to forgive. By forgiving ourselves and others, we free up a vast amount of psychic space for inspiration, creativity, love, joy and life's infinite possibilities to enter. The formula for the successful implementation of this process is written below:

> ## Forgive us our trespasses, as we forgive those who trespass against us.

These words of the Lord's Prayer are not some pious idealism devised to produce martyrs and angels; they are designed to set you free. Forgiveness and freedom are synonymous. When we blame negative childhood experience, relationship problems, financial hardship, bereavement, or some other calamity for our present misfortunes, we surrender our power to circumstances beyond our control. Subsequently, our minds become infested with negative thoughts which give rise to life-denying chemicals in our bodies that induce bad feeling: depression, fragmentation, lethargy, irritability, paranoia and bitterness. Consequently, we drink and end up back in the abreactive abyss. This whole destructive process is initiated by our refusal to let go of old wounds. But what we don't realise is that by hanging onto past pain, we are continuously wounding ourselves.

> ## Resentment is a covert method of self-punishment.
> ## The primary objective of forgiving others
> ## is to set *yourself* free.
> ## Forgiveness is not an altruistic act:
> ## it is self-serving.

Forgiveness doesn't mean pretending that no wrong occurred. On the contrary, it means that there was wrong (else there would be *nothing* to forgive) – yet, *in order to free ourselves*, we stop feeling angry or resentful towards the person.

In extreme cases, such as abuse, where forgiveness is desirable but extremely difficult, there is an effective process that facilitates release; a process that transports you from hatred to freedom.

Steve, my friend whose story appears at the beginning of the book, initially found it impossible to forgive his foster-father for the sexual abuse he suffered as a child – with good reason, you might say; but let's remember that resentment is self-effacing.

As we worked through his issues, I became aware that love and hatred were fused together, as often happens in these cases. Survivors of sexual abuse are typically reluctant to declare their love for the perpetrator as they think they will be labelled weird – *'how can you love someone after he did that to you?'*

After reassuring him that it was understandable and permissible to love his foster-father, I recommended that he separate his father's disturbing actions from the person as a whole. This enables a client to see the many different facets of a person, instead of just their negative aspects.

On doing this, Steve began to recognise the positive attributes of his foster-father and understood why he'd loved him as well as hated him. At this point I felt a shift in Steve's energy; he had mellowed somewhat. His *hatred* had transformed into *anger*.

For the next few weeks we worked on processing his anger, during which time it emerged that his father had also been sexually abused as a child (as is often the case with perpetrators of sexual abuse). By acknowledging the full impact of his foster-father's childhood experience, another shift took place; Steve's *anger* transposed into *understanding* and *compassion*.

A year later, after continuous therapy, Steve visited his foster-father's grave and forgave him. The experience is best described in his own words, *'I immediately felt a weight had been lifted off my shoulders and knew that I could now move forward.'*

The process of shifting from hatred to freedom outlined above will work for almost any problem. Not many people are able to make the shift in one quantum leap. Many don't even get as far as forgiveness, but once they attain a degree of understanding, their dilemma has a tendency to dissipate.

The logical progression through *hatred, anger, understanding, compassion, forgiveness and, finally,* **freedom** normally transpires as a result of working with a competent therapist or an excellent mentor. If you recognise a need to undergo this process, see our website for a list of approved therapists and mentors -**www.al2al.com**

Self Forgiveness

The benefits of understanding and forgiving others will only be felt if we are prepared to forgive ourselves too. Many people who abuse alcohol are so intent on self-recrimination that they feel that turmoil and hardship is all they deserve; plagued with guilt, they become obsessed with judging themselves 'bad' and 'unworthy' and sentencing themselves to a life of misery.

If you identify with this pattern of self-destruction - as I know many of you do - WAKE UP! Recognise it as the work of the Sobriety Saboteurs. Their appearance always presents an opportunity for growth – the lesson, this time is: LEARN TO LOVE YOURSELF. Guilt transpires from self-disdain, the antidote to which is self-love – *self-disdain and self-love are totally incompatible.*

At this time it may be worth reminding yourself of those famous words of Jesus:

> **'Father forgive them for they know not what they do.'**

When we were inebriated, we didn't know what we were doing either. We didn't consciously set out to harm anyone; the harm we caused was usually a by-product of our inactive conscience and suspended memory giving rise to Dr Jekyll becoming Mr Hyde.

For blame and punishment to be appropriate there has to be conscious intent to violate another person in some way, and this is very rarely the case with alcoholism. So heed the words of Jesus and forgive yourself for your indiscretions. Instead of whipping yourself and becoming an unproductive member of society laden with guilt, use your past errors as feedback to improve the quality of your life in the future.

Making Amends

This step would be incomplete without addressing the issue of making amends. Making amends to people for past transgressions is appropriate when you feel your relationship with them has been strained. If you feel it necessary and appropriate to make direct amends, then do so – it is a great house-cleaning exercise that fosters humility.

In some cases you may like to make direct amends, but the thought of doing so fills you with reticence and uncertainty. Step nine offers the perfect solution; one that will see many people benefit from your willingness to evolve into a respected, productive human being.

Step 9:
Identify Your Life's Purpose

'Don't ask what the world needs.
Ask what makes you come alive, and go and do it,
because the world needs people
who have come alive.'
Howard Thurman

Steps one to eight are primarily focused on house-cleaning – clearing up residual negative energy from the past. Step nine moves you into the present, and urges you to find out what you love to do and share it with the world. Optimal living is contingent on you being fulfilled and joyous. Living on purpose is the best way of ensuring success.

When we open to our inner guidance and flow with the current of divine intelligence which floods our being, our purpose is illuminated and our lives change *forever*.

Your life's purpose doesn't have to be some monumental feat. It may simply be a series of small things carried out with much love. But one thing is for certain - it will fill you with inspiration, enthusiasm and delight. Once you're on purpose your life will change forever. The essence of this step can be summed up in the following statement:

Love what you do, and do what you love.

Your life's purpose is relayed through the language of the heart. So feel your way into it, instead of thinking. Identify what excites and stimulates you; identify what sets you alight inside. Maybe your purpose will reveal itself in a number of stages, as it did with me – but every stage will be inspiring and stimulating, I guarantee you.

Your life's purpose is a desire of the Universe waiting to manifest through you. I cannot think of a more befitting way to relay the joys of this step other than reiterating those magnificent words of Pantajali:

> **"When you are inspired by some great purpose,**
> **some extraordinary project,**
> **all your thoughts break their bonds:**
> **Your mind transcends limitations,**
> **your consciousness expands in every direction,**
> **and you find yourself in a new,**
> **great, and wonderful world.**
> **Dormant forces, faculties and talents become alive,**
> **and your discover yourself to be a greater person by**
> **far than you ever dreamed yourself to be."**

If you have difficulties in identifying your life's purpose, the following steps are designed to help.

Life's Purpose Exercise

Take a pen and paper and answer the questions thoroughly.
Give the exercise the time it deserves.

i.   What do you thoroughly enjoy doing? Reflect on your life and identify times when you were passionate, fulfilled and inspired. What were the stimuli? Who were you with?

ii.   What kind of people stimulate and inspire you? Who are your role models? What exactly is it about these people that you admire: their outlook on life? Their values? Their determination?

iii.   If money was no object and you had all the time in the world, what would you do with your life?

iv.   What values are most important to you? (revert to the values elicitation exercise on p. 231).

v.   Revisit steps one to four, reflect on your answers, and identify any common threads.

vi.   Complete the following statements with as many answers as possible. Write freely and spontaneously.

My life purpose is . . .

The purpose for which I'm on this planet is . . . .

The vision I hold for the world is . . . .

vii. Write a brief statement about your life's purpose. Notice how you feel when writing it. If you feel effervescent and alive, the chances are you have uncovered it. If not, repeat this exercise periodically.

viii Now, find a quiet space where you won't be disturbed. Play some inspirational background music or simply immerse yourself in silence. Allow your mind to open and expand. Feel your ego and all its doubts and insecurities being consumed by your true essence: your Indwelling Divinity. Know that you are capable of achieving anything. Your true essence is the very same omnipotent intelligence which gave rise to all creation. You are creativity itself. Life is a field of infinite possibilities. Allow your mind to drift and locate the genius within. Ask the genius what unique gift it has for the world. Each of us is born with a duty embedded in our heart; our life's purpose. Let the genius within reveal this purpose. Make sure that when it is divulged you feel passionate about it - awe inspired. In silence, ask questions – pause, and feel the answers arising from the depths of your soul

ix. Finally, move heaven and earth to manifest it! The results will astound you – I promise!

Making Amends though our life's Purpose

In step eight I discussed the importance of making amends for the transgressions we carried out whilst intoxicated. Bestowing the gift of your life's purpose onto the world is a magnificent way of achieving this. Not only will your work benefit many people, but you will grow closer to God or the Universal Mind in the process. The practice of unifying with the Source of all creation through our life's work is called Karma Yoga.

Karma Yoga

The Sanskrit word *Karma* means **to do** or **action - Yoga** means **union with God.** So the practice of **Karma Yoga** is unifying with God through selfless action. Since all living things are God manifest, then Karma Yoga may be defined as the selfless use of our unique gift in service of the highest good of all we encounter. Rather than working simply for money or personal gain, a person practicing karma yoga has the well-being of others at heart. Through this service they find union with God. Let me relay my current thoughts on the subject to you:

As I write these words, I sit in solitude in the quiet ambience of the English Lake district. Although I'm alone, I am not lonely – I am intimately connected to the divine inspiration which dwells within me; I am a channel through which the Universe can express itself. In silence, I commune with the divinity which occupies my body, and realise the truth in the saying that **sometimes silence has the loudest voice**. *As silent knowing is translated into the words which I impart to you, I am filled with passion and purpose. My enthusiasm levels are peaking because the God within is consuming my ego and all negative interference is being expelled. I am at one. As I bestow my unique talents on the world, I strengthen my intimacy with God or the Universe. I allow the dreams of God to be expressed through me.*

Summary of Phase Two

- Allow your life to unfold from the facet of your being that knows the right response to every situation.
- Live life consciously
- Love the child within
- Frequently remind yourself of your goodness
- Forgiveness is the key to freedom
- Embrace your life's purpose

Phase Three: Maintaining the Magic
(Steps Ten, Eleven and Twelve)

The final phase of this philosophy for optimal living is maintenance. Rather than being a chronological process with a beginning, middle, and end, this philosophy is on-going: *it is a way of life.* To maintain and evolve your well-being, I suggest the following steps:

Step 10:
Daily Meditation

"All of humanity's problems stem from man's inability to sit quietly in a room alone"
Blaise Pascal

It is true to say that all of humanity's problems stem from an inability to sit in silence. Our urgent need to *'advance'* and fill our minds with unimportant issues has taken away our ability to discern that which is truly meaningful. *Only in silence does pure truth reveal itself. Only in stillness does clarity transpire. Only in quiet moments does our inner genius materialize.*

Withdrawing from the chaos of life to the quiet oasis of your mind is imperative to your well-being. Daily meditation not only prolongs life and radically improves psychological and physical health, but it also strengthens your connection to Source.

Here are some of the major benefits of step ten:

- **Reduced Stress**

By detaching from the field of activity – thoughts and actions - we become an impartial witness to life. From this dissociated perspective, worries and anxiety pale into insignificance: we observe them rather than own them. This practice radically reduces stress and promotes harmony and balance.

- **Replenishment**

Spending twenty minutes in a meditative state gives us the equivalent of eight hours sleep.

- **Clarity and Concentration**

Our ability to concentrate is affected by the constant chatter of our inner dialogue. Meditation promotes one-pointed awareness. In our normal state of consciousness, our thoughts are scattered and diffuse, which leads to confusion and irritability. In meditation our awareness becomes laser-like: supremely concentrated on its object of focus. Focusing solely on the present moment clears our mind, increases productivity, improves our memory, and enables us to become effective decision makers.

- **Health Benefits**

Numerous studies have proved that meditation improves our health; for example, lower levels of stress and anxiety due to meditation diminish the probability of heart disease significantly. Mind and matter are inextricably linked. Emotional turmoil often translates into physical ailments. Meditation promotes equanimity of mind which reflects in a vast improvement in physical health.

- **Control Your Mind – Don't Let Your Mind Control You**

Man has conquered some of the most difficult terrain: high mountains, the moon surface and the North Pole, to name but a few; but has he truly conquered his inner domain? How many people live life unconsciously, propelled by rigid conditioning? How often do we fall under the spell of social hypnosis?

Meditation presents an opportunity for self examination; a space in which we can review and challenge our thought processes and belief systems. This practice gives rise to the actualization of our true potential.

- **Get Out of Your Mind and into Your Senses**

Being consumed by a chaotic mind often leads to anxiety, stress, insomnia, mood swings, and depression. One method of vacating a busy mind is to concentrate solely on your immediate surroundings: look, listen, smell, taste and feel the world around you. Concentrate supremely on the present moment and allow your senses to absorb the scenery.

Meditation does not necessarily have to be an inert process; it can be achieved in a waking state. If possible go to the country and practice raising your awareness using all your senses in tranquil surroundings.

- **Happiness**

Happiness is the goal of all goals. Whatever people do, the underlying objective is to attain happiness, and happiness is an intrinsic state: we are innately happy. It is our inner dialogue which detracts from this natural state and breeds discontentment. Meditation transports us from cognitive chaos to a spiritual sanctuary that exudes peace. The result is pure, unadulterated happiness and contentment.

- **Creativity**

When our chaotic thoughts abate and silence prevails, we tap into the infinite reservoir of intelligence responsible for all creation. Great thinkers and geniuses have made all their important discoveries in this state. Remember, creativity is not the process of regurgitating that which is already known; it's the birthing of new ideas. In the silence of *non-thinking*, the Universe relays novel ideas. They arise spontaneously and set us alight inside. We experience the joy of becoming collaborators with God (Universal Mind, or whatever other term you prefer). Go into silence, discover your inner genius, and unlock your creative potential.

- **Insight**

During insight meditation we transcend the mask of matter that shrouds the material world and gain first-hand experience of the true nature of reality. To relay this experience using words is impossible, so I'll conclude this step with the following statement from the Tao Te Ching:

> **'Those who speak, do not know;
> and those who know, do not speak'**

Step 11:
Continuing Development

This step is comprised of the following five components:

i. **Stay on purpose and continue to utilize our unique talents to serve the highest good of all we encounter.**

> **When you work you are a flute through whose heart the whispering of the hours turns to music. To love life through labour is to be intimate with life's inmost secret. All work is empty save when there is love, for work is love made visible.**
>
> Kahlil Gibran

The message of this part is simple: stay on purpose. Adhering to your ultimate mission in life is a sure way of sustaining joy, inspiration, strength and meaning on a daily basis. The dark clouds of life come and go but your purpose remains forever present like the clear blue skies above. *Love what you do and do what you love.* Dedicate your finest qualities to the good of humanity.

> **To love humanity through our purpose is to be intimate with God.**

ii.   Commune with your Indwelling Divinity on a daily basis.

Throughout the course of each day, check-in with your Indwelling Divinity. Become aware of the still presence that is the core of your being. Allow life to unfold from this Wise Witness Within. When circumstances arise which knock you off balance, ask for the correct response to be revealed and act accordingly.

iii.   Frequently absorb inspirational literature with the objective of re-programming your mind.

Reading inspirational literature is one of the best ways to ensure continued success. Allocate at least fifteen minutes every day to reading or listening to enlightening and inspirational information. Constantly replenish your mind with knowledge that will stoke the fire of passion within you; knowledge that will imbue you with wisdom and bring about enlightenment.

iv.   Regularly transmit your intentions

Practice the following exercise three or four times a week:

Exercise: transmitting intentions

Sit comfortable in a quiet room.
Hold whatever you desire in your mind. Energize your thoughts with your imagination. See, hear, feel, smell and taste your desire; - act as if it's already actualized.

Let the energy of success suffuse your being. Imagine concentric circles of intelligence pulsating outwardly from your mind, propagating your request throughout

---

the universe. Double the intensity: treble the intensity. Allow the intensity to increase one-thousand fold. Immerse yourself in the contents of your mind and hold that state for fifteen minutes. Know that the Universe is listening and responding. Your request is being transmitted through a web of intelligence in which everything is connected. Your answers will appear soon. Know, with complete faith, that you are sculpting pure consciousness into the circumstances of your future.

Your mind is the womb of creation, giving birth to your requests. Now, release all attachment to the outcome and allow the universe to preside.

v.   Continually affirm positive statements

Regularly nourish your mind with affirmations.

Step 12:
Having radically transformed our lives and actualized our optimal potential, we aspire to assist others to make the journey from Alcoholic to Alchemist.

Now is your chance to shine. Throughout the world, alcoholism has reached pandemic levels. People are desperate for answers. Having experienced a radical shift in consciousness as a result of assimilating and practicing this twelve step philosophy for optimal living, you are now endowed with the psychological and spiritual knowledge with which to intervene.

You have first-hand experience of the dilemma facing people who have succumbed to alcohol abuse. As a consequence, you are ideally placed to secure their trust and guide them out of the wilderness.

Step twelve encourages you to become a burning candle, passing the flame of enlightenment to others in need; guiding people on the journey from **Alcoholic to Alchemist**.

Chapter 27

Questions and Answers with Paul and Steve

Shirley:	**Life seems intolerable without drink. Alcohol is a social lubricant. How can I socialize without it?**
Paul:	Can I ask you when you last enjoyed a social evening drinking, Shirley?
Shirley:	[*Long pause. Blank expression*] **Come to think of it - not for a long time. I've embarrassed myself so many times in black-outs that people stopped inviting me to social gatherings.**
Paul:	Precisely! A common scenario. There's a whole new world awaiting you out there, Shirley. You'll find ways of socializing that are novel and exciting. I joined meditation groups, attended self-development workshops, trained in different types of therapy and in the process met a wealth of new friends: true friends. In fact, I didn't know the true meaning of socializing until I quit drink!
Shirley:	**Do you think it's possible to drink '*normally*' after misusing alcohol?**
Paul:	To my knowledge, after a person has crossed the Abreactive Threshold, they never return to moderate drinking. Every subsequent attempt to imbibe alcohol results in an abnormal reaction.

These abreactions manifest on a mental, emotional and physical level – or a combination of any of the three. One common foible of abreaction is a compelling desire to drink more.

Shirley: **I see – thank you...... Something else's just come to mind. If the alcohol habit is caused by a person wanting to escape unresolved issues, when the issues are resolved can they resume normal drinking?**

Paul: Again, Shirley, I've never known this to happen. It seems that once the body and the mind have been purged of the effects of alcohol, then any subsequent drinking ends up in abreaction.

I drank on a number of occasions after clearing my issues. Each time I had an adverse reaction. I believe there are two reasons for this. First, my tolerance for alcohol had diminished as a result of abstaining for a good length of time, so I couldn't take it physically (I felt ill). Secondly, I still associated alcohol with lack of control and destruction and when I drank these associations came flooding back to haunt me, causing mental instability.

It appears that once the Abreative Threshold has been compromised, there is no going back to social drinking, whether we have unresolved issues or not.

John: **I drink to drown out my past. My parents fought like cat and dog and my father drank away all the money. I was ridiculed at school and isolated because of the shabby clothes I wore.**

Steve: It's often helpful to seek professional assistance in resolving such issues, John. You abuse alcohol to suppress memories of your past, but suppression is not a cure; it's simply avoidance. *The best way to escape your problems is to solve them.* I know through personal experience. My childhood was extremely difficult, too. I was abandoned at birth and sexually abused by my foster father. For years I blamed these experiences for my abusive alcohol consumption. Then I woke up! Blame, I realised, was just an argument against growth. I was entitled to a wonderful life and the only thing depriving me of it was myself. With the aid of Paul and his psychodynamic counselling skills, I resolved my childhood issues. I would recommend it to anyone; it's such a liberating experience. And now I'm truly free!

Paul: Yes, John. By suppressing unresolved experiences from our past, we give them power. Continuous suppression leads to repression; the process by which unresolved issues are banished to our unconscious mind. These experiences are not extinguished; they're highly active and find expression in our lives in various detrimental ways: neuroses, phobias, inhibitions, addictions, mood swings, the list goes on and on. As Steve says, the only way to escape our problems is to solve them. May I suggest you book an appointment with one of our therapists. They are specifically trained to assist with such issues.

John: **Yes. Thank You. Coming from you two guys, I know it's real. You've both been through it yourselves - you know how it is. If you can turn your life around after all that you've been through – then so can I!** [a renewed sense of determination now evident in John's tone]

Robbie: **I've amassed considerable debt through drinking. Lost my house, my car, and my family in the process. What have I got to live for? I may as well drink myself to death.**

Steve: That's a choice that's open to you, Rob. I've personally met many people who have taken that route out. I lost my wife and family too: when I stopped drinking! Yes, they left after I quit drinking because I wasn't the same man I was whilst drinking: I was a stranger to them. Over time, though, they realised that they respected and loved the new man who'd emerged. Transformation doesn't guarantee getting your family's respect back, but it certainly helps! Carol, my ex, and I get on extremely well today. I yearned for her return for years, Rob, but eventually we both realised we had grown apart. Today we have a great relationship and I have a new love in my life. Never thought it possible but there you go, sixty-one years of age and courting again! There are some words of wisdom I'd like you to consider, Rob:

'Attach to nothing and be open to everything'

This means don't buy into the illusion that happiness is contingent on having specific *people or things* in your life. The great mystery, that is life, has a wonderful way of surprising us when we least expect it!

As for finances, look at Paul, as part of his transformation process he decided to play double your money. He doubled his annual salary by applying his attributes to something he was passionate about, and set up a training school. He was the happiest he'd ever been.

Karen: **I drank to drown out my mother's death; she was my best friend.**

Steve: So did I, Karen; they nearly had to dig two graves. Have you ever talked about your feelings surrounding the death?

Karen: **No. People say things like '*do you think your mother wants you to be this way – pull yourself together and get on with it*' but this attitude just makes things worse.**

Paul: Hardly surprising. Most people don't know how to handle issues surrounding death, Karen. Here we have to look at process and content. The content is the story surrounding your mother's death and what you have to do to 'fix it.' The process is the underlying feelings that give rise to your upset. It is these feelings that need to be processed, Karen. Advice and solutions are of no use. You need to express the emotions that are pent up within you. As with John earlier, may I recommend one of our therapists to help facilitate the process?

Karen: **Yes. Thanks, Paul. I'll make an appointment.**

George: **What about on-going support, Paul – isn't that important, contact with other people with similar problems?**

Paul: Extremely, George. This is why I'm appealing to people to set up Alcoholic to Alchemist meetings. The more experienced members can become mentors for the new members and guide them through the processes outlined in the book.

George: **Great idea. Can I start one in my area even though I'm only three months sober?**

Paul:	Most definitely. I will help as much as possible, George. It will give you a sense of purpose and greatly enhance the probability of you being successful.
George:	[with a beaming smile] **I'll get to it as soon as I return home.**
Paul:	In addition, George, our website – **www.al2al.com** - has a wealth of on-line support for people: videos, audio files, meditations, information and there's even a forum where you can take part in discussions with other people on the journey. You could spend hours a day on there digesting wisdom that will positively re-programme your mind.
George:	**Excellent! I'll give that a go too.**

Questions and Answers with Family Members

Anne: **Living with a drunk is horrendous. My kids and I have experienced economic hardship, disruption of our domestic routine, and verbal, emotional and physical abuse. Most of our time and energy is spent trying to cover up for my husband. We ring his boss and say he's sick, when he's really hung over. We tell our neighbours that he suffers from stress. We tidy the house when he has smashed it up in black-out. Trying to keep up appearances is killing us; but what else can we do? We've got to avoid social disgrace. I've threatened to leave him; blackmailed him. I've tried everything, but I can't get through.**

Paul: First thing, Anne, is to stop the rescue mission. By making excuses for your husband, and tidying up after his outbursts, you are colluding with him. You are making it easy for him to continue drinking. When the rescue missions stop, he is forced to face the destruction and devastation he's inflicting on the family; this may lead to the motivation to do something about his problem.

Anne: **You mean just leave smashed furniture lying on the floor until he sobers up?**

Paul: Precisely. On a few occasions I threw my bedroom furniture down the stairs. The first couple of times my parents tidied it up before I'd sobered up. The last time, however, they left it there to confront me when I emerged from my drunken stupor. Broken drawers and clothes scattered all along the landing. I was baffled and asked them how it happened. They looked at me in a way that needed no words. The thing is, when they tidied up I wasn't even aware of what I'd done, but that day I was devastated. It didn't stop me drinking right away, but it gave me food for thought. Next time your husband smashes the place up, leave everything as it is. Don't approach him when he's drunk, wait until the effects of alcohol wear off and appeal to his better nature. When you do approach him, don't rant and rave, keep as calm as possible and express your grievances firmly and honestly. And finally, don't make idle threats. If you're going to issue ultimatums, make sure you adhere to them.

Laura: **What actions would you recommend?**

Paul: Each case is unique and subjective, Laura. I'm very reluctant to give specific advice. But what really got to me was this. One morning my mum came up to my bedroom. Instead of the normal ranting and raving she remained very calm. After telling me how much she and my father loved me, she told me that they couldn't stand to see me slowly killing myself. She then asked me to leave - and meant it, adding that there was always a home there for me if I quit drinking. I'll never forget that day: it was a real wake up call. In fact, that incident eventually put me on the road to sobriety.

Laura: **Hmmm, that's interesting. I rant and rave at my husband and it gets me nowhere - except a load of abuse that really hurts. I spend many nights in the spare bedroom crying myself to sleep, wondering if I'm really all the terrible things he calls me; wondering if I'm to blame for his demise.**

Paul:	Let me assure you, Laura, you are not to blame. People with alcohol habits are prone to *shadow projection*. All the things they don't like about themselves, they project onto others; that is, they see all their own faults as being situated in others and blame them - normally the people who are closest to them get the worst. It is a way of externalizing the mess that resides within them. My advice is not to take the insults personally. Ultimately, you have one major decision to make. You need to decide whether the benefits of your relationship, outweigh the deficits.
Laura:	**Yeah, I hear what you're saying – how long do I let it go on?**
Paul:	If he is going to change eventually, Laura, there is one thing you can do - gather information in advance about local alcohol treatment options. If he asks for help, get him to call immediately and make an appointment. Offer to accompany him to the clinic on his first visit.
Mary:	**Hi Paul, my name's Mary and I'm the mother of an alcoholic.**
Paul:	Can I stop you there, Mary. No – you're not the mother of an alcoholic. You're the mother of a person experiencing an alcohol habit. Labelling someone as an alcoholic is disabling. The term alcoholic denotes something that's permanent, whereas *a person experiencing an alcohol habit* denotes a temporary state. The language we use can either exacerbate or help the situation. Sorry, please go on.
Mary:	**That makes sense – thank you, Paul. That sort of answers my question too, but I'd like to clarify it anyway - Is it true that even if my son**

refrains from drinking, he will always be an alcoholic?

Paul: No it's not, Mary. It's true that he will always abreact to drink if he's crossed the threshold, but he is not an alcoholic – *he's a person*. Once he relinquishes the habit, what he will be for the rest of his life is a human being with infinite potential. Whether he embraces that potential is his choice.

Ben: **Living with an alcoholic wife is like living with a schizophrenic. She can be the most wonderful person in the world one minute, then turn at a moment's notice into the devil.**

Paul: I know, Ben; I was a perfect example. What you must remember is that your wife has probably crossed the Abreactive Threshold; therefore, unconscious issues are breaking through into her consciousness and disturbing her equilibrium. Her mind is bombarded with issues that cause severe instability.

Ben: **Is there anything I can do to help?**

Paul: Remind her of the good things she's accomplished in life. Remind her of her innate goodness. She'll be despising herself.

Ben: **OK, should I continue to pour her drink away?**

Steve: Watering down or pouring away your wife's alcohol is futile, Ben: it usually exacerbates the problem. The drinker often becomes defiant and vows to get more alcohol, which means raising funds and inviting more financial hardship. Unfortunately, drinking often has to run its natural course.

Paul: .....Yes, Ben. Your main priority must be yourself. It is imperative that you get a support network; people you can talk with openly and honestly. If you deny or suppress the problem, it will find other means of expression: depression or neurosis, for instance. Ideally, a person who can be objective would be best placed to offer support; for example, a counsellor. The problem with close friends or family is that they have a large investment in your welfare and this can impede their effectiveness. They are highly likely to condemn and berate the drinker, a course of action which, although often warranted, doesn't provide a practical solution to the situation. You need to take care of yourself, you cannot change the drinker. With the help of a good counsellor, you can put coping strategies into effect and look at your choices.

Sharon: **I feel so guilty. I've grown to hate my son after the problems he's caused us through drinking. Yet I know, deep down, I really love him. The inner conflict is unbearable.**

Steve: That's understandable and very common, Sharon. I hated my foster-father for the abuse he inflicted on me, but I also loved him. The way I dealt with it was to separate the person from the actions. You love your son, but you cannot abide his actions.

Sharon: **That makes sense, thanks Steve.**

William: **My son is only twenty-two, but he looks like an old man. He never eats and he permanently reaks of alcohol. I'm always finding bottles hidden in his bedroom and other obscure areas of the house. I throw them away, but I'm wasting my time; he always gets more.** [*William breaks down in tears*]

Steve: We must remember, William, alcohol is only a symptom. By removing the symptom we don't address the root cause. The destructive cognitive patterns etched into the unconscious mind of your

412

son are the problem. He needs a shift in consciousness to alleviate them. Our book, **Alcoholic to Alchemist**, is designed to produce such a shift. May I suggest you give him a copy. If he's ready and willing to practice the philosophy, it will produce the desired results.

Amanda: **What can I do to help my daughter? She's way out of control. It's crucifying me to watch her killing herself. God knows how much she's drinking but she stinks of it all the time.**

Paul: Frequently remind her how much you love her, Amanda. Remind her of her innate goodness. When people are in the throes of alcoholism they already despise themselves. Shouting and bawling at them just reinforces their negative self perception and heightens the need to escape. Most people experiencing an abusive alcohol habit need reminding of their innate goodness.

Summary of Main Points

- Know that your loved-one or friend's destructive drinking has nothing to do with you. You didn't cause it; you can't control it; and you cannot cure it. People with an abusive alcohol habit often revert to shadow projection, a process whereby they imagine all their own shortcomings and character defects as being situated in someone else - in this case you. This person then becomes a scapegoat. Armed with this knowledge, recognise that the aspersions they cast upon you actually define themselves.

- Develop a good support system of family and friends.

- Seek counselling and take care of yourself. The only life you exercise control over is your own. Don't exert vital energy trying to change someone else; it is a futile practice.

- Maintain your own identity. Family and friends of abusive drinkers often become so obsessed with the problem that their boundaries lapse and they forget where they end and the drinker begins.

- Don't enable the person's habit. Enabling takes various forms: covering up, making excuses, and lying on their behalf. You cannot prevent the inevitable. Attempting to do so often prolongs a person's drinking career. Focus on your own needs, not the needs of the drinker.

- Avoid major conflicts when the drinker is inebriated, but share your honest feelings when they are dry. Denying them rarely solves anything.

- If you issue ultimatums, be prepared to carry them out.

Part Ten
The Beginning

Chapter 28

The Promise

Within your depths, obscured from view
A promised land awaits for you
When stormy days, where shadows cast
Subside to bring the sun alas
This world appears, from depths ascend
And this is where you rainbow ends

Galfridus
(The Jester from my novel Spirit of Adventure)

Can you imagine going through each day without so much as one thought about alcohol? Can you imagine being imbued with so much inspiration that you feel you are floating? Can you imagine looking into the eyes of your loved ones and seeing them glisten with joy because the person they love has returned from an alcohol-induced wilderness? Can you imagine having a wealth of new friends, earning great money doing whatever you're passionate about? Can you imagine feeling healthy, vibrant and enthusiastic on a daily basis? Well these are just some of the fruits you can expect as a result of the alchemical process you have undergone.

Beyond the mask of misery which veiled your view of reality, there's always been a wonderful new life awaiting you: a life of immeasurable opportunities. Now you have taken the journey from Alcoholic to Alchemist that veil has been lifted.

I once lay in a hospital bed with tubes inserted into every conceivable orifice. My liver was grossly enlarged, my body convulsed, my complexion was yellow, and I had a toxic level of painkillers in my blood. According to the doctors' prognosis, I should be dead! Yet like a caterpillar becomes cocooned in a dark shell before transforming into a beautiful butterfly and flying into a new life, so my world was enveloped by mental and emotional debris before I awakened to a wonderful new way of being.

Today, I realize that life doesn't have to be perfect to be wonderful – but it's damn near perfect! I embrace the natural ebbs and flows, rising to the challenges and riding the crests of the waves. A deep sense of adventure steeps my mind on a daily basis and I'm always prepared to take the road less travelled.

Realizing that the Universe is full of surprises, I don't grasp at any one person, place or thing to provide happiness: *I remain open to everything and attached to nothing.* There is a never-ending source of joy that flows through me when I become a conduit for the Source of all creation. Like a detective, I live each day consciously seeking out the clues that will lead to my next adventure. I live in a constant state of awe and wonderment. Allowing each day to unfold from the wisdom and creativity of my Indwelling Divinity ensures success in every area of my life.

I recently celebrated my fiftieth birthday and I have to tell you that the last fifteen years have been unbelievable! I could easily write another book listing the wonderful experiences I've had whilst travelling the world, teaching, speaking, writing and meeting a wealth of new friends - and yet I know the best years are still to come!

I'm now in the deeply privileged position of knowing who I truly am, what I'm capable of, and what I'm here to do. Each day I undertake activities that invigorate and nourish me - activities that inspire and enrich my life. I've been given this wonderful gift called life, and I embrace every opportunity it presents.

My sincere promise to you is that strict adherence to the principles outlined in this book will bring a life beyond your wildest dreams: intimate relationships; meaning friendships; purposeful living; fulfilment; adventure; prosperity; abundance, and so much more. Your life will be enriched in ways that you've only ever dreamt about. Words are really inadequate to relay the riches I have received, so I'll leave you with this thought:

"We are all single points waiting to explode into an infinite universe"

Embrace life with complete abandon. Allow the **Alcoholic to Alchemist** philosophy to transform your life. And realize that everything you have ever wanted resides within you – *right now*.

Welcome to a new beginning, my friends,

Namaste,

Paul

The Website – www.al2al.com

www.al2al.com is a plethora of information containing guided meditations, twelve-step guidance, interviews, videos, audios, courses, and even a forum where you can share your thoughts and experience with other people following the **Alcoholic to Alchemist** journey.

Early sobriety can be a volatile period in which people are prone to relapse. Support is of the utmost importance. Visiting the site and digesting the inspirational and enlightening material is an excellent way of countering the Sobriety Saboteurs and replenishing your mind with new, life-enhancing strategies.

The site is also extremely beneficial to those of you with long-term sobriety. An eclectic mix of psychological tools will help raise your self-awareness, and the spiritual practices will enhance your understanding of the transpersonal. Your assistance in mentoring new people would also be greatly appreciated.

Most of all, **www.al2al.com**, is an on-line community where like-minded people can share their strength and hope, discuss their problems and successes, further their psychological and spiritual development, or simply relax whilst listening to a guided meditation. *Make it your home.*

Setting up a Group

Ongoing support and camaraderie is of vital importance in sustaining your well-being, evolving your knowledge, and developing your insight. With this in mind, I appeal to you to come forward and play an active role in starting **Alcoholic to Alchemist** meetings. If you want to make a difference, please contact me at **enquiries@al2al.com**. I look forward to hearing from you all.

Other Books by Paul

Spirit of Adventure:
Signposts from the Sacred Singularity

Based on an extraordinary bond between three people and three disincarnate entities, *Spirit of Adventure* combines psychology, philosophy, modern science and spirituality in a way that is designed to *inspire, challenge, enlighten* and practically *transform*.

The battleground of life leads Vi to a place of dark despair. Bereft of meaning and emotionally bankrupt, she reaches for a lethal cocktail of alcohol and painkillers. The room begins to spin as a kaleidoscope of confusion spirals through her mind. She passes out.

On awakening, her mind is strangely tranquil; something's holding her in gentle repose. Comforting words echo through the peripheries of her mind. *"Look out for the signposts,"* her *Uniqueness* concludes. Skeptical yet intrigued, Vi discards the deathly solution. Propelled by a succession of other-worldly experiences, former alcoholic, Phil, pursues a vision. Coalescing with spirit guides Theodore, Esba and Galfridus has revealed an enigma involving a novel, a development centre, and a prodigy child.

A series of synchronistic events unites Vi, Phil and Graham (a gentle giant adrift on the turbulent oceans of life). The kindred spirits embark on a challenging journey through both shadow and light. The vehicles of regression, progression, dreams, and meditation enable them to explore and cultivate their inner landscapes - whilst their ever accentuating subtle senses allow them to penetrate the mask of the material world and become conduits for Spirit.

The Spirit world's influence gradually increases and a bigger picture is revealed. Strands of consciousness spanning several spheres of existence are intricately interwoven to form a divine tapestry. A common purpose binds them as one: *Phil's vision.*

About the Author

After a life-threatening battle with alcohol in the 1980s, Paul Henderson developed a deep interest in the workings of the human mind. Subsequently, he qualified as a clinical hypnotherapist and psychodynamic counsellor, before embarking on a Bachelor's Degree and specializing in Child Development and Social Psychology.

Dedicated to promoting diversity and flexibility in the field of applied therapy, Paul recently founded the *United Kingdom Association of Integrative Therapy* (UKAIT), and its associated training school - the *United Kingdom Academy of Integrative Therapy*.

In addition to teaching psychology, Paul travels the country conducting workshops and speaking on a wide array of subjects, including Vedic Science, the Mechanisms of Consciousness, and Past-Life Therapy. His interest in the transpersonal led to his first novel '*Spirit of Adventure*,' a compelling read which combines psychology, philosophy, modern science and spirituality in a way that is inspiring, challenging and transformative.

Notes

Notes

Notes